Theater As Problem

Also by Benjamin Bennett:

> *Goethe's Theory of Poetry: "Faust" and the Regeneration of Language*
>
> *Modern Drama and German Classicism: Renaissance from Lessing to Brecht*
>
> *Hugo von Hofmannsthal: The Theaters of Consciousness*

Theater As Problem

MODERN DRAMA AND ITS PLACE IN LITERATURE

Benjamin Bennett

CORNELL UNIVERSITY PRESS

Ithaca and London

First published 1990 by Cornell University Press.

International Standard Book Number 0–8014–2443–7 (cloth)
International Standard Book Number 0–8014–9730–2 (paper)
Library of Congress Catalog Card Number 90–55115
Printed in the United States of America
Librarians: Library of Congress cataloging information
appears on the last page of the book.

⊛ The paper in this book meets the minimum requirements
of the American National Standard for Information Sciences—
Permanence of Paper for Printed Library Materials, ANSI Z39.48–1984.

For Lili

Non presumo mica d'averlo fatto io il miracolo.

Contents

Acknowledgments   ix

Introduction   1

1. Strindberg and Ibsen: Cubism, Communicative Ethics, and the Theater of Readers   17

2. Cinema, Theater, and Opera: Modern Drama as Hermeneutic Ceremony   55

3. Nestroy and Schnitzler: The Three Societies of Comedy and the Idea of a Textless Theater   93

4. The Church Militant: Audience and Spectator in *Rhinocéros*   137

5. The Trees Are Sentences: Semiotic Ceremony and Pirandello's Myth of the Theater   179

6. Approximately Five Questions on Dürrenmatt's *Die Physiker*   220

7. Conclusion: Dramatic History and the History of Drama   253

Index   269

Acknowledgments

At the risk of appearing to deny my own responsibility for this book, I want to stress the extent to which it has been a collective endeavor. Parts of the manuscript were read and criticized, in two seminars I gave, by Jefferson Chase, Joseph Doerr, Patricia Doykos, Russell Ganim, James Leva, Regina Marz, Virginia Mosser, and Anne Speare. Visitors to those seminars, to whom I am also grateful for the discussion of important questions, include William J. de Ritter, Patricia Gill, and Volker Kaiser. Richard Barr, Sveta Davé, Eva Knodt, Michael Levine, Sylvia Schmitz-Burgard, Walter Sokel, and Renate Voris, over the years, have all taken the time for long arguments on the subject matter. Peter Burgard and Robert S. Leventhal, however, have, I think, been the most uninhibited and implacable—therefore the most useful—in attacking my ideas and formulations; for them I reserve special thanks.

Early versions of Chapters 1 and 2 were published as articles in *Modern Drama:* "Strindberg and Ibsen: Toward a Cubism of Time in Drama," in vol. 26 (1983), 262–81; "Cinema, Theater and Opera: Modern Drama as Ceremony," in vol. 28 (1985), 1–21. I am grateful to the editors, consultants, and publishers of *Modern Drama*, not only for permission to use that material, but also for their criticism and comments at the time of submission. Chapters 3, 4, and 5 all began life as papers delivered at Modern Language Association sections, and brought me a great deal of useful discussion.

I am grateful, further, to the editors and consultants at Cornell University Press, to Gail Moore for help with computers, and to my

wife for all kinds of assistance, intellectual, informational, and practical. Translations from foreign languages are my own, unless otherwise noted.

B. B.

Charlottesville, Virginia

Theater As Problem

Introduction

This book is about the theory of drama. Its aim, however, is neither to establish that theory—which has been established in various
forms, along with drama itself, for over two millennia in the
Hellenic-European tradition—nor to complete it (or pretend to complete it) by insisting upon *a* theory. Its aim, rather, is to show what is
at stake in the theory of drama, to show what sort of questioning
makes up that theory, and the direction in which such questioning
leads. In particular, I am concerned with drama *as a literary type;* and
my main contention is that the theoretical discussion of drama, once
it passes beyond certain well-established but untenable preconceptions, has a profound *disruptive* effect upon the theory of literature in
general. I contend, moreover, that this disruptive effect is part of
what we mean by literature in the first place. The various stories we
tell in the name of "literary history," for example, are practically
always the story of a rupture—whether its happening is placed
between antiquity and Christianity, or at the Reformation, whether
we speak with T. S. Eliot of a "dissociation of sensibilities" beginning
in the seventeenth century, or with Roland Barthes of a division of
the writer's consciousness around 1850. I contend that the form of
drama, theoretically considered, is a uniquely revelatory locus
(which does not mean "source" or "cause") of this sense of rupture,
and that its significance and dangerous disruptive power can be
measured precisely by the extent to which literary theorists, as a
rule, avoid setting it off as an object of concentrated study.

I toyed with the idea of subtitling this book "Modern Drama and

1

Its Place in the Disorder—or (Dis)order—of Literature." I think now that this would have been dishonest. I cannot write coherently, any more than anyone else can, without either finding or making order in my material. My task as a writer, in the present case, a task which I hope the reader will accept his or her share of, is therefore above all to avoid the reductive, to bear in mind uninterruptedly that the plurality of points and arguments in the following pages aims to derive a major portion of its significance precisely from its *resistance* to the inescapable systematizing tendency of writing or reading.

1.

My focus is literary, and therefore my title, "Theater As Problem," means exactly what it says. I am concerned not with problems of the theater, but with the theater itself *as* a problem, and specifically as a literary problem. I am concerned with the problem represented by the existence of a literary type, namely "drama," which cannot be defined as a literary type without reference to the concrete extra-literary institution of the theater. For there is nothing whatever that is rhetorically or formally unique about a dramatic text; there is no characteristic or set of characteristics, or complex of "family resemblances," by which we would recognize a dramatic text as something different from a narrative text, *if we did not know about the institution of the theater,* if the theater, as an institution, were not already there to be "meant" as the text's vehicle. Otherwise a character's name, followed by a colon and some clearly fictional words, would be an entirely transparent shorthand for the sentence, "X said . . . ," and we would immediately understand that the general literary type is narrative. The association of literature with the theater, or of the theater with literature, is by no means logically or aesthetically necessary. We still have theatrical forms, especially forms of dance, that insist strongly on their nonliterary quality. But at the same time, we also reserve a special *literary* category for texts that are distinguished by nothing except what we recognize, somehow, as a fundamental association with the theater. (Nor is this recognition governed entirely by the text's outward appearance. The "nighttown" section of Joyce's *Ulysses,* for example, is ordinarily recognized as an *allusion to* the type of drama, not an *instance of* that type.)

Again, however, I am not primarily interested here in the question of *what* we recognize as drama, or in the question of *how* we classify a particular text in that category—whether by its author's intention, its public reception, its utility as a performance script, its potential effectiveness on the stage, its history of actual effectiveness on the stage, or whatever. I am interested in the problems raised by the fact *that* we distinguish drama as a literary category, that the institution of the theater (which there is no reason to regard as necessarily or fundamentally literary) still manages somehow, at least in our tradition, to carry out for itself a special segmentation of the literary universe—whereas, for example, the institution of the printed book, when it arrives, is not in the same way associated with any specific literary type.

It is perhaps possible to explain how it happens that mythical material not connected with Dionysus or any mystery religion (not to mention material that belongs to the literary genres of epic and history) comes to be performed at Dionysian festivals. But how is it that the performance texts are then understood as marking *a separate literary type?* By the time we get to Aristotle, the problem is already well developed. Tragic and comic forms are classified alongside epic and dithyramb as types of mimetic "poetry" (*Poetics*, 1447a); and the effect of tragedy (for instance) is defined in a way that makes it fully available even to the reader or hearer of the tale in narrative form (1453b). But at the same time, the distinction in "manner" of imitation, which separates dramatic from nondramatic genres, is insisted upon (1448a); and this distinction, as it applies to drama, is strictly nonliterary, since it arises entirely from the question of *who*, here and now, is doing the imitating, whether a direct representative of the poet, or actors in a scene. *Is* drama a literary type? Or is it the result of a nonliterary distinction among methods of presenting literary texts?

Anne Ubersfeld begins her discussion of the general question of drama and theater by saying:

> Le théâtre est un art paradoxal. On peut aller plus loin et y voir l'art même du paradoxe, à la fois production littéraire et représentation concrète; à la fois éternel (indéfiniment reproductible et renouvelable) et instantané (jamais reproductible comme identique à soi).[1]

> Theater is a paradoxical art, or can be seen in fact as the very art of paradox, at once both literary product and concrete representation, at

---

[1]Anne Ubersfeld, *Lire le théâtre*, 4th ed. (Paris, 1982), p. 13. Further quotations by page in parentheses.

once both eternal (indefinitely reproducible and renewable) and momentary (never reproducible as identical to itself).

There is, it seems to me, a slightly misplaced emphasis here; for the paradox in question is more fundamentally literary than it is theatrical. It does not operate in the case of ballet or mime, or in the case of extraliterary theatrical rituals such as the mass; and it does operate in the case of nontheatrical literature, for example in the hermeneutic tension between meaning as a function of the text and meaning, here and now, for a particular reader or audience. But the perception is still accurate. The theater is a uniquely intense focus of paradox, the place where a significant, or indeed constitutive paradox of literature becomes an art in its own right, the art of drama, "l'art même du paradoxe."

And therefore the theater is a problem. Without actually belonging to literature, it still manages somehow to be crucial to literature, a concrete historical reality without which literature could not be the particular (but nonconcrete) intellectual reality that it is—without which, again, it seems to me that the hermeneutic difficulties that mark our sense of the very happening of literary meaning would be dismissible as mere abstract quibbles, would lack the quality of ingrained experience that sustains our whole interest in the literary. And without the theater, more especially, not only the reality, but also the immensely fruitful *idea* of "drama" would be missing from the literary universe.

Drama, I maintain, does belong to literature; but I also maintain that the attempt to make sense of drama, as a type, in strictly literary terms, in terms of nothing but the structure of rhetorical or discursive possibilities, is futile. Especially the customary triadic division of literature into epic, lyric, and dramatic genres is futile, no matter how attenuated or subtilized. Northrop Frye says: "For all the loving care that is rightfully expended on the printed texts of Shakespeare's plays, they are still radically acting scripts, and belong to the genre of drama."[2] What does "radically" mean here? "Words may be acted in front of a spectator; they may be spoken in front of a listener; they may be sung or chanted; or they may be written for the reader." But these are all open possibilities, always available for practically any words, any text, whatever; to call them "radicals of presentation" (Frye, pp. 246–47) is to assume precisely the structure of types they

---

[2]Northrop Frye, *Anatomy of Criticism* (New York, 1966; orig. 1957), p. 247. Further quotations by page in parentheses.

are meant to establish. Nor does the idea of "the rhythm of decorum" (p. 268) help much. It is reasonable enough to assert, as a rule of thumb, that "as style is at its purest in discursive prose, so decorum is obviously at its purest in drama, where the poet does not appear in person." But it does not follow that "drama might be described . . . as *epos* or fiction absorbed by decorum" (p. 269). For that "absorption"—the perfection or at least maximization of which is a *theoretical* necessity, if "drama" is to have meaning as a strictly literary term—does not actually happen, beyond narrow limits, for a reader, does not actually happen except in an actual theater, depends therefore upon an *accidental* quality in my present relation to the words, and so brings us back to the problem. (Nor will it do to object that what "actually" happens is not the issue here. For if the actual were irrelevant, then it could be argued, for example, that in some ways the demands made by decorum are less stringent in drama than in the form of philosophical dialogue, where each speaker must be made to represent adequately, vis-à-vis the others, not only himself or herself but also the alert critical reader. Philosophical dialogue would thus be more dramatic than drama, its discourse, so to speak, more absorbent.)

Perhaps, therefore, we should simply discard the notion of drama as a "literary type" altogether, or at least not worry about it. Perhaps this line of thought is inherently fruitless, leads nowhere but to its own self-complication and perversion—which is perhaps part of what Antonin Artaud has in mind when he insists that the literary or textual violates theater's real cultural business. And perhaps, finally, it will seem paradoxical if I now say that I have no disagreement with Artaud, that I regard precisely the energy of his assault on the textual as an index of the importance of theater as a literary problem. In any case, Artaud does not hope, and cannot hope, actually to sever the connection in our culture between theater and literature. We do think of drama as a literary type; we cannot erase our minds and start over.

2.

This is a book about the theory of drama. But it is also specifically about modern drama; the reasons for this particular combination of concerns will appear in detail in Chapter 2. For the time being, let it be noted that in a book of this sort, the choice of focus is a considerable problem. On the one hand, a theoretical argument in the field

of literature—especially if that field is thought of as radically irreg-
ular—requires a certain breadth of historical scope to avoid being
dismissed as mere speculation. On the other hand, my point about
the *disruptive* operation of drama as a form, and of dramatic theory,
requires a relatively narrow focus, since the radical sense of the
"disruptive" that I have in mind necessarily excludes the possibility
of historical regularity over large periods. The disruptive is what it is
precisely by never being what it has been, by defying generaliza-
tion.

This problem is not unique to my particular version of the theory
of drama. We can sense it, for example, even in a statement as
apparently innocuous as the one with which Austin E. Quigley
opens his first chapter: "One of the more obvious characteristics of
modern drama is the sheer diversity of plays that have earned an
important place in the field."[3] "Diversity," strictly speaking, has not
the character of a "characteristic" to begin with, since only the arbitrary choice of perspective keeps it from being a characteristic of
anything whatever. The proverbial peas in a pod can be looked at in
a manner that shows diversity as their most "obvious characteristic." But Quigley has no choice here. As a theorist, he *must* think
in terms of characteristics; as a theorist of drama, he must *resist* just
this type of thinking—which he then does very effectively, for example, in his critique of "'Theatre of X' categories" (Quigley, p. 6).

The problem is a powerful one, and Quigley's response to it is to
place himself, or to find himself, under the obligation to maintain a
special kind of balance between theoretical concentration and empirical openness. He manages this task (with the aid, especially, of
Wittgenstein and Nelson Goodman) by insisting on the idea of
"worlds" and "theaters" in the plural, thus mobilizing the perennial
theoretical force of the world-theater metaphor, while also stripping
it of its apparent totalizing ambitions. The result, along with several
illuminating readings of individual plays, is neither theory, nor *a*
theory, so much as it is a general critique of theory, which produces
some ideas of great theoretical potential—such as "drama of inquiry" (p. 262), to which I will return later. But Quigley's undertaking
tends also, in its concern for its balance, to avoid some of its own
most interesting ramifications, especially as these have to do with
the philosophical notion of theatricality that the world-theater metaphor brings with it.[4]

[3]Austin E. Quigley, *The Modern Stage and Other Worlds* (New York, 1985), p. 3.
Further references by page in parentheses.
[4]Precisely a theory of drama concerned with the relation of "world" and "theater"

Peter Szondi's response to the same basic problem is diametrically opposed to Quigley's. Szondi plunges with reckless abandon (or what must at least seem such from an empiricist point of view) into a thoroughly systematic Hegelian theory of drama and its history.

> Drama in the modern European sense originated in the Renaissance. It was the intellectual venture of a humanity that had come to itself after the collapse of the medieval world-picture, that humanity's attempt to construct a world-reality in which it might confirm and mirror itself, a reality based solely upon the representation of interpersonal related-ness. . . . The exclusive dominance of dialogue, of interpersonal utter-ance, in the drama reflects the fact that drama consists only of the representation of interpersonal relatedness, that it knows nothing but what is illuminated in this sphere.[5]

When Szondi says, "Drama is absolute" (p. 15), we are tempted to respond that he is perceiving only his own absoluteness, an abso-luteness that produces such statements as "quotation has as little place in drama as variation" (pp. 16–17), which runs roughshod over the whole European tradition of dramatic parody. And the gulf be-tween this attitude and Quigley's appears especially in Szondi's re-mark, "The relation spectator-drama admits only the forms of com-plete separation and complete identification, not a penetration of the spectator into the drama, nor his being spoken to by the drama" (p. 16), not, in other words, a relation of "inquiry," not a flexible interplay of "worlds" and "horizons."

But on the other hand, Szondi is interested mainly in "modern" drama, from the late nineteenth century on, which he claims is marked by precisely the crisis and collapse of the rigid theoretical model he starts from. Whether the model is interpretively valid, therefore, or how generally applicable it is, does not concern him, as long as it provides him with intellectual leverage for carrying out his main task. His "Introduction" states that in his book, "only one particular form of literary work for the theater will be called 'drama.' Neither the religious plays of the Middle Ages nor Shakespeare's

---

opens the possibility of coordinating the thought, for example, of Frances A. Yates, *Theatre of the World* (Chicago, 1969); of Marian Hobson, "Du Theatrum Mundi au Theatrum Mentis," *Revue des Sciences Humaines*, n.s., no. 167 (1977), 379–94; and of Suzanne Gearhart, "The Theatricality of Nature and History," in *The Open Boundary of History and Fiction: A Critical Approach to the French Enlightenment* (Princeton, 1984), pp. 234–84.

[5]Peter Szondi, *Theorie des modernen Dramas* (Frankfurt/Main, 1966; orig. 1956), pp. 14–15. Further quotations by page in parentheses.

histories belong to this form. The historical mode of observation entails even that we leave Greek tragedy out of account, since its nature would require a different intellectual horizon in order to be understood" (p. 13). And if we ask why this particular idea of drama should be privileged in this particular argument, the answer can only be "historical": "History [as happening] is restricted to the chasms between established literary forms; but only the reflection upon history [history as account] can erect bridges over these chasms" (p. 12). The argument is therefore circular, in the Hegelian manner that calls into question the boundary between *res gestae* and *historia rerum gestarum.* "Drama" is the name of an absence; it means that idea of drama which is presupposed—if not, indeed, called into being—by the late nineteenth-century "crisis" which has already left it behind but still requires it in order to be (or become) the historical crisis it is.

If Quigley is made wary by the permeable boundary between theory of drama and drama itself, Szondi is made overbold. Since the historical element in which we operate is inescapable anyway, why *not* go ahead and make the supposedly inevitable historical move of laying down a clear system of concepts with which to operate—the type of system that a more circumspect approach merely conceals, or blinds itself to, hypocritically? No attempt, after all, is made to deny the historical relativity of the system. Our concepts, precisely in wearing proudly the implied quotation marks that never fail to enclose them, cut through all "diversity" and free themselves for the business of making definite categorical statements, applying maximal interpretive leverage to texts. And if Szondi's approach is thus an anticipatory criticism of Quigley's, Quigley's implies in turn an equally valid criticism of Szondi's. For Szondi, in the very process of ostensibly acknowledging the historical relativity of his procedure, also places himself strictly *above* history by brushing aside the traditional (thus historically sanctioned) force of what we generally mean by "drama" in the first place—what we after all cannot help but mean by it—a field of meaning in which it is historically dishonest *not* to recognize the quality of "diversity," however questionable that concept may be in a theoretical context.

Or to look at the matter differently, the ambitious definiteness that gives Szondi's statements both their systematic and their heuristic value, in order not to collapse into mere inaccuracy, requires (as a justification) that those statements bring with them precisely the implied quotation marks that undermine their definiteness. What we have, then, are statements that try to be both there and not there at the same time, statements "under erasure." And in the case of dramatic theory, it is an open question whether this radical procedure is to be preferred over Quigley's equally "historical" acceptance of existing language-games as a basis for development—especially the game represented by a nontotalizing use of the word "world," which looks over its own shoulder by both inhabiting and standing back from its own implied perceptual center. In the case of most narrative, where we may feel it necessary to acknowledge that our theory is itself a telling of stories, we shall perhaps naturally tend to operate in a manner closer to Quigley's. In the case of poetic types that show a stronger analogy with spatial representation, we shall perhaps be better justified in taking Szondi as a model. But drama, in the dependence of its definition (or lack thereof) on the real institution of the theater, is not sufficiently well defined in rhetorical terms to guide us in establishing a rhetoric of theory. Again, therefore, the theater *is* a problem.

3.

I think it is obvious that there is no very fruitful middle ground between the positions I have associated with Quigley and Szondi. Any attempt at compromise would probably find the defects of both positions unavoidable, their virtues unattainable. But there is at least one other possibility for approaching the theory of drama that has been experimented with extensively, the idea of "semiotics of the theater." The object of study is now not drama as a literary type, but rather the whole of the theatrical happening (or as close to the whole as possible), which is analyzed as the combined operating of various sign systems and various types of sign, and analyzed in a manner that specifically avoids privileging the linguistic sign. As in much semiotics, definite scientific pretensions are at work here. The semiotician claims, at least by implication, to have avoided the pitfalls of critical or theoretical rhetoric by going back to the smallest systematically distinguishable units of the theatrical experience, units from which a maximally objective model of that experience can be constructed.

The trouble is that semiotics is not a science in the sense that its claims to validity are discussible on empirical grounds. There is no such thing as semiotic evidence or a semiotic experiment. On the contrary, semiotics in truth exists *for the sake* of the paradoxes and aporias it ostensibly arrives at, whether they arise, say, from C. S.

Peirce's notion of the "interpretant" and the infinity of signification, or from the Saussurean recognition that the only actual happening in the isolable domain of signification is the happening of difference. Semiotics in systematic form does not merely arrive at paradoxes. It is *aimed* at them, aimed at revealing ever anew their inevitability and ramifications, aimed at developing and refining the self-critical depth of our conscious situation in existence, our situation as sign-users, or more especially as the users and creatures of language.[6] Jonathan Culler sets forth the dramatic or fictional plot of semiotics, as it were the myth of semiotics, when he says:

> In so far as literature turns back on itself and examines, parodies or treats ironically its own signifying procedures, it becomes the most complex account of signification we possess. . . . Because literary works do have meaning for readers, [however,] semiotics undertakes to describe the systems of convention responsible for those meanings.
> This is a coherent and necessary program: since communication does take place we must discover how it occurs if we wish to understand ourselves as social and cultural beings. But literature itself, in its continual pressure on and violation of codes, reveals a paradox inherent in the semiotic project and in the philosophic orientation of which it is the culmination.[7]

This account is reasonable in the abstract; but the actual intellectual process moves in the other direction. It is only because we *already* know of our paradoxical situation with respect to language, only because this situation *already* reveals itself in the practice of literature, that we undertake the general "semiotic project" in the first place. A semiotics that seeks to circumvent the literary altogether, or to avoid strictly the recognition of any uniqueness in the linguistic sign—as semiotics of the theater sometimes pretends to—is therefore a semiotics that makes nonsense of itself.[8]

---

[6]There are various ways of developing this basic insight, not all of which lead into the field of language and literature as traditionally delimited. For example, Julia Kristeva, Σημειωτικὴ. *Recherches pour une sémanalyse* (Paris, 1969), pp. 31–32, stresses the revelation of the ideological quality (in my terms, the quality of our being not only users, but creatures as well) of our situation with respect to "science" comprehensively understood: "Toute sémiotique donc, ne peut se faire que comme critique de la sémiotique. . . . On pourrait soutenir que la sémiotique est cette 'science des idéologies' qu'on a pu suggérer en Russie révolutionnaire, mais aussi une idéologie des sciences."

[7]Jonathan Culler, *The Pursuit of Signs: Semiotics, Literature, Deconstruction* (Ithaca, 1981), pp. 35–36, 38–39.

[8]The by now classical formulation of this position, that semiotics cannot avoid privileging language, is the "Présentation" by Roland Barthes in *Communications* 4

Yet semiotics is useless if it does not also maintain an inner distance, a position of analytic leverage, with respect to its own crucial linguistic or literary component. And the balance, the needful internal irony, that thus arises is perhaps most elusive, but also most significant, in the case of semiotics of the theater, where the subject matter is neither clearly literary nor clearly distinguishable from the literary, where, consequently, neither the systematic aspect of the argument, nor its content, is alone sufficient to establish the distance required.

It is in semiotics of the theater, therefore, that we expect to encounter a book like Ubersfeld's *Lire le Théâtre*. This book is as much a symptom as a solution of the problems it brings up, and is full of insights that bear a curious relation of irrelevance to the very argument from which they spring. The theater, for Ubersfeld, becomes a venue where language revels in its own paradoxes, especially as these have to do with the operation of reference: the status of the theatrical sign that is both signifier and referent, and in a sense its own referent (Ubersfeld, pp. 34, 150), in a concrete space that is *"construit pour être signe"* (p. 151), "constructed precisely in order to be a sign"; the corresponding tension between identification and distance in the spectator's situation (pp. 41–45); the curious non-reference of the notions "I," "here," "now," precisely *in* the here and now of the stage (pp. 251–52); the manner in which the idea of the character ("personnage"), once it is rescued from its technical and ontological untenability by a process of reference on the stage, then reenters the linguistic domain by providing a focus of the poetic as such, *"un lieu proprement poétique"* (p. 113). But when this idea of language as the essential player on the stage is made more systematically explicit, in the discussion (using A. J. Greimas) of "le modèle actantiel au théâtre" (pp. 53–107), which conflates the categories of action and syntax, the argument becomes relatively superficial, trivializes the texts it treats, and arrives at a notion of "dialogisme" (pp. 96–97) that approaches the narrowness of Szondi's definition of "drama," but without Szondi's scrupulous historicistic self-limiting. There is, it seems to me, not merely an accidental or occasional inconsistency, but a *structural* inconsistency at work here, which, while in a sense perhaps damaging the argument, also makes room

---

(1964), 1–3, which is both developed and criticized by Jacques Derrida, *De la grammatologie* (Paris, 1967), p. 75. Both a key passage from Barthes and Derrida's response are found, in English, in *Of Grammatology*, trans. Gayatri Spivak (Baltimore, 1976), pp. 51–52. Barthes, however, in suggesting that semiology will eventually appear as *part* of a "translinguistics," insists on more than I do.

in it for precisely its numerous moments of brilliance. Ubersfeld's whole approach obliges her to take a stand against the autonomy of the "chose littéraire" ("literary object") in drama (p. 111). But this stand does not prevent her from capturing the miraculous insight to which she is led by the ostensibly antiliterary idea of "theatrical space," the recognition that

> l'espace scénique concret . . . est médiation entre différentes lectures possibles du texte: l'espace scénique (de la représentation) est ce qui permet de lire *à la fois la poétique du texte et son rapport à l'histoire*. L'espace scénique étant devenu objet poétique, c'est-à-dire lieu de combinaisons de réseaux, d'une certaine façon la lecture qui en est faite par le spectateur se reverse sur le texte littéraire. La lecture de l'espace textuel du texte dramatique passe d'une façon décisive par l'espace scénique de la représentation. [P. 163]

> The concrete scenic space mediates among different possible readings of the text; the scenic space (of performance) is what makes it possible to read simultaneously *both the text's poetics and its relation to history*. Once the scenic space has become a poetic object, a locus of interaction among systems or levels, the spectator's reading of it is in a way turned back upon the literary text. The reading of the textual space of a dramatic text is conditioned decisively by its passage through the scenic space of performance.

The "chose littéraire," that is, becomes truly itself, truly a "thing," *only* in the theater, where its various possible readings or uses do not clamor for precedence in mental time, but rather coexist in a concretely available spatial pattern of potentialities that includes, and so relativizes, every particular act of readerly appropriation.

As a stance, therefore, adopted by someone who has something important to say, as Ubersfeld does, semiotics of the theater can be made to yield powerful results. When, on the other hand, it is promoted as a method, as a system for finding things to say, it produces nothing of consequence, as in Keir Elam, *The Semiotics of Theatre and Drama*. Elam's presentation is by no means unintelligent. But in attempting to set forth theatrical semiotics as nothing but method, and in his care to avoid the sort of inconsistency that at once both plagues and benefits Ubersfeld, he sees no reason for any greater precision than is exemplified by his equation of the scenic "signified" with the "class of objects" to which the prop belongs, and no reason to develop the notion of "the spectator's semiotic initiative" beyond a point at which even the audience's presence in the theater—a fact of enormous historical and generic significance—is still only one of a number of "audience signals."[9]

4.

I suppose I have by now put myself under an obligation either to explain in detail the method I propose to employ in the following, as it differs from the other methodological attitudes I have discussed, or at least to explain why I am not going to explain. My aim, as I have said, is to set forth *the* theory of drama, in the sense of the pattern of significant philosophical or literary-theoretical questions that are raised *by* drama as a literary type. But strictly speaking, there is no such thing as the mere raising or formulating of questions in a field such as literary theory or theory of drama. The question receives its contour and significance only in the course of a concentrated attempt to deal with it, a focused theoretical initiative of the sort that I have suggested is missing in Elam. This does not necessarily mean, however, that one must pretend to have *answered* one's questions, as I think Szondi does. Quigley's attitude here is more reasonable.

> To think of a category or of a generalization as a measuring rod is to change both the way in which we construct it and the way in which we use it. And to use it as Wittgenstein suggests, as a means of continuing an inquiry, is to locate in the framework with which we study modern drama a feature that is characteristic of the drama itself: a commitment not to conclusions but to improved means of inquiry. [Quigley, p. 61]

Quigley is right; "inquiry" is a useful idea by which to arrange modern drama. And he also *must* in some sense be right, since, in any humanistic field, there must be some basic continuity between the object of study and the act of studying. What is still missing in this statement, however, is an attentiveness to the matter of what *type* of question needs to be dealt with, what type of question will respond to a focused attack without becoming either merely answerable or merely impenetrable. And it is with regard to this mat-

[9]Keir Elam, *The Semiotics of Theatre and Drama* (London, 1980), pp. 8, 95–96. Another frequently quoted attempt to treat semiotics as a method for dealing with the theater—hence another failure to understand Kristeva's point about semiotics and its critique—is Patrice Pavis, *Problèmes de sémiologie théâtrale* (Montreal, 1976), which avoids important issues less obviously than Elam, but in basically the same way.

ter that I think I have not so much a method as an idea, an idea that distinguishes my approach from the three main methodological programs I have outlined.

I am not primarily interested in the supposed uniqueness of drama, in what separates drama from literature (or from the rest of literature). I maintain, rather, that the crucial question is, What does drama do *for* literature? What is the role—in the broadest sense, the historical role—of drama in the literary universe? Only in response to this sort of questioning does theater reveal itself as the problem, the fruitful and self-renewing problem, that I think it undoubtedly is. And only this sort of questioning, which has as its goal not an answer or a resolution, but a further questioning, a perennial self-questioning in literature itself, can hope to avoid both of the twin methodological pitfalls of dogmatism and indecisiveness.

In particular, I will suggest that drama is the *church* of literature— the church, fastened down in space and time by its theater, not merely the religion—that drama is not merely one literary type among others, but rather is to literature as literature itself is to the whole of language, a focus of maximally intense self-reflection, a place for the taking of thought and the ever repeated beginning of self-renewal. But the reader must not expect a kind of hymn to drama, as if either drama as a form or any particular drama were in any sense perfect. On the contrary, I use the term "church" advisedly; for drama, like every church, is also the sign of a defect, and is itself a defect (a defect marked, for all to see, by its categorically unstable relation with its theater) in the larger historical entity to which it belongs.

The specific arguments I will make fall into three main groups, although the divisions among them do not correspond to chapter divisions. I will try to show, first, that the form of drama unmasks the quality of *reversibility* in certain crucial hermeneutic and semiotic relations that appear, by nature or by definition, to exclude it. The whole order of literature in which those relations operate is thus called into question, but not in the sense that the possibility of an alternative order is suggested; the argument proceeds by way of common and familiar theoretical concepts, and does not pretend to occupy a revolutionary position. What drama does, I mean, is to sustain and repeatedly exhibit, in literature as a whole, the paradoxical character of an *inherently* questionable or self-undermining order. One corollary of this discussion is a questioning of the status of the word, the linguistic sign, as a privileged signifier. But this aspect of the argument must not be confused with the assumption, prevalent in "theater semiotics," that the use of nonlinguistic sign systems in the theater automatically strips language of its semiotic privilege. The actual situation is a good deal more complicated, and more interesting, than Elam, for example, makes it appear.

The second group of arguments has to do with the relation between fascism and the aesthetic notion of universal uniformity of response, hence with what I contend is a political danger built into the whole operation of literature as we know it. Readers will differ in their opinion of the explanatory power, with respect to the actual Fascist and Nazi movements, of the literary-aesthetic sense of the word "fascism" that I propose. But disagreement on this matter need not affect the substance of the argument: that the idea (or postulate or requirement or dream) of universal uniformity of response develops a specially insidious power in the history of literature; and that the form of drama—despite the theater's apparent control over its audience, by contrast with a reader's supposed freedom—operates within literature as a counterforce to that idea and its baggage, as the repeated prevention of a threatening historical closure of the literary field.

The third area of argument, finally, has to do with the role of literature in sustaining our sense of history as a problem, as the paradoxical coincidence of structure and task, and with the corresponding role of drama within literature. The argument here, which is less concentrated than in the other two categories, touches on such matters as the special historical background of modern drama, especially the premodern conventions I call "theater of readers" and "textless theater," and the historically relative operation of "boundary effects" by which our sense of genre and meaning is shaped. In the concluding chapter, I suggest that the dramatic theater is the sign of a disruption in the very idea of "history," whether applied to drama itself, to literature, or to human affairs in general.

5.

Once again, this book must not be read as an attempt to contribute to theater history, or theory of the theater, in the sense that these fields of study are separate from literary studies. I talk a great deal here about "what happens" in the theater, or on the stage, in connection with particular works. In all cases, the reader should recognize that I am treating those happenings, those visible physical events, as *literary* happenings, in the light of questions arising from literary theory and interpretation. My approach is based on the question, What does the theater do *for* literature? And it is based on the assumption that this question makes sense, that the theater, at least in our tradition, has taken root mainly in the domain of the literary, and has developed its own special habits and functions accordingly. I assume, in other words, that what happens in the theater, for all its unrepeatable physical particularity, *is* after all always a literary event, and that precisely the radical tension, the categorical disparity, that thus arises, is a crucial structural feature of what we mean by literature to begin with. The detailed arguments in the following chapters should be regarded as a test of this assumption.

In any case, given my assumption, I have not felt obliged to remain within what may by now perhaps be claimed as the canon of modern theatrical literature. The authors I treat are all, I think, widely recognized as major; but in choosing particular works for discussion, I have not been guided by the question of whether these works are regarded as good theater, or can be regarded thus, or have left a mark on the theater. Not the short-term operation of the theater in a particular society, but rather the relatively long-term operation of the theater in the history of our conception of the literary, is my present concern. And the texts I have selected for discussion are simply those that, as far as I know, lend themselves best as examples in the arguments I want to make—except that in some cases I have favored texts that do not figure prominently in my *Modern Drama and German Classicism*, to which this book is in some respects a sequel. If it is shown later that a text I have ignored would have served my purposes better, I will gladly concede the point.

CHAPTER ONE

Strindberg and Ibsen: Cubism, Communicative Ethics, and the Theater of Readers

In some ways the relation between August Strindberg and Henrik Ibsen is entirely obvious. The echoes of *Peer Gynt* in *Lucky Pehr's Journey* and the attack on *A Doll's House* in *Sir Bengt's Wife* require no comment; nor does it seem to me unlikely—even though the original titles are not as similar as their usual English translations—that *The Ghost Sonata* has to do with *Ghosts* in an oblique manner. In both the visionary and the realistic mode, the attempt to surpass Ibsen is a constant factor in Strindberg's dramaturgy, and binds him to Ibsen in the very process of separating him. My immediate aim is to trace this complicated relation on the level of the history and theory of drama as a form.

1.

I want to suggest an analogy between time in drama and space in painting. It must be recognized, first, that a dramatic scene does not actually contain time in any more than the limited sense in which a painting contains space. A certain amount of time is required for performance; but the sharp formal boundedness of the scene, its containment between a beginning and an end beyond which it simply does not exist, fails to satisfy our notion of time as an unceasing and uninterruptible flow. The scene, or the play as a whole, has the character of an interlude, a discrete segment of existence devoted to a ritual or vision or evoked reality that is recognized as different from the world in which we live the rest of our lives.

But if the representation of reality, in any reasonable understanding of this concept, is aimed at, then it follows that drama must create an illusion of unrestricted time comparable to the illusion of unrestricted space created by the painter on a two-dimensional surface. This necessity produces what I will call temporal perspectivism in Western drama. Just as the painter gives the impression of planes situated *behind* the plane of the canvas—by using lines that are assumed to be parallel in reality but converge in the drawing—so the dramatist, by making a plot depend on events in a relatively distant fictional past, gives the impression of temporal planes *behind* the scenic present, the impression of a temporal continuum extending beyond the limits of what is performed. Not all Western drama employs temporal perspective in the same degree; some representational dramatic conventions operate differently. In French classical drama and in German Classicism, the past is as a rule clearly overpowered by a present action to which our attention is drawn. The sense of unrestricted time is produced here by way of an analogy between precisely this focusing of our attention and the imagined focusing of subjective time, for the fictional characters, upon a moment of crisis; thus a shadow of our own belonging-in-time is projected back to us from the stage. And even in conventions where temporal perspective operates, there are widely different ways of achieving it. In ancient and in Renaissance drama the procedure tends to be formal, as it were geometrical, corresponding to the use of architectural outlines to define space in Renaissance painting. The past is narrated by a chorus or prologue, or revealed in measured steps, as when Oedipus questions witnesses. But in the wake of nineteenth-century literary realism—especially the genre of the novel, where reality is understood to mean substantial periods of time—neither the classical concentration of time nor the quasi-architectural perspective of ancient or Renaissance tragedy is an acceptable convention. Hence the emergence of what is usually called indirect exposition. The present is dominated by an oppressive, looming past, which is revealed only gradually, in realistically motivated conversation and action. And the skillful use of this technique, the evocation of vast temporal depth, with an entirely seamless transition between depth and foreground, is a major part of what was and is prized in Ibsen.

But Ibsen's strictly perspectivist phase is transitory. Drama inevitably concerns itself less with long periods of time as such than with the past as an immediate presence in our mental and social life, which suggests the question of *how we see* the past; and this question leads to the dramatic equivalent of impressionism. The impressionist painters do not reject perspective; they do not neglect to show distant objects on a smaller scale than nearby objects. But they do question whether our perception of space is as objective and geometrical as perspective painting suggests: do we really see lines and contours, or do we, rather, simply see light (or Cézanne's "volume and color") from which we then infer lines and contours? Ibsen, like the impressionists, without neglecting to indicate a past history for his plots, questions whether there is such a thing as *the* past in our lives. Is it not rather a pattern of private mental and emotional stirrings for which we merely infer an objective cause? This sense of time emerges in the theme of Hjalmar Ekdal's ineradicable illusions. If an illusion is ineradicable, hence irrefutable, is it an "illusion" to begin with? It emerges in the relation between Rosmer and Rebecca, which takes the form of a counterpoint built on differing and developing *ideas* of the past. In *The Lady from the Sea*, an ominous past is suddenly rendered innocuous—and so in a sense loses its quality as "the past"—by a simple mental development in those who perceive it. Then Hedda Gabler attempts actually to repair her past, to force Lövborg back into what she considers his proper place in it. And in *The Master Builder* it is not possible to establish beyond doubt even the bare facts of the past relation between Solness and Hilde. Just as the impressionists turn away from the direct conventional representation of space, and seek rather to represent the combination of data and process from which we infer our idea of space in reality, so Ibsen turns from the representation of time to the adumbration of the mental processes by which an idea of time arises in us.

Strindberg's first major achievements are similarly impressionistic, in showing the relativity of the idea of time by a clash between the temporal or historical universes of different characters. This technique is applied consistently in *The Father*, down to the level of the minor characters; and in *Miss Julie* it is developed into a collision not merely between differing ideas of the past, but between fundamentally different *types* of temporal experience: Julie has a past but no future, Jean a future but no past. Then, in *Creditors*, precisely the similarity between two characters' views of the past, not the difference, creates doubt about the existence of *the* past. Adolf's idea of his own past is obviously influenced by Gustav; and Gustav's past relation with Tekla, as we hear of it, is primarily an idea that he reinforces in himself by compelling Adolf to confirm it. Therefore precisely the area of agreement between Adolf's memory and Gustav's is suspect, and I think it is clear that we are meant to generalize from this. Even where the agreement between individuals, between witnesses, gives the past a kind of legal objectivity, still the dialectical operation of memory is such that this evidence itself must cause doubt; the past as an objective entity remains as unattainable, in effect as nonexistent, as ever. Impressionism is a natural approach to the theater for Strindberg, and it is a mode he never entirely abandons. Even after the expressionism of the first two parts of *To Damascus*, we find *The Dance of Death*, in which impressionistic technique is developed with unprecedented intensity, in which the past is not merely called into question but whipped about violently like a flag in a storm, utterly subject to the particular human situations in which it is made to function.

Let it be noted, finally, that the stylistic terms here borrowed from painting are applicable to drama in a way that they are *not* applicable to other literary genres. Verbal narrative, especially, does not possess any feature directly comparable to the "picture plane" in painting, despite the frequent (and justified) use of such terms as "scene" and "scenic" in narrative theory. Narrative, by its use of tenses and by other devices, can operate subtly with temporal *relations*, but can never establish an absolute *present*, a temporal picture plane, in the sense that what is now actually being said or done on the stage constitutes such a present. The stylistic history we are speaking of, from perspectivism to impressionism, expressionism and cubism, is thus, within literature, specific to drama as a type.

2.

Neither Strindberg nor Ibsen remains satisfied with impressionism as an artistic approach; and in Strindberg's case the reasons for dissatisfaction are clear. If our idea of time, hence a crucial component of our idea of ourselves and the world, is conditioned by our particular situation and lacks all objective validity, then mimetic realism can no longer be justified as a theatrical convention. If a drama seems to present itself as imitating reality, while in the very process it demonstrates the relativity of its characters' idea of time, then the audience—since mimesis presupposes that we do see things as they are—are placed in the position of imagining themselves exempt from precisely the all-infecting relativity they are asked to acknowledge. This danger of logical conflict between style and meaning impels Strindberg toward expressionism.

Whereas the impressionist, in questioning our idea of space, is still guided in overall composition by the mimetic conventions under criticism, the expressionist allows the mental or emotional content of the picture to distort the composition, and so confuses the idea of imitation to the point where we cannot accept it as a valid aesthetic category. Distortion of this type characterizes Strindberg's quest and dream plays. Stage settings no longer represent simple locations (as distinct from what happens in them) but become symbols emanating from the consciousness of a character; certain figures, like the Beggar in *To Damascus*, know more about the central character than they have any right to, and so unmask the whole fiction as a reflection of that character's inner life; by such devices as the past relation between the Stranger and the Physician, the fictional universe is subjected to an anguished constriction which in *To Damascus* we associate with the constrained inner anguish of the Stranger himself. But above all, time is distorted. In *To Damascus I* the manner of time's movement, the shape of temporal experience, is in doubt: is it linear (progressive, cumulative, nonrepeating), or oscillating on a path marked by the seaside, the hotel, the Physician's house, the street corner? Or is it a circle of repetition? Then, in *To Damascus II*, temporal continuity is simply exploded, especially by the banquet and prison scenes. And in *A Dream Play* time is made to move at bewilderingly different velocities, even with respect to itself, like eddies, pools, currents in a swift, shallow stream.

Of course this idea of expressionism is theoretically questionable. The sense in which mimetic conventions "presuppose that we see things as they are," in any art form, is at best tenuous. What is actually presupposed, at most, is the possibility of comparison between certain details of a fictional world that is spread out visibly before us and certain details of a quotidian world that we find ourselves gropingly in the midst of. Once we look at the matter in this way, it is evident that expressionism (as defined earlier), far from eliminating the mimetically required possibility of comparison, itself still requires it. How else do we perceive "distortion," if not by comparing? Even if we follow Szondi and speak of "ego-dramatics" in Strindberg's expressionism, the problem remains.[1] It is true that

---

[1]Peter Szondi, *Theorie des modernen Dramas* (Frankfurt/Main, 1966), p. 40, who quotes Strindberg: "I think that the life of a single individual described in length and depth is truer and more enlightening than the life of a whole family. How can one know what is going on in someone else's mind? . . . There's only one person's life that we really know and that one is our own." This English translation is from August Strindberg, *The Son of a Servant*, trans. Evert Sprinchorn (Garden City, N.Y., 1966), p. 6.

in Western tradition, the absence of a directly expressive or assertive authorial voice is characteristic of drama as a form, so that the influence of the authorial ego, when it is felt, can have the effect of a formal rupture. But authorial absence in Western drama, while more or less a formal constant, varies widely in signification; it completes and preserves (refrains from intruding upon) the *presence*, in various styles, of God, of truth, of nature, of history, of a representative subjective dynamics, and so on. And in the dramatic idiom presupposed by Strindberg, an idiom deeply affected by narrative realism, the absence of the author corresponds to the presence of the *real*. That absence is thus absorbed into the mimetic endeavor, which means that its revocation, the author's sudden "expressionistic" presence, is recognized (and so functions) only by way of precisely the convention it pretends to supersede. Or yet again, how do we recognize certain features of a dramatic text or performance as reflecting the influence of an authorial ego in the first place? How else but by carrying out a version of precisely that impressionist critique of perception whose illegitimate point of view, whose untenable pretensions to knowledge, expressionism supposedly unmasks and dispenses with?

We must therefore not expect too much from the concept of expressionism in itself; but we can still speak of a *stylistic dynamics* tending in the direction of the expressionistic. Temporal perspective in drama raises questions that are acknowledged in the development of impressionist style, which however brings with it a problematics of its own that is responded to gropingly by stylistic devices we recognize as expressionist. And once we understand that this progression, this dynamics, is what we observe in Ibsen and Strindberg, at least one interesting question arises. Why does Ibsen not follow the same path taken later by Strindberg? The impressionism of his later plays contains a definite tendency along that path. In *The Master Builder* there are several possible ways of accounting for the conversations Hilde "remembers" with Solness; but in her immediate effect Hilde is close to being one of those typical expressionist figures with mysterious inner knowledge of the hero. She is a projection of Solness, as the Rat Wife is a projection of the creeping things that inhabit the Allmers's psychological household. In *John Gabriel Borkman*, by contrast with an obtrusively strict temporal continuity, space (which is ordinarily less flexible than time in drama) suddenly becomes fluid in the last scene, when Borkman takes his walk; and this relaxation of theatrical conventions is evidently a projection of the internal change taking place in Borkman. In *When*

We Dead Awaken, the quadrangular pattern of characters is a kind of moral coordinate system by which Rubek attempts to chart the posi- tion and contours of his own true self.

For Ibsen, as for Strindberg, dramatic impressionism produces a tendency in the direction of expressionism; but Ibsen, to the end of his career, remains much closer to a consistently mimetic style. Why? Surely the author of *Peer Gynt* was not incapable of radical stylistic experimentation. My point is that the absence of a fully developed expressionism in late Ibsen makes sense only when recognized as the result of a *deliberate resistance* to the stylistic dynamics described here, a deliberate avoidance of the untenable expressionist position.

3.

The expressionist tendency in Ibsen is explained by stylistic dynamics; but the reasons for a resistance to that tendency are *ethical,* and are reflected in thematic patterns in the late plays. Ellida Wangel, given the free choice, prefers a thoroughly prosaic reality over the "terrible and alluring life" of poetic possibility offered by the Stranger.[2] A similar choice is made by Alfred and Rita Allmers at the end of *Little Eyolf;* after discussing various possible ways of poeticizing or tragedizing their existence—death, separation, infidelity, revenge on the poor who live below—they finally arrive at what seems to them a momentous decision: simply to go on living, and to try being decent to the people around them. In both cases, if with a certain irony in each, the ordinary, orderly operation of domestic or social reality is presented as the result of a serious ethical choice, not merely as unthinking routine. *Hedda Gabler* stresses the negative aspect of the same idea by showing that normal human existence, if we consider it disinterestedly (that is, aesthetically, in terms of what Hedda calls "beauty"), is simply not tolerable. I do not mean that Hedda's attitudes are a prescriptive model for the audience's response; but a quite improbable degree of bourgeois complacency would be required to assert that there is no truth in her perception of things. Normal, everyday human life, from the point of view of aesthetic disinterest, is an unthinkably tedious affair,

---

[2]The Ibsen quotations are from *The Lady from the Sea,* trans. Frances E. Archer, and *When We Dead Awaken,* trans. William Archer, in *The Collected Works of Henrik Ibsen,* vols. 9 and 11 (New York, 1923).

which means that the disinterested aesthete (like Hedda) cannot regard such a life as "normal," cannot lead such a life except by making the free and extraordinary choice to do so. For an individual with any degree of detached perspective on his or her existence, as for Ellida or Allmers, normal human life cannot happen except as the result of a *free decision*, a deliberate subjection of aesthetic disinterest to ethical commitment.

This point explains, in something like personal terms, Ibsen's resistance to the expressionistic tendency in his own development. We are meant to sense the latent expressionism in the last plays; and we are meant to understand that by resisting that tendency (by not returning to the theatrical idiom of, say, *Peer Gynt* or Goethe's *Faust*), by remaining close to the conventional limits of mimetic style, we and the author together are participating in an ethical decision similar to the decision suggested on the level of theme. But the reason for this decision, on *our* part, is not yet clear. Hedda Gabler's suicide, considered as the result of her lack of ethical decisiveness, and contrasted with the apparently successful commitment of characters in other plays, is still only an admonitory fable, whereas what is required of us—if my basic argument is valid—is a decision at once crucially historical and immediately personal, a decision that is in the process of being taken here and now, in the theater considered as a focal point of both our personal existence and the historical movement of our society. Learning, or knowing, what the right decision would be, is not enough. The decision must be immediate and ethically urgent, a decision taken here and now.

I contend that a sufficient basis for *our* decision, in this sense, and a direct connection to the question of style, is established with perfect clarity in at least the final four plays. Solness, Allmers, and Borkman all make a conscious effort to believe that they are devoting their lives to other people—Solness to the happy families he imagines living in his houses, Allmers to his son, Borkman to those whose prosperity he had dreamed of creating—and all three projects possess a certain logic. But each of the three men, as Solness puts it, must pay a price for his supposed altruism; and it becomes clear in each play that the reason for the exaction of this price is that the project had in truth always been self-directed, that it had never been a genuine approach to other people. This moral lesson concerning the ideas of self and other, however, is also an allegory of the artistic situation at which the author has arrived. The stylistic dynamics leading toward expressionism can be understood as an attempt to achieve profound contact between drama and its audience, an attempt to provide the audience not merely with a conventional picture of the world, but with an immediate intuition of the process by which our ideas of world and time are generated. As in painting, a questioning of the objectivity of perspective gives rise to dramatic impressionism; and the recognition that impressionism is not strictly consistent, since its retention of the basic mimetic idiom conflicts with its lesson about the nature of perception, leads onward to expressionism. If this progression is interpreted as a striving for communication, a striving that begins by attempting to lay hold of the objective (that which is there in exactly the same way for everyone) but now, having despaired of objectivity, seeks at least to show forth the necessary (therefore shared, communicable) conditions of our experience, then expressionists can claim that by distorting images into symbols of an individual's inner life, they are carrying out their communicative task more scrupulously and with greater effectiveness than their stylistic predecessors.

But in attempting to benefit us by establishing communication, the expressionist, like the series of insidiously dominating male characters in the plays, overshoots his mark. He aims for a communication based on the assumption that no true communication is possible, that each of us lives in a strictly self-created world. We follow the expressionist, therefore, and learn from him, only by submitting to him, by surrendering to his vision, just as those myriads whom Solness or Borkman dreams of making happy would in truth only be contributing to their benefactor's self-magnification. The expressionist can teach me how *he* sees things, and perhaps even in a sense how *I* see things, but he has not grasped the secret of how *we* see things, the common ground where people meet and deal genuinely with one another. This is the ethical dimension of the logical and artistic difficulties that attach themselves to the notion of expressionism. The necessary continuance of mimetic convention in expressionism, as a means of shaping and focusing the endeavor, is now interpreted as a kind of dishonesty, a duping of the audience rather than a genuine communicative move.

But once the problems of the progression from perspectivism toward expressionism have been given a new center in the ethics of communication, it becomes in a sense possible to solve them. What is needed is a *common ground* for genuine communication; and precisely the radical expressionist critique of mimesis reveals the possibility of such a common ground *in the discredited conventions of the mimetic,* in a type of social realism, to which Ibsen now steadfastly adheres despite the expressionistic pull of his stylistic development.

That the mimetic is *only* a convention, without objective validity, is insisted upon by the strong expressionistic undertow in Ibsen's late plays. But precisely the conventionality of the mimetic implies its nature as a *communal* initiative, a way of seeing that we now more or less arbitrarily agree to keep in common with other people; precisely this arbitrary quality is now the source of ethical value. The objective or experiential validity of artistic conventions has become irrelevant; our task is to understand reality in such a way that real contact with others becomes and remains possible. The conventionally mimetic does not reveal truth or even demonstrate facts; but it is a ground or medium of communication, and functions the more perfectly as such when its lack of objectivity is generally recognized. If we imagine that "realistic" drama shows us reality, then our philosophical doubts about reality necessarily imply doubts about the communicativeness of such drama; but if the realistic begins by being discredited, if it is recognized from the outset as mere convention, then the conscious decision to accept that convention *is* undoubtedly communicative, shared with others, a communal process.

This argument, though perhaps abstract, is not at all speculative, for Ibsen himself incorporates it into his last play, *When We Dead Awaken*. The relation between Rubek's finished statue, with its supposedly hardheaded acceptance of the truth, and his original ideal conception, is the same as the relation between the expressionistic and the mimetic. From the expressionist's point of view, mimetic representation is philosophically naïve, like Rubek's orginal style; for it assumes the existence of universally comprehensible entities or objects that can be imitated. The expressionist, with what he thinks of (in Rubek's words) as his greater "experience of life," has therefore discarded the mimetic fallacy. But as in the case of the expressionist, Rubek's striving for truth is ultimately only a form of narcissism; the focus of his work is now a self-pitying vision of himself, surrounded by those human animals whom he despises and subjugates in his art. We must not be misled by any apparent connection between Rubek's late pretensions to "realism" and what we are accustomed to think of as Ibsen's own "realistic" style; the latter, as we have seen, is not realistic so much as impressionistic, with a tendency toward expressionism, embodying the recognition that mimetic theatrical conventions do *not* communicate a true "experience of life." The mimetic, or the avoidance of the expressionistic, in late Ibsen—like Rubek's *original* statue, which he must now learn to reaffirm—is an ideal, a proposed rallying point for human communication in a genuine and joyful form (whether or not it agrees with "experience"), thus the hope for an awakening from our "death" as the encapsulated envisioners of narrow private worlds.

The quality I am attempting to lay hold of in Ibsen is an elusive one, but the idea of opposed forces in the late plays—an expressionistic tendency then countered by a tendency that resists it and cleaves to the mimetic—can be supported by parallels with other simpler ideas that have the same basic structure plus a more easily established interpretive applicability.[3] In fact, the present argument is not strictly an interpretive one to begin with. I do not claim that the opposition of expressionistic and mimetic tendencies, or the ethical implications of that opposition, can be understood as part of the meaning of any one of Ibsen's late plays, as a kind of sudden truth revealed to the audience. My point is that Ibsen is not attempting to reveal or contain truth in the structure of the *work*, but rather is attempting to create, over the span of a number of works, a new dramatic or theatrical *idiom*, in which that stylistic tension, which is realized in the audience as the tension of immediate ethical decision, will be an ingrained characteristic. The decision in question, after all, our decision in favor of the communal or communicative over the supposedly objective or the supposed truth of experience, is not a decision that can be taken at one time and then simply allowed to determine our further existence. For the basis of communication is recognized as arbitrary, without objective validity. The act of decision, therefore, *is* itself the communicative stance in favor of which we decide, and therefore becomes invalid if it is not repeatedly and unceasingly reenacted. And the temple devoted to this needful quasi-religious reenactment is the theater, provided the theater learns to speak the language Ibsen would teach it. What is crucial is not meaning, but *style* as the token of an ethical decision repeatedly taken in the theater.

The problems inherent in the development of representational theater, in the progression from perspectivism toward expressionism, are thus at least provisionally dealt with by the envisioning of a new theater in which they function not as problems but as coordinated elements in an ethically significant structure. Ibsen's theater, understood thus, is in no sense either nostalgic or retrogressive. The impressionist critique of temporal perspective, and the expressionist

---

[3]See my *Modern Drama and German Classicism* (Ithaca, 1979), pp. 299–302, on the "dialectical" in Ibsen—an idea that is supported by arguments of Robert Brustein and Brian Johnston—and on the mutual "impairment" of individual and communal tendencies.

response to the problems of that critique, are both fully present. Even the "ego-dramatics" of expressionism remains a factor, except that now the authorial ego is detectable in the force that *opposes* expressionist style for the sake of exploiting the mimetic as a communicative medium. Without our sense of mimetic convention as representing not mere conformity, but a *free act* (hence requiring an agent, an "author"), the ethics of the late plays does not hold together. The author is no longer the source of a particular and ultimately inexpressible anguish that twists the theatrical idiom out of shape; the author has become person-as-such, the other half (with the spectator) of the decisive communicative act that constitutes the theater, the spectator's partner in a communication that has primarily only itself and its ethical value as a content. The authorial function that operates here is merely a normal presupposition in narrative, whereas in drama it must be *made to appear*, must be brought into focus, by something like Ibsen's device of creating the *counter*movement to a clear stylistic tendency.

In any case, the spectators in Ibsen's theater thus find themselves very much in the situation of *readers*, confronted with an authorial person whose individual peculiarities, in the very process of being identified, must be recognized as masks, forms of self-presentation, behind which that person itself retreats toward the quality of person-as-such, or intention or meaning as such. Ibsen's theater is *a theater of readers*—but not in the sense that Szondi might have given this formulation, not as if the dramatic theater were here contaminated with qualities properly belonging to the "epic" or narrative genres. For Ibsen's theater is still strictly and traditionally a theater, a place of communal ritual. When we actually read those late plays in a book, we are simply readers, whereas for the spectator, in the theater, the situation of being a reader in this sense (communicating directly with an "author") is *exceptional* and thus the potential object of an entirely radical reflection. In particular, I claim that *the ethics of reading* is at issue here, the accomplishment of reading not as an individual exercise but as a communal and community-forming act. I stress the idea of "accomplishment." The actual reader, in the contemplative solitude that is normally our state when reading, can perhaps be made to understand in the abstract that the conscious self-adjustments he or she undertakes in reading may be regarded as a social act, a decision for the communicative. But that decision becomes more than a mere abstraction, is actually accomplished, actually happens here and now, only in the theater as Ibsen imagines it, only when the individual *discovers* himself or herself a reader

while actually participating, together with other people, in a concrete communicative endeavor.

4.

Ibsen the socially oriented artist, intent on understanding and
communication; Strindberg the self-preoccupied expressionist, rescuing himself from insanity only by the repeated effort of re-creating
his tortured inner life in the cool material of art: the argument so far
thus flatters some common opinions on the two men. But I contend
that the resistance to expressionism, hence also the authorial function, as in Ibsen, is found in Strindberg as well, and in an even
stronger form. Strindberg directly proposes a need for resistance to
the expressionistic in his preface to *A Dream Play*, when he speaks of
the dreamer's need to awaken, to rejoin and be reconciled with
reality. The description of the dream play as a type, in that preface,
reads like an expressionist manifesto: space and time are exploded
or overcome in the theater; mental or inner realities assume physical
shapes; the stage becomes the projection of a single governing consciousness. But still, we are told, even from the point of view of that
governing consciousness, ordinary daylight reality is preferable to
the dream or expressionist vision.

This tendency toward what appears in Ibsen as the ethically based
avoidance of expressionism is also discernible in the very fabric of
Strindberg's expressionist style. *To Damascus III*, for example, is still
basically expressionist. The scenic visions are obviously symbolic;
shapes and spaces, especially in act 3, scene 1, are permitted to
change fantastically in accordance with the Stranger's inner needs;
entrances and exits are determined not by external causes but by the
development of moods and thoughts in the central figure. But a
number of touches are stylistically incongruous. The Tempter, for
instance, who of all the characters is most exclusively a projection of
the Stranger's inward state, is suddenly endowed, in act 3, scenes 1
and 4, with a detailed past history, as if he were a human being in
his own right. It is as if the dream were struggling back toward
reality, as if the mental figments were striving to reveal themselves
as real entities after all, as if the expressionistic were turning away
from itself toward the mimetic. Or we think of Caesar, who is introduced in *To Damascus I* as a projection of the Stranger's monomania,
but who now, as the Pilgrim, also receives his own three-dimension-
al being. Indeed, the whole use of plot complications in *To Damascus*

bears thinking about. That there had once been a relation between the Confessor and the Lady, or that the Stranger and the Physician had known each other as boys, tends to make the work's apparent expressionistic structure not more cohesive but less so. The symbolic or philosophical connections among these characters are quite sufficient to bear the weight of the work's development; if the work were merely expressionistic, the connections via past history would be superfluous. The function of those connections is thus antiexpressionistic; they repeatedly suggest the possibility that the dream is merely a dream, the possibility that *all* the inner connections that make up the play's desperately pessimistic philosophical structure are merely the morbid mental distortions of simple facts in a solid real world to which we might conceivably awaken. Plot complication is here a counterforce to the expressionist conviction that our world is never anything but our own mental construction.

Still more significant is the nature of time in *To Damascus III*. In Parts I and II of *To Damascus*, time is treated expressionistically; the suggestion of chronological reversibility or circularity is prominent, and inconsistent action sequences are made to collide. But in Part III, despite the generally expressionistic style, time becomes strictly linear and cumulative. The action begins at the foot of a mountain and ends at the top, if with some delay. Earlier scenes, to the extent necessary, are recollected in scenes that follow, and later scenes are prepared for in what precedes. Things happen one after the other, building toward the conclusion. And it is clear that this relatively mimetic ordering of time is related to the development of the Stranger's character; as the Stranger grows toward self-conquest, the time in which he lives straightens itself out into something approaching a conventional idea of time as progression. The counterforce operating against expressionism, in Strindberg as in Ibsen, is thus basically ethical in nature. The existence of a reality that is more than just the anguished projection of ourselves, the operancy of reality as a medium of communication and understanding, may not be taken for granted; such reality arises only as the result of an ethical growth or resolve on our part.

As in the case of Ibsen, moreover, the commitment to a stylistic development in the direction of expressionism is not merely retracted. Precisely the movement *away* from expressionism in the temporal structure of *To Damascus III* is still itself an expressionist feature of the work, a quality of style understood to be the manifestation of subjective processes in a fictional character, in that it reflects the Stranger's growing self-mastery. Like Ibsen, Strindberg thus uses expressionist technique as a means of dealing with the very problems it generates, and so seeks to preserve in dramatic style the epistemological insight that produces expressionism in the first place. And like Ibsen, he employs to this end a strategy that involves the introduction of ethical categories into the aesthetic and epistemological domain of style.

The sense of a struggle between expressionist style and ethical or communicative resolve becomes central in Strindberg's later development. In some plays it is perfectly obvious, as in *Easter*, where Lindkvist's sensible directness and generosity dissipate the atmosphere created by our sense of his shadow as a relentless avenging force in Elis's inner life. In some plays, for example *To Damascus*, it is woven more subtly into the artistic texture. And in some plays it is elaborated in the direction of a new style. The basic opposition in *A Dream Play*, for example, is between the visionary and the practical, between the claims of the Poet and those of the Attorney, between a world of truth, where the dreams of poetry are more real than reality itself, and a world of cause and effect, where coal heavers, lawsuits, and university faculties are at home. It is suggested repeatedly, however, that precisely the world of cause and effect, in which we are miserable, is the indispensable vehicle of our true being, that only suffering can impel us toward truth; and this idea must be applied to the work's form. What we see on the stage, after all, is a poetic vision; its expressionist style insists upon its freedom from the laws of space, time, and causality. But rather than make use of its freedom, rather than turn away from the world of our misery, the play does exactly the opposite; like the Daughter of Indra, who descends to earth by free choice, the play freely chooses to focus on the harsh reality of cause and effect, of senseless repetition, of imbecility in the form of strict logic. And it is this choice that is suggested to *us* as an ethical imperative. If we open the door and attempt to experience truth directly, we discover nothing; we must choose freely the way of suffering, the real world composed of necessities and conventions that never answer our inner needs, for only in this way can we progress beyond the narrow darkness of the self. When we awaken from the theatrical "dream," we shall find ourselves in exactly the same intolerable reality that the play has sketched; and yet, as Strindberg suggests in his preface, our awakening will still represent a step upward, beyond the tormenting expressionist fluidity of the stage vision, toward something that has become more solid and communicable by virtue of the knowledge—which we receive precisely from the vision's expressionist quality—that it must be our free, arbitrary choice.

Thus the tension between expressionist and mimetic styles, as it appears in Ibsen and even in *To Damascus,* has in a sense been left behind; but the idea of an ethically founded affirmation of the real is unaltered. Strindberg is now aiming for something new, but without turning his back on the complex of problems and responses involved in the development from a perspectivist to an impressionist and then toward an expressionist dramatic style.

5.

I use the term "cubism" in a relatively narrow sense, to refer to the artistic technique by which different aspects of an object or scene are combined into a single cohesive composition. When we observe a cubist work, we find ourselves occupying, at the same time, several *different* points of view with respect to the same object; and I take it that this exercise is meant to reveal the true nature of our perception of space. We do not "see" space as that series of receding planes which the perspective painter constructs, but neither is there quite so much discontinuity between our actual perceptions and our awareness of space as the impressionist or the expressionist imagines. Our awareness of space, for the cubist, is simply our *knowledge* that different points of view exist with respect to the object we are observing, a knowledge that is fully integrated with our sense experience, not merely abstract. "Seeing" an object already *means* recognizing its situation in space, which in turn *means* envisaging, or in effect "seeing," its other possible aspects. Cubist art redoubles for us a mental process we always engage in anyway. In the mere act of seeing, we repeatedly create the same kind of artistic synthesis that a cubist creates on the canvas. We do not *first* see an image and *then* infer other aspects of the object, but rather we combine the supposedly original and supposedly only implied aspects of the experience into a mental composition (like the artist's physical composition) which is so thoroughly unified that we have the impression of simply "seeing" an object in space.

If these ideas are accepted as a working definition of cubism—and I make no claims concerning their validity in art history—then cubism has in common with impressionism and expressionism the recognition that space is essentially a mental construct, not a directly perceived reality. But whereas the impressionist thinks of space primarily in terms of its unverifiability in perception, and whereas the expressionist shows space as an involuntary projection of our inner life, the cubist regards space as a repeated intellectual or artistic *achievement* on our part, comparable to the achievement of creating a unified composition from different points of view. Thence it follows that something like cubism in drama, a stylistic correlative to the idea of the simply real as an *achievement* of ethical resolve, would provide a radical solution to the problem of dramatic style as both Ibsen and Strindberg encounter it.

The solutions we have already discussed are ingenious and significant. But they have the effect, so to speak, of shifting the *scene* of dramatic style from the particularity of the work into the generality of history. To understand the play of force and counterforce that arises from the thought behind expressionism, even to be aware of that interplay, we must already understand in detail the historical situation of expressionism. The history of dramatic style has itself become the shape of dramatic style (which to some extent is always the case with artistic styles, but not in the relatively crude sense that a particular view of stylistic history is needed to read the present style as an ethical message). It is this crudity—which must lead ultimately to the swamping of the very concept of style by that of message, hence to a reductive idea of communication as message-transmission, hence to the collapse of precisely that concept of communication which *is* the message of the counterexpressionistic tendency—that compels Ibsen to concentrate on the development of an idiom rather than the articulation of a meaning. For Ibsen's new theatrical idiom, by its very nature *as* an established idiom (assuming it were successfully established and accepted), would be pregnant, so to speak, with its historical filiation, yet without needing to exhibit that filiation on the level of message. The transition from stylistic history to communicative ethics would already have been negotiated, and would with every performance be renegotiated, in the idiom's very quality of being established for the community.

Even here, however, there are difficulties. For the success of Ibsen's theatrical enterprise would also in a sense entail its failure. The meaning of any particular work, at the hypothetical goal of the process, would be fully absorbed into the character of the idiom (as happens, but not yet fully, in Ibsen's own last plays), which means that the tension between work and idiom, or between text and theater, would vanish. Thus the quality of drama as drama (as a form at once both literary and theatrical) would vanish, and this event not only makes nonsense of the development that produces it, but is also irreconcilable with the constitutive function of what I have called Ibsen's "theater of readers." The theater would become *nothing but* ritual, and the principal meaning of any work, being contained in the idiom, would be independent of anything articulated in the work itself—more or less as the meaning of the mass is independent of the content of the homily.

A response to this difficulty would be cubism. If a cubist drama is possible, then its style will not allude historically to expressionist style, but will replace it. Temporal experience will appear as a mental creation, but no longer as an (at best) involuntary or (at worst) solipsistic mirroring of the individual. It will have the character, rather, of an objectifiable artistic achievement, and this character will satisfy the ethical imperatives of communicativeness and self-conquest that become stylistically crucial for Ibsen and Strindberg. There is already a movement toward such cubism in *A Dream Play,* where the sense of the vision as an individual's convulsive self-projection is much less pronounced than in *To Damascus.* The Daughter of Indra is less the absolute center of the vision that turns about her than the Stranger is of his vision; the vision, while still expressionistic, is shifted in the direction of the objective. Or we think perhaps of the change of perspectives between Foulgut and Faircove, which suggests spatial cubism. But in a fully developed dramatic cubism, cubism in the medium of time, not space, it seems clear that the "aspects" of an object or event will include its past, present and future, and that the effect of cubist style will be to remind us that when we perceive something as existing in time, what we really do is create a unified artistic composition, essentially a dramatic composition, that integrates those aspects with one another. How will such a style work in drama? It has been suggested that the shift in focus from imagery and experience toward something more like pure structure characterizes a relatively cohesive tendency in modern literature that can be compared to cubism;[4] but such a focus on the structural will not by itself neces-

---

[4]Walter H. Sokel, *The Writer in Extremis* (Stanford, 1959), designates "cubism" as one of "three schools of modernism" (p. 30), the others being surrealism and expressionism. In particular, "Cubism aims at 'surreality' and musicalization primarily by intellectual means. It is more radically experimental than Surrealism, but at the same time much more objective. . . . It emphasizes the structural element rather than the striking visual detail. Literary 'cubism' experiments with language rather than with imagery and metaphor" (p. 29).

sarily satisfy the ethical demands that arise in Ibsen's and Strind-berg's development. Rather than attempt an abstract answer to the question of dramatic cubism, let us turn directly to Strindberg's last plays.

In *The Ghost Sonata*, as in *The Dance of Death*, the past is thoroughly obscure. When Hummel describes to Arkenholz the complicated relations among the people in the apartment house, we naturally expect analytic drama in the manner of Ibsen's *Ghosts*, in which all the past complications are delicately coordinated and brought to bear, in a kind of crescendo, on the present action. But actually, only the fact that the Young Lady is Hummel's daughter has any direct influence on what might loosely be termed the plot. The rest of the past and present complications serve mainly as a general atmo-spheric explanation of why the "ghost suppers" take place, and of the Young Lady's *taedium vitae*. There are any number of strong hints about the past that are never developed: Johansson's history, for example, and the Baron's career as a jewel thief. And at the moment when Hummel is about to lay everything out, he is sent off to the closet to die.

In *The Dance of Death* the obscurity of the past is associated impres-sionistically with our understanding that the past is really nothing more than an idea that shapes itself differently in each person's mind. Thus, even without knowing it in detail, we still sense that the past determines the present in a relatively logical manner, via people's evolved attitudes, just as we sense depth in an impression-ist painting even without being able to compare exactly the scale of receding planes. In *The Dance of Death*, the past still exerts its influ-ence from a position as it were behind the present; and in *The Ghost Sonata* this is no longer the case. Here the logical or chronological relation between past and present is broken. The scattered details that we do learn do not operate as limits or causes, but affect the present action only by way of atmosphere; the past is thus simply fused with the present, as a mysterious but inexhaustible source of suffering, like the household servants in the life of the Young Lady. "I'm going now—but I am staying just the same," says the Cook (p. 491),[5] and it is just so with the past, which stays even in its going. The implied depth of impressionism, with past behind present, is replaced by an immediate fusion, as full-face and profile might be fused in a cubist painting.

---

[5]*The Ghost Sonata* and *The Great Highway* are quoted from August Strindberg, *Eight Expressionist Plays*, trans. Arvid Paulson (New York, 1965).

The Ghost Sonata is a cubist tragedy. It has an ethical dimension that appears especially in the words of the Mummy: "But I can stop time—I can wipe out the past and undo what has been done—but not with bribery and not with threats . . . but through suffering and repentance" (p. 484). Cubist style, the fusion of present and past, suggests the possibility of moral freedom, of breaking the apparently unbreakable causal relation between past and present. The past is still with us, like the Milkmaid in the doorway or the ghosts around the table; and yet it has also in a sense been "undone," for it is no longer a distant and unalterable determinant of the present. It is no longer "behind" us, no longer out of reach, no longer simply that dread "It was" which Nietzsche's Zarathustra calls the greatest enemy of the will, but rather it has become fused with the present, and has thus entered the domain of our will, our moral decisiveness, after all.

The ethical dimension is not yet fully developed, however; the focus is upon the magnitude of suffering (of living in the presence of the past) by which our moral freedom is purchased. If we do not live the past uninterruptedly, and suffer for it, if we shrink from the past, as Hummel shrinks from milk wagons, then the past will slip away from us, out of our control, and again become a distant, irresistible determining force in our existence. That this, moreover, is a general law of life, not merely a result of actual guilt, is shown by the final scene between the Young Lady and the Student. Hummel attempts to rescue his daughter from the suffering of the ghost family by rescuing her from the retributive logic of time, to which end he seeks out Arkenholz, the Sunday's child, for whom past and future, the Milkmaid and the collapsing house, are immediate realities. What Hummel does not understand is that the state of being rescued from time, of living in the unchanging immediacy of the past, is *already* the very substance of his daughter's suffering, as of the Mummy's and of the other ghosts'. Therefore the appearance of Arkenholz, with his relentless candor about the true nature of human life, only makes the Young Lady's condition intolerable to the extent of destroying her. Either we live chronologically, at the mercy of time and causality and retribution—like Hummel, who does not understand that any other possibility exists—or else we achieve freedom in the immediate presence of the past, by suffering unbearably: these alternatives describe the whole of the human condition as seen in the mirror of cubist tragedy.

6.

But tragedy as represented by *The Ghost Sonata* does not realize the whole potential of cubist style. Only *The Great Highway*, it seems to me, develops fully the ethical force from which dramatic cubism is born. There are a number of clear points of contact between this play and *The Ghost Sonata*. The idea of controlling someone, of "taking" or stealing a very self, by knowing about it, and especially by knowing about its past, is prominent in both works. In both there are a number of references to possible plot complications that are rooted in the past but now lead nowhere, thus producing a sense of a breakdown in the causal relation between past and present, hence the possibility of fusion. Both works are basically cubist in style. But *The Great Highway* incorporates a more complete ethical justification of cubism.

At least three of the other main figures, first of all, are in some way identical with the Hunter, expressionist projections of him. In the case of the Wanderer—who appears when the Hermit asks the Hunter, "Who are you?" (p. 413)—this relation is obvious, especially since the Hunter later identifies himself metaphorically with the Wandering Jew. But the case of the Japanese leads directly into the work's complex time structure. The Japanese says he has been living in Tophet for more than fifteen years, which would mean, if time operated logically, that he had been there when the Hunter had made a public spectacle of himself. Yet he seems to know nothing whatever of this event, or of the Hunter's later efforts to expose Möller; he acts as if he had never before detected a spark of true humanity in Tophet. And the Hunter, even though the spot represented on stage had been one of his haunts, and even though he remembers the other shops vividly, apparently has no recollection of the tea shop or its owner. Clearly we are meant to be puzzled by this anomaly, for the exact number of years separating the various events is mentioned no less than three times in scene 4. And it must occur to us, then, that if the conversations between the Hunter and the Japanese were taking place, say, thirteen or fourteen years in the past, *before* the Hunter's crisis, the two men's unawareness of each other's existence would be no problem. But these conversations are also made continuous with the conversations between the Hunter and Möller, which definitely belong to the present. Thus, at least on a relatively superficial level, a sense of fusion between past and present is created.

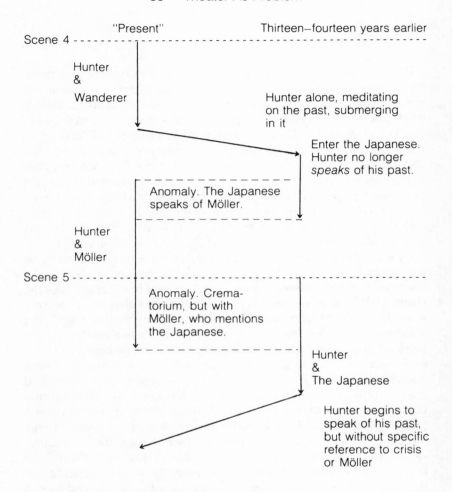

"Present"   Thirteen–fourteen years earlier

Scene 4

Hunter
&
Wanderer

Hunter alone, meditating
on the past, submerging
in it

Enter the Japanese.
Hunter no longer
speaks of his past.

Anomaly. The Japanese
speaks of Möller.

Hunter
&
Möller

Scene 5

Anomaly. Crema-
torium, but with
Möller, who mentions
the Japanese.

Hunter
&
The Japanese

Hunter begins to
speak of his past,
but without specific
reference to crisis
or Möller

In any case, the association of the Japanese with the Hunter's past, in another way, is made by the Hunter himself when he says to Möller that he had "committed hara-kiri" twelve years ago (p. 441). If the Japanese is not a real figure from the past, then at least his ritual suicide is the reenactment of an event in the personal past of the Hunter. The Japanese *is* the Hunter at an earlier stage of his life, and the significance of this form of identification becomes clear when we recognize that it applies to the Wanderer as well. The Hunter himself had once been trapped into an unsatisfactory marriage; he had apparently played out the early phases of his love at exactly the spot where the Wanderer is ensnared; and at the beginning of scene 6 he implies that he, like the Wanderer, had known in advance the disastrous absurdity of the situation in which he had been involving himself. In the Wanderer, as in the Japanese, the Hunter encounters an epoch of his own past self; and those curious conversations between them, where each repeatedly takes words out of the other's mouth, are a dramatization of the inner interwovenness of past and present. In our words, in our very thoughts, we are constantly forestalled by a ghostly intruder who is insistently identical with ourselves, yet still also intractably alien, alien in its very familiarity, which is the familiarity of our own at once completed and uncompleted past. (There is, to be sure, a similar conversation in scene 2, with the Girl, who is apparently *not* a projection or past state of the Hunter. I will take up this point later, in discussing the alterity of the Self and the corresponding nonalterity of the Other.)

The third figure who represents an element of the Hunter's past is Möller the Murderer. Only by way of this identification does the Hunter's tirade make any sense, in which he enumerates acts and achievements for which Möller took the credit and he the blame. Möller is that component of the self which (like Hummel, another murderer) lives chronologically, affirms its achievements, strives forward in time, attempts to leave the past behind; the Hunter, like the Mummy, is that component which lives its past uninterruptedly and suffers for it, thus renewing itself and "shaking off" the "vermin" of guilt (as Möller puts it, p. 442), but only at the price of unceasing anguish. The Wanderer, then, is the Hunter's inevitable past entanglement in the world, despite his foreknowledge of what such entanglement would lead to; Möller is the Hunter's actual participation in society, his attempt to fashion an identity for himself by occupying a solidly determined position with respect to others, thus in effect using others for his own ends and so robbing them of *their* identities, as it were murdering them; and the Japanese is the Hunter's hara-kiri, his anguished crisis of self-appraisal, self-rejection, and self-renewal.

To the extent that we merely recognize other figures as projections of the Hunter, however, even if we identify them as belonging to the Hunter's past, we are still treating the work as if it were expressionist, not yet cubist. In *A Dream Play* and *The Ghost Sonata*, again, the sense of cubist style arises precisely from a decentering or unfocusing of the structure of projections grouped about a main figure; and this type of decentering is carried out even more strongly in *The Great Highway*. What makes this play cubist, rather than expressionist, is that the principal projections themselves, in the pattern they form and in their operation, constitute an analysis of the whole idea of temporal experience, an analysis that does *not* preserve the integrity of the self on any level. The expressionist projections function here as *objective* or impersonal temporal aspects because, in their quality as projections, they unmask the problematics of the very concept of a "projection" or a "temporal aspect" relative to a given subjective or personal center.

In particular, I maintain that the Wanderer represents *the past as such*, the entrapment, by the world, of the supposedly free or undetermined or "wandering" self, that entrapment which never *actually* happens because it has always *already* happened, because the very idea or experience of the self includes the idea or experience of its determination, its having been entrapped or entangled in a world, because that original free self, which first *becomes* entangled, is never our actual self, but always merely a projection or image which, for all we know, could as well be fiction as recollection. The past, that is, is the explanatory myth-of-origin with respect to our experience of an unaccountably entangled condition, and the Wanderer embodies this myth. He represents what we always *mean* by "the past" in the first place. And once this is understood, it becomes clear, correspondingly, that the Japanese represents what we always *mean* by "the future," namely, the vision of an eventual disentangling of self from world, an eventual reattainment of the mythical free self, an eventual state that can become real—though not within our experience—only in the ever impending future event of our death. If the past, in our relation to it, assumes the quality of myth, then the attitude of hope or resolve with which we approach the future is a form of ritual, reducible ultimately to the ritual of hara-kiri.

The role of Möller in this pattern has to do with the idea of *the present as such*. For the present, suspended between regret for the past and resolve or hope for the future, is not the center, but precisely the negative or enemy of the self, "the one we do not want to be." The past as such is the (fictional or mythical) process of our becoming determined, the future as such is the (mortal or ritual) process of our escaping determination; and the present as such, accordingly, is the *state* of being determined, of being entrapped in fixed relations to other people—which relations necessarily also determine those other people, and so as it were "murder," for them as well, that free or original self which is the object of both regret and desire. The present as such, whether we will or no, is thus also the state of being a murderer. I say, however, only that the figure of Möller "has to do" with the present as such, for the situation is evidently complicated by the figure of the Hunter, and by Möller's distinctness from him.

This complication is both explained and developed by yet another, by the suggestion of *reversibility* in the categories of past and future. The Japanese, who represents future as such, is also the single figure who is made to belong most completely to the Hunter's *past*, by the chronological anomalies in scenes 4 and 5 and by the motif of his death. The Wanderer, on the other hand, who represents past as such, is also clearly projected into the Hunter's *future*. He and the Hunter agree in scene 5 on the inevitability of their meeting again; and at the end of the play the Hunter is on his way back to the Hermit, where he had first met the Wanderer. Thus, moreover, a sense of temporal circularity is introduced—the first scene could easily follow the last—which implies, from another direction, an interchange of past and future.

But the reversibility of past and future has to do here mainly with the distinction between the self as subject and the self as object. The past-as-such (happening of determination) and the future-as-such (escape from determination) are past and future, respectively, from the point of view of the state of *being* determined, which is the present self considered as an object. The self as subject, however, is precisely that free or undetermined component of the self which, in the process of self-consciousness, takes the self as its object, and in so doing detaches itself from (occupies a conscious distance from) the object-quality of the self. It follows that the future-as-such, from the point of view of the self as subject, becomes the *past*, since an escape from determination must be posited as the act by which the present (free) subject has constituted itself to begin with, vis-à-vis the determined object that it contemplates. The very nature of the self-aware subject, contemplating in memory a determined self that it has been identical with, yet is now detached from (in a position to be dissatisfied with, as the Mummy and the Hunter are dissatisfied), involves the idea of an escape from determination as its founding act. And the past-as-such, the happening of determination, from the point of view of the strict subject clinging precariously to its freedom, to its quality as nonobject, becomes a constantly impending and threatening *future*. Indeed, the process of self-consciousness itself, by which the subject is constituted, is also an act of self-objectification (a constant entering of precisely the *free* subject into the quality of object) that makes that threatening future inevitable.

Now we can understand the relation between the Hunter and Möller as aspects of the present. Möller is the present self as object, which in its own determinedness entails the related determination or "murder" of other people. The Hunter is the self as subject, doomed to unending self-dissatisfaction, doomed never to be "the one I longed to be" (p. 456)—doomed in fact never to be "one" at all, in the sense of one determined entity—yet also preserved *as* a free subject by precisely that doom. The style of *The Great Highway*, at least in its representational aspect, is thus strictly cubist, not expressionist. The mere showing of past or future relative to a central figure does not necessarily overstep the limits of the mimetic, or of the expressionistic, depending on the extent to which that past or future is recognized as a subjectively conditioned vision. What *The Great Highway* presents, however, is a working model of the ceaselessly dynamic constitution of past and future as experiences, hence of the very structure of our living in time, in the same way that cubist painting analyzes our being and perceiving in space.

From the point of view of . . .	the past is . . .	the future is . . .
Self as object (Möller)	past-as-such, happening of determination (Wanderer)	Future-as-such, escape from determination (Japanese)
Self as free subject (Hunter)	separation from determined self, from self as object of consciousness (Japanese)	threat of determination, operant in self-consciousness as self-objectification (Wanderer)

There is, moreover, an ethical component to this model, in the figures of the Hermit and the Tempter, who represent the choice between what I will call *living for* the self as subject and *living for* the self as object. The latter alternative, the acceptance of one particular determined existence as a form for the self, is the tempting prospect of indulging and enjoying our subjectivity by setting a determinate end to the tension, the problem, the anguish of self-consciousness. The individual still suffers, as Möller does from his conscience, but his suffering is not the whole, knowing, self-imposed and therefore compoundedly self-reproachful suffering of the human condition as experienced by the Hunter, who cannot accept determinacy even to the extent of being photographed or purchasing a seashell. Living for the self as subject, on the other hand, is an implacable insistence upon the strictest freedom conceivable (whether or not one is verifiably or demonstrably "free"); it is not so much the making of a choice as the keeping open of choice, of tension, of anguish. And it is this paradoxically less "selfish" alternative, this endless decision-against-decision, in which the audience of *The Great Highway* is implicated. Just as the spectator at Ibsen's late plays is implicated in the communicative resolve that produces a resistance to expressionist style, so the spectator of *The Great Highway,* by having the maddeningly complex dynamics of temporal existence unfolded before his or her eyes in a kind of diagram on the stage, is implicated in the ethical attitude (living for the self as subject) that repeatedly confronts us with just that hopeless labyrinth.

Nor does it follow, incidentally, that this argument now expressionistically centers the structure of *The Great Highway* after all, by focusing it upon the Hunter. The Hunter—in the significance of self-as-subject, or of "living for" the self as subject—*is* the play's center, but only, so to speak, "under erasure." For to understand the Hunter as representing self-as-subject is to understand a contradiction, to recognize the strict or free subject in the one form it cannot assume, that of a representable object. Or perhaps it is this contradiction itself that represents the free subject, as the victim of an inexorable process of self-objectification, whereupon the focus of representation has been shifted in the direction of the spectator, who himself, in the very process of understanding the representation, now enacts or undergoes what is represented. And this shift, in turn, does not result in the establishment of a new ultimate center for the artistic structure, except insofar as the center is now constituted by an incessant shift or loss of center. State or center thus constantly disintegrates into process or paradox. And the same applies to the ethical notion of living for the self as subject, which, paradoxically, entails a condition of unceasing indecision between itself and its own opposite, between the Hermit and the Tempter.

7.

I contend that the cubist ethics of *The Great Highway,* like the antiexpressionist ethics of late Ibsen, is at base a *communicative* ethics, an ethics governed by the need for a ground of genuine contact with other individuals. We must recognize first that the basic relations among the Hunter, Möller, the Wanderer, and the Japanese are established on three separate levels. On level 1, the four figures together (along with the Hermit and the Tempter) form a dynamic model of temporal experience as seen *from within*. In facing this model, in the theater, it is as if we were engaged in analyzing *our* experience in time; to the extent that the model refers to the Hunter's experience, since he represents the one type of life (living for the self as subject) for which such experience unfolds in its full complexity, the Hunter is a projection of the spectator. On level 2, however, each of the three other figures is simply identical with the Hunter, in representing a past epoch or crisis in his life. The stage in this sense offers us a cubist portrait, a model of the manner in which we "see" an individual (the Hunter) in time, not by knowing his past in the form of a linear history, but by seeing him in the actual multiple presence of his past. These two levels of structure, moreover, are clearly dependent on one another. Without the experience of the full complexity of our own situation in time (level 1), we have no basis on which to form the cubist perception of another individual (level 2). But on the other hand, our own experience of time does not unfold fully without contact with others, without the possibility of reducing other individuals to objects that bear fixed relations to the self-as-object (Möller); or rather, our own experience of time depends on both the presence and the *avoidance* of this possibility, on our ability to take people as something *other* than mere objects, which is to say, on our practice of cubist perception. We cannot resolve to live for the self as subject (i.e., fully experience our temporality) if the alternative (murder, or living for the self as object) is not available to be decided against.

And on level 3, finally, the Wanderer, the Japanese, and Möller are presented as individuals clearly distinguishable from the Hunter. The Hunter's past, to the extent that we learn of it, could not have happened without Möller's having functioned as a separate individual; and the reaction of the citizens of Tophet to the Hunter's question appears to confirm what he says about Möller. The Wanderer is given a specific location in the chronology of the Hunter's life by the revelation (assuming we can credit it) that the Waitress is the Hunter's daughter, which places a definite number of years between the two men's entrapment in marriage. And the Japanese is distinguished by the details of his culture and language, which give clear individual contours to his being. As with Caesar and the

Tempter in *To Damascus*, we are shown figures who are obviously expressionist projections of the central character, yet also individuals in their own right. But in *The Great Highway* there is none of the tension between different styles that had characterized the earlier play. In *To Damascus III* expressionist time laboriously struggles back toward mimetic time, whereas in *The Great Highway* not only the incompatibility of the Hunter's chronology with that of the Japanese, but also the chronological conflict between scene 6 and scenes 4 and 5, and the motif of chronological circularity, maintain an expressionistic, strongly antimimetic quality of style to the very end. In *The Great Highway*, then, mimetic style is not even a possibility; and the question of the significance of those figures who hover between independent individuality and the state of subjective figments must therefore be raised yet again.

Level	Hunter	Möller	Wanderer	Japanese
1	present, self-as-subject	present, self-as-object	past-as-such (subject's future)	future-as-such (subject's past)
2	central figure	self-definition in society = murder	entanglement with others = self-loss	self-rejection, hara-kiri = self-renewal
3	individual	[	other individuals	]

Once we understand the structure of *The Great Highway*, however, that question is not especially difficult. We have already seen that from the point of view of the spectator, levels 1 and 2 (so to speak) are superimposed, that the experience of our own situation in time is equivalent to the act of cubist perception by which we recognize others as temporal beings. From the point of view of the Hunter, levels 1 and 3 are analogously superimposed; for it is in relation to the Hunter that Möller, the Wanderer, and the Japanese arrange themselves into a model of subjective temporal dynamics, while at the same time the Hunter confronts them as distinct individuals in the play's action. And levels 2 and 3, in turn, taken together, yield a kind of detached expressionist diagnosis of the Hunter's plight, of his inability to distinguish clearly between other people, as they themselves are, and the tormenting projections of crises recurring in his own subjective existence.

A single main theme runs through all these structural possibilities: the idea of a relation of superimposition, of mutual dependence, interwovenness, boundary blurring, a relation tending ultimately toward *indifference*, between the perception of self and the
perception of others. The last two superimpositions mentioned
above (levels 1 and 3, 2 and 3) can themselves be superimposed in
this sense, for they combine a view of the Hunter's situation from
inside, from his own perspective, with an objective diagnosis of that
situation. And it follows, I think, that in *The Great Highway*, the
hovering of dramatic figures between identity and alterity with respect to a perceiving subject (whether the Hunter or the spectator)
no longer suggests a striving toward mimetic style, a struggle to
awaken from the dream, but rather reflects a general epistemological condition of our existence. Such hovering characterizes *all*
human beings as we encounter them in "real" life. Other people
always are, at the same time, both reflections of our own self and
strictly distinct persons. This idea incorporates the expressionist
tenet that all reality is essentially a projection of the self, while also
taking account of the Hunter's perception that social reality, our
encounter with other people, nevertheless always confuses us, that
our very self is stolen from us when we deal with others, that despite all our efforts to remain spectators, we are always drawn into
the stage-action of life and, in the process, forget who we are (p.
413). This is why the windmills are named Adam and Eve; no sooner
do two human beings exist than they interfere with each other, take
the wind from each other's sails. Other people, as we experience
them, are always projections of ourselves, the continued presence of
our own past, the unfolding of our own temporality; but they are
also always "other," alien, confusing, challenging.

This state of affairs—that reality, in the very process of expressing
and reflecting us, also confuses us—implies the presence of a fundamental confusion or disharmony in our own being. And while this
disharmony may be regarded as a defect (in the Hunter's last words,
for example, about not being able to be the one he had longed to be),
it may also be regarded as a virtue, a source of human stature. For it
is clear that "murder" as practiced by Möller, the insistence upon the
object quality of others in relation to the self-as-object, is precisely
the *denial* of that hovering quality in others which reveals our own
defectiveness and confusion. The Mummy in *The Ghost Sonata*,
moreover, refers to the same defective inner state, the state of not
being the one we want to be, when she claims that she and her
fellow ghosts have the *advantage* over Hummel (the murderer) of
being able to experience dissatisfaction with themselves; or we think

of the portrait gallery in *To Damascus III*, where the Stranger is urged to accept and affirm man's two-headedness. That other people are "other" in the very process of being images of ourselves thus corresponds not only to life lived for the self as subject, faced with the whole tormenting dynamics of temporality, but also to the capacity for suffering by which we are enabled in a sense to overcome time and live a voluntary, rather than a merely passive existence.

Again, the combination of sameness and otherness in other people reflects a basic epistemological condition of our existence. But it is not a condition we can simply *accept*; it is not a condition *for us*, in our experience, unless we achieve it by an active resolve. If we accept as merely given the otherness of others, then both self and other assume the status of *objects*—since that which is "given," that which is there to be accepted, is by definition an object—and we have committed what Strindberg calls "murder." The hovering quality of other people is then trivialized; their identity with us is reduced to our sharing the quality of a mere helpless object ("an ordinary, normal human being" [p. 453], says the Tempter), their alterity is reduced to the difference between different objects. The mere acceptance of other people's otherness is in truth not altruistic but selfish, not a social but an antisocial attitude. The realization of our defective condition as altruistic virtue (which it in truth is) requires more than acceptance; it requires an affirmative resolve that consists not in our accepting the otherness of others as given, but in our constant giving of otherness *to* others. And this action, in turn, is made up of *two moves*, exactly the two opposed moves that characterize the reception as well as the creation of cubist art (whether painting or drama). For the cubist process by which we perceive other people involves (1) the imposition of our own thought and experience, our own inference of temporal aspects, on those people, while at the same time (2) we relinquish our claim to that thought as *ours*, and instead acknowledge its effects as part of what we "see." Genuine intersubjective relations, in which "murder" is avoided, require unceasingly these combined cubist moves of self-imposition and renunciation, which are the positive enactment of our defective condition. Social existence in its fulfilled form, as a genuine ground for communication among independent subjects, is a work of cubist art constantly in the making.

And yet, what is the *aim* of the artistic endeavor by which we, as individuals, institute and maintain social existence in this sense? What I have called the giving of otherness to others can be understood as the effect of this endeavor, or as its final meaning; but if we posit it as an aim, then we have taken the other, yet again, as a kind of object. Clearly, the aim in question must be reflexive, an operation of the self upon itself that loses its object in the very act of grasping it; it must be an aim similar to the Hunter's at the very beginning: to "collect myself, my thoughts— / and be myself again . . . / the self that has been stolen" (p. 410). Or in terms we used earlier, social existence depends on the individual's aiming to live for the self as subject; the basic social virtue, the Hunter's virtue and the Mummy's, the only way to avoid "murder," is the striving to organize our own self into a cohesive unity, to integrate past with present, that the objective component of the self (the "it was") be as it were engulfed by our fully realized moral and volitional being. To the extent that we thus succeed in overcoming our subjection to time, we are also directly confronted (level 1) with the tormenting riddle of our temporality, with the tantalizing but hopeless vision of being "the one" we want to be; and the correlative to this perfected suffering in the self is our cubist experience of others (level 2), which in turn is the only genuine social or altruistic initiative of which we are capable.

Again, however, this ethics is not altruistic in the sense of advocating self-denial or even compassion. Denial of self in favor of another presupposes exactly that objective relation to both self and other which constitutes "murder"; even the subtle stirrings of a supposed compassion remain fruitless, cannot be translated into action, without generating that objective relation. The ethics of *The Great Highway*, like that of Ibsen's late plays, is a strictly *communicative* ethics, aimed at a communication that has no objectifiable content, a communication whose content is entirely exhausted in establishing the ground of communication. The social reality imitated in late Ibsen is valuable not because it is real or objective or verifiable, but solely because we carry out together the act of insisting upon it in the face of an alternative that tempts us (like Strindberg's Tempter) with its *greater* fidelity to the "experience of life." Likewise, in late Strindberg, the value of living for the self as subject lies solely in our insisting upon it together; only thus do we become and remain, for each other, the hovering cubist images that express our renunciation of those more palpable interpersonal relations which tempt us with the promise of participation in the ordinary or normal, but are in truth mere murder, the negation of community.

8.

The social component of this advocacy of intense self-preoccupation, its quality as a communicative ethics, is suggested in the action of *The Great Highway* by an exactly symmetrical pattern of incidents involving the Hunter and the Wanderer. In scene 2 the Wanderer seeks to ferret out the Girl's inmost secrets, to organize and dominate her existence by knowing it, and he fails; in scene 4 he attempts exactly the opposite, to break contact with the Waitress, to have nothing to do with her, and again he fails. The point is that we may never either approach other people too closely or sever arbitrarily our relation with them; neither the move of self-imposition nor the move of renunciation may be carried out to the exclusion of the other. That the Wanderer's blundering is possible, however, implies that the hovering cubist vision of other people, the balance between approach and separation, between self-imposition and renunciation, between identity and alterity, is a social *achievement*, as it is presented in the two contrasting scenes involving the Hunter. After the Wanderer leaves, the Hunter and the Girl do successfully approach each other, to the point of carrying on a conversation that is essentially a monologue; but they achieve this only by insisting, in what they say, on a strict separation. And the identification of the Waitress as the Hunter's daughter makes a connection with scene 6, where the Hunter, with his daughter in another form, again keeps a precarious balance between approach and separation.

The ceaseless artistic endeavor by which we strive to lay hold of our own true self is a genuine social act, not merely an exploitation of others for our own ends. Precisely by carrying out that endeavor in the way that profits us most, that brings us closest to both the whole misery and the whole merit of our condition, we also find ourselves carrying it out in such a way that it becomes a medium of communication with others, which preserves others' identity while also making contact with it. We neither dominate nor submit, but we maintain a balance between the two that enables the other person to share the *shape* of our own experience, to share precisely that keeping of balance, that double move, that quality of our experience *as a shaping act*. When we experience other people as hovering between independent individuality and the status of mental projections of ourselves, when we experience them as a cubist achievement—and only when this happens—community becomes possible, not in the sense that we know each other, but in the sense that the possibility is opened of our working in concert toward the creation of human existence as a work of art by which our subjection to time is overcome, if at the price of maximum suffering under our temporality.

In *To Damascus* and *A Dream Play* the resistance to expressionist style arises from a mistrust of the self-investigating and self-project-ing individual; the individual's preoccupation with realizing his or her own being must be overcome in favor of a more self-mastered and outward-directed attitude. But in the fully developed cubism of *The Great Highway* an entirely new ethics emerges, as a *result* of the style, not as a reason or an excuse for it. The doctrine of pity or compassion, the idea that we must deny ourselves in order to accept the feelings of others, is now rejected by the Hunter in his conversation with the Woman; indeed, it had already been rejected earlier, by implication, in scenes 2 and 3. No sooner do two human beings exist than they impede each other, like the windmills; but if we therefore resolve not to impede each other, if we insist on yielding to others, the result is mere absurdity, like the society governed by the Smith in scene 3. What we must do is not give up our quest for self-realization, but prosecute that quest with ever renewed tenacity, for then we discover that our closest approach to our own full self is itself the only possible source of genuine community. This is the meaning not only of the Hunter as a dramatic figure, and of the hovering cubist style, but also of the work's implied circularity. Precisely by resolving to return to the Hermit, to *leave* human society in favor of the ice and snow of pure self-contemplation, the Hunter is returning to the beginning of the play, whence he will *enter* human society, descend yet again into that precarious balance by which we are always in the process of creating, communally and artistically, a human world for ourselves.

And yet, even this argument, in focusing on the individual's aim, threatens to present the communal or the social, the otherness of others, as secondary, as a mere symptom or by-product of the individual's ethical resolve. Once more, therefore, as in the argument on structural levels (in the dependence of level 1 on level 2), it must be emphasized that a valid individual aim or resolve, in the terms of this ethics, cannot arise except in the presence of a community that *already* functions more or less in the sense of cubist art. There is no end to the process of creating; we never are "the one" we want to be. And yet we must always strive uncompromisingly to achieve that state. The Tempter therefore suggests to the Hunter that he *knowingly* live his life in accord with the endless circularity of his fate, by becoming Tophet's architect once again; and the Hunter drives him off, rejects his suggestion, by asserting a simple faith in "the Creator" which (we recognize) *will* lead him in a circle, down from the mountain again, in spite of himself. The Tempter suggests that the Hunter live his life as a pattern of circular return; the Hunter refuses, but in a manner that shapes his life into a pattern of circular return. This is as it must be. Our existence can never be anything more than an endless cycle of self-approach, dissatisfaction, and resumption of the quest. But this cyclic process depends precisely on our striving to go beyond it, on our faith in the absolute realizability of our true being; the process must happen *in spite* of us. For if we assent to the cycle, then we no longer fully believe in the attainability of the true self; our resolve, our commitment to the quest for the self, is then no longer strong enough to produce even the cycle, and not even an approach to true human community, to full self-realization, is then possible. *Hence the indispensability of the otherness of other people*, the dependence of level 1 on level 2, the need that society always already be there. By becoming confused about ourselves, by "forgetting who we are" *in society*—and only by this path—we also repeatedly forget the impossibility of actually attaining our true self; thus we can be moved once more to commit ourselves to the quest, which in turn makes social existence possible and leads us yet again into our salutary confusion, into the eternal cycle.

Society, moreover, functions in this manner not only in its degenerate form—where the Hunter in us rebels against the threat of being made a mere object, of having his self "stolen"–but also in its more or less perfected form. For the correlative, in our personal life, to the cubist perception of other people in a relatively communicative society, is a constant confrontedness with the whole of our temporality, a state which, if we could exist in complete isolation, would represent not temporality or contingency at all, but a maximum of self-wholeness and self-realization, a kind of divine self-presence—which cannot happen in reality. What enables this state to be itself, this living in the presence of the past, what transforms it into a condition of maximum suffering and self-dissatisfaction, is exactly its inevitable correlativity with the social, the inescapable web of relations with other people, which gives rise to the chimerical and infinitely tormenting idea of "the one" (the particular individual, measurable against others, with particular qualities and relations) who we had wanted to be and never can be.

9.

This ethics of maximum commitment to the quest for the true self, as I have said, is not merely expressible via cubist style, but a direct natural outgrowth of that style; and the result is an extraordinarily complete fusion of the ethical and the aesthetic, which to my mind represents Strindberg's culminating achievement. Modern literature in general tends to exclude prescriptive ethics from the aesthetic realm. In earlier historical ages, when (we suppose) ethical values were more widely agreed on, the ethical could be incorporated into art by a normal mimetic procedure; but modern authors, if they adopt a specific ethical position, must justify it abstractly and in effect preach it, to the detriment of their works' artistic integrity. For both Ibsen and Strindberg, however, the separation of ethics from art is a problem, not merely a fact; and the response, in both cases, is a strictly communicative ethics, an ethics aimed solely at the establishment of a ground for the type of communication, the type of community, in which a rebirth of unified ethical and aesthetic sensibilities is possible.[6] The very idea of a communicative ethics in this sense, however, has two telling consequences. First, the work's ethical purport must be entirely present, entirely contained or expressed, on the level of style or dramatic idiom, since no prior communicative ground can exist that would support a message on the level of content. And second, the new ground of communication that is envisaged can be established only by being constantly reestablished; it exists only in the process of being created or asserted anew. Otherwise the style in which it is contained ceases to be itself ethically pregnant; the ground of communication, to the extent that it is taken as preexisting, is not the goal of our ethical commitment but a mere basis for it, and the ethics in question is no longer strictly a communicative ethics. The new ground of communication in Ibsen, again, is not mimetic style as such, but rather the act, which we carry out together, of *asserting* mimetic convention in the face of its own historical untenability, in the face of an inexorable expressionist tendency that the play itself refuses to let us forget about.

We have seen, however, that these considerations bring out problems in Ibsen's enterprise. In the new dramatic idiom toward which Ibsen's late work apparently strives, the struggle between expressionist insight and mimetic convention would eventually become constant and would be the whole meaning of each work, like the struggle against sin in the mass. The result would be the end of

---

[6]This is, essentially, the problematics of Goethe's *Faust*, the idea of the work of poetry as itself constituting (or at least instituting) a new human "land," a new community that has no specific qualities except its being a community, in the sense of an ever renewed creative act on the part of its members. See my *Goethe's Theory of Poetry: "Faust" and the Regeneration of Language* (Ithaca, 1986), esp. chaps. 6–8, 11.

drama, or the return of drama to the bosom of religious ritual. But in Strindberg's late plays this problem appears to be solved. Cubist style does not require the expressionist tendency as a foil, since it is itself built on the idea of perception as a constantly repeated synthetic achievement, hence on the idea of the social as a sense of our carrying out that act together. And at least in *The Great Highway*, the problem of the absorption of content into style appears to be circumvented by the shaping of the work's content into a layered structure that does nothing but reflect and develop the stylistic quality of cubism. What we have here, then, is not merely the adumbration of an as yet unrealized dramatic idiom that will one day set the seal upon our quality as a community, but rather a huge unified dramatic ceremony in which that community, at least for a short while, *is* ecstatically realized, a ceremony whose aesthetic and ethical dimensions are indistinguishable, a work, therefore, that assumes classical proportions in its historical context.

Even the theatrical medium is exploited, in Strindberg's last plays, with a radical simplicity and efficiency. In such plays as *To Damascus* and *A Dream Play*, the theater is a kind of collective dream struggling to awaken from itself. The ethically crucial moment, for us, the audience, occurs not *in* the theater, but at the moment of our *leaving* the theater and returning to face that mundane reality which the expressionist vision has taught us to value. In *The Great Highway*, by contrast, the theater itself, as we sit in it, becomes the model of a maximally communicative society. Our sitting side by side with others, facing the stage—not facing each other, not pretending to know each other directly—corresponds exactly to the idea of a community established by each individual's striving for self-realization to the point where he or she is confronted (as the audience is by the stage vision) with that complete experience of temporality which is in truth both the goal of our individual striving and the whole of what we have in common. Indeed, to the extent that the spectator recognizes his or her *own* temporality in the stage vision, the theater not only imitates but *is* a maximally perfected human community. And our leaving the theater (or our undeniable remaining aware, during the performance, of the world outside the theater) is now not a return to reality, but merely that other aspect of true community in which we face each other, "forget who we are," become confused by the idea of "the one" we want to be, and are thus lured once more into the quest for the self by which our ground of communication is established.

And yet, for all their ceremonial completeness, Strindberg's last cubist works are still infected with a fundamentally problematic quality that I think we shall come to associate with drama as a type. For Strindberg's theater, like Ibsen's, can in the final analysis be considered a theater of readers. The destiny of drama, if we use Ibsen's work as a basis for speculation, is to become a ritual exercise in the ethics of reading, the ritual center, as it were the church, of a community in which reading is practiced as a genuine communal act, rather than a gratifying or at best edifying pastime for the individual. The dramatic theater, in which a story or a specific meaning is enacted, would no longer be necessary if we once knew truly how to read, if we recognized in our reading not merely a receptive process, but the constant active creating, along with others, of a ground for communication. And very nearly the same sense of drama as a form is derivable from *The Ghost Sonata* or *The Great Highway.* Is the reader, in contemplative isolation, not at least potentially a *better* recipient of these plays than the spectator in a theater? Does the situation of the reader not represent more perfectly the situation of the lonely self resolutely in quest of itself? Is this not therefore also a theater that exists mainly in order to be superseded by reading?

The drama of Ibsen and Strindberg, in other words, accepts from the outset an ancillary function with respect to literature as a whole. There can be no such thing as a perfection of dramatic form, because the very existence of drama is the symptom of a fundamental defect in the general literary situation to which it belongs, a communicative defect that interferes with perfected reading, with reading as the committed and energetically visionary participation that poetic literature appears to require of us. Is this sense of drama as an inherently imperfect form, as itself always the sign of a defect, applicable *only* to authors like Ibsen and Strindberg, only in periods of what Szondi calls "crisis," or does it have a broader theoretical validity?

CHAPTER TWO

Cinema, Theater, and Opera:
Modern Drama as
Hermeneutic Ceremony

The theater of readers in Ibsen and Strindberg is an inherently *temporary* theater, possessed by an evolutionary instinct, a kind of Nietzschean or Shavian desire to be superseded. It does not look back longingly toward the conventions of nineteenth-century narrative; it prophesies, it heralds a historical epoch in which drama will no longer be necessary, in which the condition of being a reader will be alone sufficient as the ground for a newly perfected community. But the problem of reader and theater (or of the reader *in* the theater) is not exhausted in this historical vision. In this chapter, we will approach it from a different direction.

1.

No significant work is done in the criticism of literature that does not include or presuppose a discussion of genres or types or modes, an analysis of the artistic universe into units compact enough to provide a basis for characterizing, differentiating, and comparing particular texts or features of texts. Even in the case of broad theoretical attempts to explain the artistic endeavor or the aesthetic experience as such, some basic notion of types is necessary to identify, in the first place, what the philosophical or political or psychological argument is meant to account for. But our manner of carrying out this analysis into types has undergone considerable historical change. Not only generic definitions themselves, but also the form, status, and significance of such definitions, are increasingly at issue;

55

and by the middle of the twentieth century, this development reaches something like a climax of self-critical subtlety. We think of Emil Staiger's understanding of the terms *epic, lyric, dramatic* as the "literary-critical names for fundamental possibilities of human existence as such"; or of Northrop Frye's overlaid grids of mode, genre, and radical of presentation; or of Käte Hamburger's idea of a linguistic dynamics in which literary types represent prominent structural deviations from a basic subject-object discourse of "reality statements."[1] These initiatives (and any number of others) are clearly significant; and they are also futile, at least with respect to the goal of establishing adequate and reasonably exhaustive definitions of literary types. In each case, the philosophical suppositions required by the argument are far too specific and precarious to support the idea of a structure which, if it existed, would be a prior conditioning factor in all philosophical discourse anyway. This difficulty, in the abstract, is perhaps not absolutely insurmountable; but the pattern of futility at least casts doubt on the whole notion of defining literary genres.

I think it is fair to say that as a result, definition in this area, as a foundation for understanding individual works, has now for the most part been abandoned in favor of a procedure perhaps best called *discrimination*—by which I mean not the establishment of supposedly firm boundaries between types, but rather the focus upon cases where it is evident precisely that a firm boundary cannot be drawn, and the examination, then, of the nature and significance of whatever more complex form of differentiation is insisted upon nonetheless in intellectual tradition. The problem of discrimination, for example, does not arise until we recognize clearly how uncertain the boundaries are that separate such types of writing as literature, history, philosophy, and criticism. Only then are we compelled to ask, not what literature is, but *what we mean* by literature, what sort of intellectual act is represented by our drawing of the distinctions. Only when we recognize the inadequacy of the obvious definitions of, say, autobiography, biography, biographical fiction, and the novel, are we in a position to undertake the more fruitful task of discriminating, of asking *what our stake is* in distinguishing among those types. Or to put it differently, definition is interested in boundaries, boundaries between entities presumed each to have a

---

[1]Emil Staiger, *Grundbegriffe der Poetik* (Zurich, 1946), p. 226; Northrop Frye, *Anatomy of Criticism* (New York, 1966); Käte Hamburger, *Die Logik der Dichtung* (Stuttgart, 1968), also published as *The Logic of Literature*, trans. Marilynn J. Rose (Bloomington, Ind., 1973).

nature prior to being distinguished, whereas discrimination, in the sense I mean, concerns itself with *boundary effects*, with the problematic state of affairs that accompanies the very happening of boundary, boundary considered as a primary, not a secondary event.

This manner of posing the question of genre evidently parallels the development of semiotics, of philosophical strategies for understanding "difference" as a strictly primitive notion. But I will try to avoid the complications of these strategies by insisting on the formulations I have suggested, by asking "what we mean" by drama (or any genre designation), by asking "what our stake is." For in the first place, the system of literary genres is both relatively constant as a terminology and thoroughly historical as a phenomenon. If genres—or the relations among them or the boundaries between them—had in any degree the quality of *objects*, then the terminology would not be constant, but would change radically with developments in analytic technique, like the terminology used to describe physical matter. And the nonobjectivity of genres, in turn, is obviously the nonobjectivity of the historical, of entities that *include* our own perceptual and formulative activity, and never stand over against us in a completed form. (Nor will it do to say that genres are "given by tradition"; for if we are in a position to be "given" something by a particular tradition, if we are sufficiently detached, then the tradition is not strictly ours to begin with, not a determining factor in our world-view, and so can "give" us something only in a very limited sense.) That is to say, the system of genres depends for its very existence (in a manner as undeniable as it is indeterminable) on our assent to it, on our active participation in its shaping. When we ask what a genre "is," we are always in truth asking what we have *already* "meant" by occupying a position from which the question can be raised. Hence the critical importance of boundary effects, where the illusion of objective distinguishability becomes minimal and the question of "what we mean" emerges clearly enough to be addressed.

In the second place, the particular question of drama especially favors a discussion in the terms I am proposing. For it is in relation to drama that the idea of our "stake" in literary genres comes most to the fore. The nature of our stake in the whole system of genres is probably something most of us could agree on. That system provides us with an indispensable ground of communication, or in literary terms, with a ground for the intelligibility of texts, a preunderstanding without which the process of understanding a text (or for that matter, the process of producing a text) could not even begin.[2] But this idea is relatively abstract and does not clarify the nature of our relation to any particular system or particular genre. Nor does it clarify the general questions that are already inherent in the metaphor of a "stake," especially the question of how it is permissible (or if not, then avoidable) to think of the system of genres as representing a kind of conscious decision on our part, comparable to the communicative decisions we make routinely within an existing system of genres, but subject to the impossible condition that it be not itself grounded in such a system. This is the question of origin: how can a system of genres come into being without requiring a prior system as its ground? And it implies a theoretical correlative to the vision, in Ibsen and Strindberg, of a ground of communication maintained only in the form of a constantly renewed communicative act.

There are a number of reasonable theoretical responses to this question. But my point is that the form of drama represents a response which, so to speak, is built into the system of genres itself, a focus at which the system itself takes account of a crucial difficulty in its own constitution. For the idea of our stake in specific literary genres, while extremely common, is in general also extremely abstract and tenuous, little more than a fond hope. We imagine that ancient epic was the vehicle of a type of collective identity that we begin by conceding we know nothing about from experience; we suggest that the realistic novel functions as a kind of social conscience, and in the process we show precisely our own lack of conscience, our aesthetic detachment from the social committedness we admire; we insist, with a degrading lack of both precision and conviction, that there is a somehow specially humane or humanizing force in poetry. But in the case of drama we are at least certain, on concrete evidence, *that* we have a stake in the form. For drama owes its very existence to a type of decision, to a purposeful collective expenditure of effort that is comparable to the collective decision envisaged whenever we think of our stake in genre as such, an expenditure, a decision, that is repeatedly manifested *in the institution of the theater.* Drama does not grow, slowly or organically, in the bosom of a culture or language; drama is *established,* at specific times and places, and requires not only a specialized architectural setting,

---

[2]A very clear discussion of the relation between the notions of "genre" and "pre-understanding," at least since F. D. E. Schleiermacher, is given by E. D. Hirsch, Jr., *Validity in Interpretation* (New Haven, 1973; orig. 1967), pp. 258–64. Hirsch's polemical insistence upon "authorial intention" as a primitive notion must be allowed for, however.

and not only a large number of trained personnel, but also, as a rule, considerable economic and publicity organization in the society as a whole.

At the same time, however, drama is strictly a *literary type*. A piece of writing will be immediately recognized as drama, and interpreted in the light of expectations historically associated with drama, even by a reader who has never been in a theater. In a sense (a limited sense, which we will discuss), drama can dispense with the theater, even though there would be no such thing as drama if there were not (or at least if there had not been at some time) such a thing as the theater. Drama, then, is a literary type that owes its existence to a *concrete* act of collective decisiveness, an act in which even those of us who are only spectators still participate. Nor does it matter that the actual origins of the theater are nonliterary, that the theater was not first invented for the sake of drama—although a large number of European theaters, since the Renaissance, in fact were founded for the sake of drama. If the theater were merely an extraliterary institution that literature uses for its own ends, there would be no such thing as drama—just as there is no single literary type specifically associated, in its structure, with the printing industry. The theater, rather, has been *appropriated* by drama, incorporated into the very nature of the form as a basic structural condition. As far as the literary audience is concerned, the theater belongs to drama and at least represents (even if, in strict historical fact, it is not) the concrete collective act by which drama is founded.

This representation is crucial. We still cannot say *what* our stake is in the genre of drama. In fact, no matter how exact and subtle our formulations, it is never possible to specify precisely what our stake is in *any* particular genre. An exact and satisfying answer to a question of this sort would require a metadiscourse that cannot exist, a discourse prior to the genre distinctions that ground its own intelligibility. The question is thus strictly unanswerable, but the *questioning* is of vital significance. For if we stop asking *what* our stake is in this or that genre, then we have in effect stopped knowing *that* we have a stake, whereupon the genre in question (and in the end, literature as a whole) assumes the quality of nothing but an object, and so stops being literature in the sense of a definitively human activity, *our* activity.[3] Hence the importance of what I have called

[3]The circumvention of this point keeps Austin Quigley's book (*The Modern Stage* [New York, 1985]) from being as sound in its overall structure as it is perceptive in detail. The insistence on what Quigley calls "common-core" similarities is *not* of necessity merely a "mode of categorization" of objects (p. 61). If the categorization of objects, or more especially the manner in which we commonly use words, is what we

discrimination, or the study of boundary effects, where the asking of what we mean, or what our stake is, is prosecuted. But how do we *know* to keep asking? How do we *know* that the asking of these finally unanswerable questions is worthwhile? My point is that the site or vessel of this knowledge is nothing so intangible as tradition or racial memory or the constitution of the human spirit, but exists in the domain of historical fact as the genre of drama. The representation, in the institution of the theater, of a concrete and purposeful collective act by which a literary type is founded, I contend, is our indispensable ritual *recollection* of the truth that we do have a vital stake in literary types as such. Drama, that is, is the memory and the conscience of literature.

I do not claim to have established this point yet. I do not claim even to be able to establish it conclusively, for to do so would be to know exactly what our stake is in the genre of drama. But I will develop the idea in various arguments to follow, and make, as best I can, a kind of case for it. Drama, I insist, is the church of literature, the collective ceremonial thinking of a crucially human thought that torments us by defeating in logic its own theoretical formulations, the repeated ritual enactment of the truth that the whole array of literary types—hence, by extension, the very existence of intelligibility, of communication, of a human world—is a single huge human work of art constantly in the making.

2.

And yet, from the point of view of discrimination, the case of drama presents special difficulties. Within the general area of drama—as within the general area of written or potentially spoken texts—any number of illuminating discriminations are possible.[4] But when we try to apply the technique to drama as a whole, as itself a single basic type, we encounter trouble; for the boundaries

---

are interested in, then Quigley is justified in preferring a method, for example the one suggested by Wittgenstein's "family resemblances" (pp. 60–61), which goes out of its way to accommodate "both similarity and difference." But if we treat literary genres in this way, if we do not insist on a stronger form of identity (whether or not we can achieve it), then we lose sight of the very nature of what we are talking about, of our crucial and constitutive "stake" in the genre or genres under discussion.

[4]The taxonomy of modern drama suggested in chap. 9 of my *Modern Drama and German Classicism* (Ithaca, 1979), for example, is generated by discrimination rather than definition, although this distinction is itself only groped at, in that book, by the concept of the "heuristic" (p. 314).

separating drama from other poetic types of the same order, especially the traditional boundaries with lyric and epic—curious as
this may sound—are not *sufficiently* fluid or uncertain or questionable. Strong affinities can be established, hence discriminations undertaken, between various dramatic and nondramatic genres, with
respect to such specific qualities as imagery, character, fictional
structure. But at least one primary distinguishing characteristic of
drama *as drama* does not participate in those affinities and discriminations: I mean the ontological defectiveness of the dramatic text as
merely written or printed (and merely read); I mean our sense,
when we read a dramatic text in a book, that we are not receiving
the *whole* work, that a crucial element of the work (or if one prefers,
of the work's intention) is missing in our actual experience as readers, as solitary readers conjuring up mental images in response to
the words, rather than spectators dealing with real, palpable images
and sounds in the festive atmosphere of the theater.

I have said that drama is strictly a literary type, that in a sense it
can dispense with the theater. But drama cannot obliterate our consciousness of its historical affiliation with the theater, and it is this
consciousness that produces for a modern reader the sense of ontological defectiveness I am speaking of. When we read a fictional or
expository or poetic text, we are convinced that we are receiving the
whole of what we are supposed to receive. If we detect a lack in
the text, then we assume normally that it is a technical lack, a lack in
the way the text is made, not in the way it *is*. Or if we recognize that
our own relation to the text is inadequate, then what we mean is that
we lack sufficient knowledge or training or experience, or are perhaps
just not in the right mood, to receive an intact whole that would
otherwise be available to us. The difficulty, again, does not lie in the
way the text *is for us*. But when I read a drama, when the dramatic text
is (for me) an object of reading, part of my understanding of its
quality as drama is the recognition that it *could be* (for me) something
quite different, a kind of shadowy, inferred presence governing the
action and speaking of ceremonially disguised figures in an open
space before a restrainedly festive crowd of which I would be a
member. I recognize, moreover, that if the text were now, for me, that
shadowy theatrical presence, then it would never need to be an object
of reading; I would be satisfied, or at least I would be meant to be
satisfied, with its theatrical mode of being. When I read a novel in
book form, I know that I am doing exactly what is meant to be done
with the work. When I read a play in a book, I am much less confident
in this regard; I recognize that the work's present mode of being, for
me, is secondary or subordinate with respect to another mode of

being, for me, is secondary or subordinate with respect to another mode of being that the very idea of drama compels me to envisage.

Perhaps this point can be refined a bit further. When I say that the dramatic text shows a marked ontological defectiveness by comparison with other types of text, I do not mean that every non-dramatic text is ontologically perfect, or is so in the same degree as every other. I have approached the matter by way of the relation between text and reader, and I concede that this relation is never perfect, never utterly completed by the placing of a *mere* text (the words and sentences, plus a somehow strictly circumscribed system of their significations) before a *mere* reader (who manages to segregate a portion of his or her mind as containing nothing but that prescribed and circumscribed system of significations). Henry James, for example (using, incidentally, a theatrical metaphor), suggests that the novelist's job is to strive "to live and breathe and rub shoulders and converse with the persons engaged in the struggle that provides for the others in the circling tiers the entertainment of the great game."[5] And we too, in reading a text that is written in this spirit, will feel the need to "rub shoulders" with the characters in the fiction, will find ourselves striving (at least in the mind, the feelings) to leave our high readerly seat and actually move about on imagination's stage, with the result that our actual situation as readers, when it impresses itself once more upon our consciousness, must seem a defect in our relation to the text. But it is not an ontological defect. Our sense of exclusion, as readers, from the beckoning world of a novel's fiction, is a normal and expected feature of the genre; we never *really* expect to find ourselves, even in imagination, wholly submerged, actually present, in the fictional world we read of.[6] We *can* really expect, however—it lies fully within the realm of possibility—that we might be actually present in the theater at a performance of the drama we are reading. Our exclusion from the theater as mere readers, therefore, is *not* a normal feature of the genre. It is for us an ontological defect of the text.

[5]"Preface to 'The Golden Bowl,'" in Henry James, *The Art of the Novel: Critical Prefaces*, ed. R. P. Blackmur (New York, 1934), p. 328.

[6]Wolfgang Iser, *The Implied Reader* (Baltimore, 1974; orig. 1972), comes close to actually disputing this point when he says that "the novel . . . is the genre in which reader involvement coincides with meaning production" (p. xi). He of course hedges constantly in this matter, attempts to walk what I think is a nonexistent tightrope between the reader's "subjectivity," in its production of "configurative meaning," and "certain controls" that must somehow be exercised by the text (p. 46). My response is that the reader's supposedly meaning-producing involvement in a "new reality through fiction" (p. xiii) is always understood by the reader as his or her own generically appropriate *gesture*, that "meaning," in any reasonable sense, only begins to happen in this distanced self-understanding.

I have made this point as strongly as I can, because I think it is important and valid. But it also has a historical dimension by which its range is limited. For the ontological defectiveness of a particular sort of text cannot be experienced unless the corresponding ontological integrity of certain other texts is recognized as a possibility. And this possibility, it seems to me, does not arise until after the institution of the *anonymous reader* has been established, which means not until well into the age of printed books. If a text is to be thought of as having anything like its own integral existence, if it is to have existence *as a text,* then it must be able to exist *for* (that is, to be read *by*) anyone at all—which is what Luther, for example, insists on in the case of the Bible. Even in the age of printed books, and even in the case of literary texts (which we, in the wake of post-Romantic criticism, think of as universal, accessible to anyone sufficiently educated), this condition is not as obviously satisfied as it might seem. It has been suggested, for instance, that in the eighteenth century there was a specific *resistance* to the idea of the integral text and the anonymous reader.[7] Perhaps it is not until the advent of the systematically self-integrating philosophical text, after Kant and especially in Hegel, that these ideas are fully established.[8]

[7]Eva Knodt, *"Negative Philosophie" und dialogische Kritik: Zur Struktur poetischer Theorie bei Lessing und Herder* (Tübingen, 1988).

[8]See Anne Ubersfeld, *Lire le théâtre,* 4th ed. (Paris, 1982), p. 140, on the "non-dit du texte." Paul de Man, "The Rhetoric of Blindness," in his *Blindness and Insight* (Minneapolis, 1983; orig. 1971), pp. 102–11, discusses the organic metaphor for the text and its effect in criticism very neatly; but later in the same essay, when he says, "What happens in Rousseau is *exactly* [my emphasis] what happens in Derrida" (p. 138), his emphasis not upon rhetoric in general, but upon a particular *kind* of rhetorical process comparable to the sense of sight, a process that is isolable as the generative principle of different texts, reflects the *persistence* of that same organic metaphor, a persistence that is testified to by precisely the sudden incongruous injection of the idea of authorial intention—"The pattern is too interesting not to be deliberate" (p. 140)—that is meant to deny it. What I mean to suggest is that the organic metaphor *cannot* be excised or fully suppressed in any critical-theoretical genre of writing. For a genre always brings its history with it. Consider the frequently trivialized notion of intertextuality, which emerges, in all its particular uses, from the recognition that text is in truth never anything but "intertext," that the space of operation between texts is where the text actually happens—or most simply, that every text is made entirely of other texts, which means that we never arrive at the point of a single integral text's operating on its own principles. "Si on admet que toute pratique signifiante est un champ de transpositions de divers systèmes signifiants (une inter-textualité), on comprend que son 'lieu' d'énonciation et son 'object' dénoté ne sont jamais uniques, pleins et identiques à eux-mêmes, mais toujours pluriels, éclatés, susceptibles de modèles tabulaires" (Julia Kristeva, *La Révolution du langage poétique* [Paris, 1974], p. 60). The trouble is, how shall we lay hold of this notion *in* our study of texts, since it is still *texts* that we study? Kristeva, *Recherches* (Paris, 1969), pp. 143–73, starting with Bakhtin, suggests that the "polyphonic" (or dialogic or carnivalesque) novel manages to account maximally for its own intertextuality. But she cannot avoid (any more than de Man can, or Bakhtin) presenting the

But for us at least, for the twentieth-century reader, it is evident that these ideas do definitely belong to the conception of the literary, and that the unique ontological defectiveness of the dramatic text has therefore become a factor in our literary experience, which means in turn that drama, for us, is separated from other literary types not by a boundary but by a gulf. Drama, for us, unless we abstract from its affiliation with the theater—which would mean abstracting from its quality as drama—is thus *too* clearly differentiable from other poetic types for the purpose of discrimination. Attempts have been made to develop a notion of "performance," or of "reproductive art," that would embrace both the reading of a text and the performance of a play; but such notions are too abstract to be really useful here.[9] In the first place, there is too fundamental and too insistent a difference between something that happens in the individual's mind and something that happens out there in the presence of witnesses, in actual human community. In the second place, the supposed similarity between the act of reading and the undertaking of theatrical performance, as far as I know, is nowhere actually anchored in the history of either reading or theater; boundary effects arising from that similarity would have to be manufactured by the same process of discrimination that pretends to study them. With regard to the form of drama, therefore, especially modern drama, discrimination presents a problem. It is all too easy to answer the question, What is drama? But it is correspondingly difficult even to pose the question of what we *mean* by drama, what stake we have in distinguishing it as a poetic type, hence, ultimately, why we practice it in the first place.

Although I have myself already said a certain amount about what I think we mean by drama, none of the points made in this or the preceding chapter approaches the definiteness we require. We do

---

"polyphonic" as an organizing principle in particular nameable texts, which leads at least to the brink of the old error. We can say, or shout, the words "text" and "intertext" all we please; that action is still understood as a not-saying (thus a saying after all) of "oeuvre littéraire" (Kristeva, *Recherches*, p. 16), which brings with it all the old baggage of literary study, going back to scriptural exegesis and beyond. I do not mean that we *cannot* think the "intertextual," or think beyond the organic metaphor. We undoubtedly do think in these ways. But the question is, *where*? Is there a locus in our literary experience where the possibility of this thinking is preserved more or less permanently? And I contend that the intractable defectiveness of the dramatic text provides just such a locus, that the promise, as it were, of our ability to maintain the needful theoretical perspective of the intertextual, is thus established in the real theater, the church of literature.

[9]See, for example, Hans-Georg Gadamer, *Wahrheit und Methode*, 2d ed. (Tübingen, 1965), pp. 140–61.

not, in any significant degree, know what we mean by drama, unless relatively clear boundary effects, susceptible to study by discrimination in the sense just discussed, are an integral part of our
literary or aesthetic experience. And the consideration that the problem we thus face may well be a peculiarly modern one, that dramatic
boundary effects operative, say, in late eighteenth-century Germany
may no longer be available to us, does not make the problem itself
any easier.[10] Perhaps, in fact, it can be argued that the *temporary*
quality of the theater of readers in Ibsen and Strindberg is either a
response or a capitulation to this specifically modern problem. We
will return to this matter in the next chapter.

3.

The method by which I propose at least to map out a circumvention of the difficulty I have suggested involves a discrimination between drama and cinema. If it is objected that there is no obvious
justification for regarding drama and cinema as separate entities, I
respond by repeating that my purpose is neither to define nor to
classify, nor in any sense to effect a conclusive separation, but rather
to discriminate, and that discrimination begins precisely where the
drawing of clear boundaries becomes impossible. I therefore make a
point at the outset of conceding various degrees of validity to the
various possible views of drama and cinema as aspects of but a
single phenomenon, views ranging from the idea of cinema as not
much more than a device for propagating drama, a mere electric
stage, to the idea of cinema, or indeed television, as the inevitable
destiny of drama in our time. But by the same token, I claim for my
argument its own degree of validity, commensurate with the degree
to which it relieves a clear difficulty in our view of modern drama,
and does this in a manner that also illuminates certain otherwise
troublesome aspects of the whole idea and practice of drama in
European tradition. One question I will not deal with is that of the
exact boundary, or the extent of overlap, between the cinematic and
the dramatic.

---

[10]See my *Modern Drama and German Classicism,* esp. pp. 18–19, 41–42, 58–64, 100,
112–16, 208, 211–13, on drama's representing *the literary as such* in late eighteenth-
century Germany, so that more generally literary or poetic boundary effects perhaps
there have the effect of discriminating drama. Or perhaps the genre of the "Novelle,"
especially as developed by Heinrich von Kleist, serves to articulate specific boundary
effects for drama. See Sveta Davé, "The Flow of the World: Genre and the Social in
the Works of Heinrich von Kleist" (Diss., University of Virginia, 1985).

To begin with, it is evident that cinema provides a useful focus for dealing with the relation of drama to the general array of literary types. Despite cinema's tendency to rely less upon verbal expression than live theater does, certain prominent features of cinematic art place it *between* drama and literature, in the vicinity of narrative. It has long been recognized that cinematic images, by being mere images—not the real people and things, however disguised, that appear on the live stage—have something closer to the mental or dream quality that we suppose also characterizes the more or less eidetic effects of verbal narration in the mind of a reader. And this quasi-mental quality of cinema can be developed by techniques of film editing that produce for the viewer instantaneous changes of image scale, or of point of view, comparable to the changes that can be produced for the imagining reader by an adroit use of language. Perhaps more important, however, is the quality of the camera in cinema as a controlling presence of roughly the same sort as the controlling authorial presence that we cannot help inferring when we read a text, a controlling presence that we do not experience, or at least do not experience in the same way, at the performance of a play. Among the glittering courtiers who crowd onto the stage in the second scene of *Hamlet*, for example, there is one gentleman attired incongruously in black; and even if we pay him no special notice until he makes himself heard, still we acknowledge with no hesitation that he has *been there* before us the whole time. For the reader of the text, on the other hand, Hamlet is in effect simply *not* there until, in due course, his name and the first words he speaks are arrived at, in the same way that he is not there for a cinema audience until the camera picks him out.

These affinities between cinema and verbal narrative must be borne in mind. But if we rely upon them exclusively as a basis for discriminating between cinema and drama, we shall find ourselves relying too heavily on the psychological assumptions they involve. Therefore I propose what seems to me a more solid basis. In cinema, namely, the performance is *identical* with the work, whereas in drama we recognize that the performance we are attending is one of a number of *different* actual or possible performances, that it represents a particular and inherently questionable *interpretation* of the work. It is beside the point that there can be differences among screenings of the same film, or that different versions of the same film are sometimes made in order to comply with local laws and the requirements of exhibitors. When we sit down in a movie theater, we do so in the confident assumption that what we shall see, as Hart

Crane has it, is exactly what has been "Foretold to other eyes," just as we assume that other copies of a book are the same as our own; and what we then do see in the cinema is the work itself, in at least as strong a sense as the printed book can be said to contain the novel itself.

This point is unaffected by my earlier argument concerning the ontological defectiveness of the printed dramatic text, even though that argument implies that theatrical performance tends to *complete* the dramatic work, to bring it more fully into existence, rather than merely to interpret it. If we agree that there is such a thing as the "work" (the *opus*, the whole culturally effective entity), and that the dramatic text by itself is markedly defective, falls markedly short of adequately representing the work, then it follows that performance in a theater contributes to *constituting* the very object (the work) of which it is an interpretation. This is a paradox, but not a difficulty. It in fact reflects a fundamental paradox of hermeneutics: that the object of interpretation is always in part constituted by the act of interpretation. Surely the novel, considered as a work, includes the activity of reading and understanding that its sign system anticipates, just as the film as work includes the activity of viewing. And that activity of reading or viewing, upon analysis, is easily seen to be interpretive in nature. The case of drama is different only in that this paradoxical situation is deployed on the level of conscious experience; drama, so to speak, acts out the hermeneutic paradox. When we participate in a theatrical performance, even if only as spectators, we *know* that we are interpreting, whereas we generally experience our reading or film viewing as if it were nothing but a *reception* of the work.

Crucial, again, is the difference between different performances of a play, which enables us to form the mental habit of *detaching* the performance, as interpretation, from whatever we suppose the work itself is. When we detect a flaw in the acting or directing of a film, we count it a flaw in the work. When we detect a similar flaw in the performance of a play, we count it a flaw in the performance alone, leaving the work untouched. When we reread a novel, or go back to a film we have seen before, we do so in the expectation of repeating as exactly as possible what we remember as our first experience with the work; when we see a play again, we expect rather to receive a *new* perspective upon it. Dramatic performance, while in a strong sense indispensable to the very existence of the work, is still, in every particular instance, strictly detachable from the work, as an interpretation of it. And it seems to me that this strongly marked, as it were theatrically exaggerated paradox echoes or replicates another strong paradox that we have discussed: that drama is strictly a literary type, yet somehow also indissolubly associated with the concrete institution of the theater, and indeed crucially influenced *as* a literary type by this association.

Exactly how this compoundedly paradoxical phenomenon arises need not concern us. An explanation could probably be offered in terms of the historical development of conventional anticipatory attitudes; and this sort of explanation, incidentally, would leave open the possibility (which I do not dispute) of further historical change in the future. But whatever the explanation, and whatever the degree of historical invariance involved, it remains generally true, for us, that we experience the reading of a novel or the viewing of a film as a direct reception of the work itself, whereas at the performance of a play, our experience is that of coming to grips with an interpretation of the work. Needless to say, certain cases cloud this distinction: film remakes, cinematic versions of narrative or dramatic works, "live" television, and perhaps mime or dance, where the idea of the "work" becomes maximally problematic. But my purpose is not to draw a diagram showing exactly where or what either cinema or drama is; that there can be no such diagram is clear from the basic hermeneutic parallels anyway. My immediate aim, rather, is to discriminate between what we mean by cinema and what we mean by drama; and I think that the idea of interpretation, especially the distinction between interpretation and understanding, provides a useful basis for this undertaking.

4.

I claim, first of all, that this view of the form of drama as the acting out of a basic hermeneutic paradox, while it is brought into especially sharp focus by the discrimination of drama from cinema, is also anchored in both the tradition of the form and the invariable epistemological or semiotic structure of theatrical experience. The first point emerges immediately from the observation that drama as we know it has always manifested an awareness of its essentially self-interpretive structure, that the question of our stake in drama—the question of what we are doing in the theater, of why (or whether) the theater is needed, a question that could conceivably discredit the whole endeavor—is also a prominent and recurrent motif in dramatic tradition itself, to an extent to which I think no corresponding question is thematized in the tradition of any other poetic type.

The tendency of the dramatic stage to question its own function and value, by such techniques as the play-within-the-play, is already fully developed in Greek theater: in the complex relation between chorus and action, which, especially for Aeschylus, acknowledges that the play is never "about" any action that is not already itself a form of public theatrical representation; in specific Sophoclean touches, for example the cruel little drama staged for Odysseus by Athena at the beginning of the cruel drama *Ajax* that is staged for us, or the arrival of Oedipus, as the *Colonus* opens, at once fictionally and literally upon Athenian soil; in Euripides' constant ironic distancing of generic expectations. And in later European drama the variety of devices becomes enormous, but the theme, the questioning, is constant. The world-theater metaphor, for example, when invoked *in* the theater—on a large scale in Calderon, or in any of the smaller-scale versions devised by Shakespeare—produces an abyss or infinite regress of self-interpreting. Or there are brilliant little flashes, for example Philinte's allusion to *L'Ecole des maris* in the first scene of *Le Misanthrope*, which, along with Alceste's response, "Mon Dieu! laissons là vos comparaisons fades," places us in a double bind with regard to *our* sense of the comparability of world and theater. Or there is the repeated dramatization of dramatic theory in German Classicism—in Kleist's *Prinz Friedrich*, for example, where the Elector presents his political vision to the Prince in a kind of theatrical interpretation which the Prince *mis*interprets but, precisely in doing so, fulfills the original vision.[11] And if, in modern theater, comparable techniques are more extreme or more highly refined, this is merely a development of existing tradition. We think immediately of Pirandello, where the replaying of a scene in *Six Characters*, for example, calls our attention to the possibility of a replaying of the entire work, hence to the quality of the performance we are watching as a particular interpretation of the work—a train of associations that would be incomplete if the work were a film.

The second point involves the whole semiotic theory of drama (which I discuss in detail in a later chapter). Let it suffice to note here the significance of the relation between words and *things* in drama, which is affected by the special quality of the stage as a situation where the sign (the word) and its referent can be made actually to confront each other, in a way that is possible neither in writing nor even in cinema, since even in a photographic image the quality of

---

[11]See my *Modern Drama and German Classicism*, chap. 1, on Kleist, and also chaps. 3 and 4, on G. E. Lessing and Goethe.

sign (not referent) is dominant.[12] This point can be illustrated by a pair of paradigmatic examples. In *Waiting for Godot* we hear:

> ESTRAGON: *(violently)* I'm hungry!
> VLADIMIR: Do you want a carrot?
> ESTRAGON: Is that all there is?
> VLADIMIR: I might have some turnips.
> ESTRAGON: Give me a carrot. . . .[13]

Vladimir then produces an object that Estragon identifies as a turnip only after he absentmindedly takes a bite of it, whereupon Vladimir insists he "could have sworn it was a carrot." Even in response to an expression of elemental animal need ("I'm hungry!") Vladimir and Estragon find themselves struggling clumsily with the relation between words and meanings, especially between words and things.

But finally, at least for the time being, they get it right. Vladimir continues rummaging in his pockets until he does find a carrot, which he presents to Estragon with the words, "There, dear fellow," and which Estragon proceeds to eat with some enjoyment. The point is that when Vladimir finally pulls out the long-awaited carrot, even before anything is said, we in the audience find ourselves thinking: yes, that is a carrot. At the same time, however, in the context of this play, where not even the simplest possible statement is ever firmly established, we also necessarily *question* the thought, "yes, that is a carrot." How can we be sure? Is it a carrot, or is it only that we "could have sworn" it is a carrot? What does the thought— or indeed the question—mean? We seem to know that what Vladimir holds in his hand corresponds to the word "carrot," but the knowledge is no longer a simple registration of external fact. What counts, rather, is that we and Vladimir and Estragon, and presumably the other spectators, evidently *agree* about the carrot; we experience our factual knowledge as *a significant communicative achievement*. Simple recognition and naming have become an achievement for us, just as the simplest action on stage becomes a comically complicated achievement for the characters; we are aware, for a moment, of how much daring and determination and trust are necessary in order to think: yes, that is a carrot. In spite of overwhelming contrary forces (which are the play's main theme), we and the actors and the rest of the audience have managed to assert our belonging-together as a

[12]See Ubersfeld, pp. 34–36, and Michael Issacharoff, "Space and Reference in Drama," *Poetics Today* 2, no. 3 (Spring 1981), 217.
[13]Samuel Beckett, *Waiting for Godot* (New York, 1954), pp. 13–14.

reasonable community; our quality as a community hangs on that small yellow root we insist on agreeing about, and the affectionate little address with which Vladimir completes the transfer is a manifestation of this communal feeling. Such an experience, obviously, is not available to the reader, for whom even the carrot that Vladimir eventually finds is still only the verbal sign "carrot." And for a cinema audience, if the play were on film, it would be only the iconic sign for a carrot, an *invariable* sign, the same in every showing—*not*, like the carrot Estragon eats, consumable; *not*, as Vladimir assures us about that carrot, the last of its kind; *not*, in other words, the occasion for an unrepeatable communal achievement. On a movie screen the carrot *has* to be what it is; in the theater there is always the risk of its not being what we mean at all, of its not being, say, what it had been yesterday.

The other example I have in mind is in some respects exactly the opposite: the invisible knife, the knife that is not there, in Eugène Ionesco's *La Leçon*. What interests the audience in this case is the manner in which the monotonous ritual repetition of the word can be seen to *generate* the actual object. For the purposes of the play's action, such as it is, the bit of empty space that the Professor grips and brandishes and wields *is* occupied by the physical reality that the word "knife" insists on. The actual absence of the knife in the theater thus presents the spectator with *the power of the word "knife,"* whereas for the reader, as soon as he or she reads the word "knife," even with the adjective "invisible," the knife is *not* in any reasonable sense absent—it is as present to the reader as the things referred to by the words "Professor" and "chair"—and the word has no special power. Even if the director uses a real knife, as Ionesco suggests might be done,[14] it remains clear, in the theater, that the word is not a response to the object, not a token of recognition, but rather a force in its own right, to which the object *owes* its either visible or invisible being. And even in a cinema version this is no longer true. For on the screen we would perceive that *there is no knife* (or as the case may be, that there is a knife), once and for all, whereas in the theater we understand that *the knife is not there*—but with no "once and for all" about it, since (as that stage direction makes clear) the knife could just as well be there after all.

In the theater, the word is a force that generates the thing. This is the condition of which the Pupil's pains, as the Maid puts it, are a "symptom"; in feeling pain, and in running her hands over her

[14]Eugène Ionesco, *Théâtre I* (Paris, 1954), p. 87.

aching body, pronouncing the name of each part she touches, the Pupil desperately attempts to sustain her sense, and ours, of at least these most directly experienced objects (parts of our own body) as primary realities, which the words merely refer to. But her struggles are hopeless. Words do not respond to the prior existence of things; on the contrary, words fix, govern, generate things. And the triumph of language over the Pupil's body, or over the bodily or material in general, can be understood in two ways: as the expression of an insidious philosophical glottocentrism, of the easily abused truth that it is language that generates our sense of the identities of things, not vice versa; and as an acknowledgment of the simple fact that not only the knife, but all the actual things and people on the stage, *are* generated by words in the sense that the words of the play's text are prior to them and require them, an acknowledgment, therefore, that we, the audience, merely by going to the theater, are collaborating in a form of ritual glottocentrism practically equivalent to murder, that we—whether we intend it or not—are implicated in the subjugation to language of an innocent physical reality (the actual things on the stage, which could just as well be doing something other than functioning in a play), a sheer physical reality which our verbal corruptness no longer even permits us to experience as such.

These two examples are opposites not only by depending in one case on the presence, in the other on the absence of a particular physical thing, but also by revealing opposed aspects of the idea of interpretation. The non-innocence of interpretation, that interpretation is never strictly detached, but always implicated in the nature of its object, is the center of focus in Ionesco, whereas in Beckett it is the manner in which interpretation repeatedly lurches free of the problematics of text, word, sign, free of its ever compromised and ever renewed object (this last represented perhaps by the speech of the temporarily untethered Lucky), into moments of immediate communicative clarity. Our inevitable and now theatrically exaggerated interpretive situation is understood in one case as constraint, in the other as freedom, both of which it in truth is. And precisely as opposites, the examples thus form a paradigm that illuminates from opposed quarters the depth to which critical self-consciousness is involved in the very structure of the dramatic stage, in that the difference between words and things provides a compelling transition to the problem of interpretation and its object.

It may be true that we never perceive a thing in purity, as somehow nothing but itself; but it is equally undeniable that there is a difference between the word or the cinematic image, in which the thing has undergone measurable intellectual digestion, and the thing in drama, which perhaps bears a clear relation to the words of the text and the sensible totality of the stage, but would also be capable of existing in completely different relations, should the occasion arise. For the reader, the carrot in *Waiting for Godot* is "the carrot in *Waiting for Godot*"; for the spectator, it is—*a* carrot, which could just as well do any of the other things carrots do. For the reader, the word "knife" in the text of *La Leçon* denies that knife the possibility, which it regains on the stage, of existing in the relation of not-being-there. And this difference matters. I do not claim to have shown that drama is—in "essence"—self-conscious. I do maintain, however, that the reflection on the structure of text plus interpretation which emerges from the discrimination with cinema is not only verifiable in tradition, but also engaged in the form itself at what we recognize as an entirely fundamental level, that in fact, therefore, it is part of what we mean by drama.

5.

But the difference between reading a play and watching a performance is not a strict disjunction. In fact, it follows from the argument so far that the tension between text and performance exists *for* the dramatic spectator, that the experience of reading the text is an integral part of the experience of watching a performance. If this were not so, we should have no way of recognizing the performance as an interpretation in the first place, since we should have no conception of *what* is being interpreted. The text, when we are actually reading it, is ontologically defective and markedly fails to represent the whole "work" for us. But when we are in the theater, when we are confronted with an actual performance that we recognize as a *mere* interpretation, the text, the now absent, shadowy, obscured, abandoned text, now paradoxically does represent the object of interpretation (the work) after all, precisely *by* being absent, shadowy, obscured.

The recognition that the performance is a particular interpretation thus already suffices to make us *virtual readers* of the text, even if we have never actually read it; even in the theater our experience includes the distinction between interpreting and understanding (the latter being what we suppose we would do as readers), and this distinction locates the text for us. This is not an obscure point. It can be tested by recalling that even if we have never read a particular play, we are capable, after seeing it, of making *distinct* judgments on the work and the performance, of recognizing the good performance of a bad play or vice versa. Even while under what we like to think of as the "spell" of the performance, we have formed our own intellectual conception of the work (represented by the text), and have been measuring the performance, considered as an interpretation, against it. The showing of common experience in this matter is supported by written tradition; the idea of the dramatic spectator as a virtual reader is, for instance, not much more than a reorienting of Diderot's thought in the *Paradoxe sur le comédien*.

Even in the theater, then, we do not escape our situation as readers of a written text. And this point brings us back to the question of our stake in drama, of our need, if we have one, for a literary form yoked to the concrete unliterary labor of the theater. Why do we bother to go to the theater? Or why, when we go, do we consider the activity anything more than a diversion? If understanding is available to us as readers, and if, even while sitting in the theater, we *remain* understanding readers of the text, presumably capable of forming our own interpretations, why do we require the interpretation represented by performance? In precisely what sense is theatrical interpretation more an integral part of the work than the interpretations we might arrive at mentally?[15] I have mentioned specific features of plays by Pirandello, Beckett, and Ionesco which require performance for their realization. But are such moments of communicative illumination enough to establish a necessary bond between the theater and a particular type of poetry?

At a certain limited depth, the answer to all these questions is obvious. Hamlet's words, "while memory holds a seat / In this distracted globe," are a familiar theatrical metaphor, suggesting (1) the seat of consciousness in the globe of the head; (2) the attentiveness of spectators in the Globe Theatre to what passes before them; and (3) the idea of all humankind as the bearer of memory, therefore as the bearer of a duty to assert order, in the great globular world. The first two of these suggestions correspond to the tension between virtual reader (individual consciousness, an individual head, understanding a text) and actual spectator. But if there is to be a sufficient reason for drama, as opposed to mere reading (or, for us, cinema), then there must be a correlative to the third suggestion as well. Somehow the theater must open onto the whole of human

---

[15]See my *Modern Drama and German Classicism*, pp. 52–73, on Lessing, especially on the question of the "drudgery of dramatic form" (p. 59).

space and time; and it must do so not merely as an institution, but as a vehicle for the particular work that is apparently only interpreted in it. In other words, the ancient *ceremonial* quality of drama must be retained or renewed; the performance must not only interpret the work, but also realize it as a ceremony that asserts human order on a universal scale.

The limitations of this idea can be understood by way of a discrimination between drama and opera. (Again, the issue of definition does not arise, and there is no need to worry about the distinctions among opera, oratorio, *Singspiel*, music drama, operetta, various types of comedy with song, and so on.) The whole text of an opera, insofar as it is available for reading and understanding, includes the musical score as well as the libretto, and therefore prescribes the actuality of performance (pitch, volume, pace, rhythm, duration) much more exactly than the merely verbal text of a drama. The performance of an opera is thus more a *realization* of the text than an interpretation. The listeners, like the spectators in a theater, are virtual readers; to varying degrees they know and understand the text (including the music), and are aware of the multiplicity of possible performances. But whereas the various performances of a drama, as interpretations, are felt to *diverge* from the basic understood text, in opera, by comparison, we have the sense of a *convergent* movement by which various performances approach the sort of ideal or perfect realization that is not ordinarily inferable from a verbal text alone. That is, we have a sense of the individual performance as a ceremony, as the foreshadowing of a timeless and invisible human action.[16] The "perfect" performance of a play is an unusual concept; at a dramatic performance we are ordinarily impressed by what the director and the actors have "done with" the work. But the idea of a perfect or definitive operatic performance is not at all unusual. This point can be understood in part by way of common experience, the relatively more conservative and indeed sometimes almost religious attitude of "opera lovers" toward their art, their quality as connoisseurs, equipped with an incorruptible mental standard of perfection, like the lovers of wine or purebred dogs.

The discrimination between drama and opera, to be sure, is no more conclusive than that between drama and cinema. But provided

---

[16]This argument, in a slightly different form, appears in more detail in chap. 14, "Art by Accident," of my *Hugo von Hofmannsthal: The Theaters of Consciousness* (Cambridge, 1988). Hofmannsthal's work is of course an especially appropriate area for the discrimination of drama from opera.

we agree that it represents a significant aspect of the way we think about drama and opera, it enables us to ask an uncomfortable question. If the ceremonial quality of performance is as essential to drama as I have suggested, then why has dramatic tradition as a whole not tended more strongly in the direction of opera? What stake have we, again, in an art form of which every individual work is constituted for us, in part, by particular divergent interpretations of itself, rather than realized for us by a musical ceremony? Especially in this century, of course, there have been a number of theoretical and practical initiatives tending toward ceremonialized drama: *Parade*, Artaud, Max Reinhardt, Salzburg. But drama nevertheless remains something different from both the visualized narrative of cinema and the aesthetic ceremony of opera. Why have these other two forms not simply divided the functions of drama between them? What is the function of drama itself? What do we mean by drama?

6.

My point is that precisely the discriminability of drama from cinema and opera, precisely our acknowledgment, in the dramatic theater, of a separation between understanding and interpretation, makes possible the ceremonial quality of drama, especially modern drama, in a sense entirely different from the sense in which opera may be thought of as ceremony. For the theatrical self-consciousness of modern drama, the necessity of performance (whether actualized or not), not only establishes but also *reverses* the distinction between understanding and interpretation. On the one hand, we understand the work as virtual readers, while as actual spectators we receive an interpretation of it. But on the other hand, since the performance generates meanings that belong to the work but *are not there* for the reader—we recall those moments in Pirandello, Beckett, Ionesco—we are compelled to recognize that true understanding occurs *only* via performance, whereas the situation of the reader makes available, at best, a defective, verbally conditioned *selection* of meanings, which is to say, something very like a particular interpretation of the work. To the extent that the performance interprets the text, we understand as separate individuals and interpret as a community in the theater; but insofar as the work requires performance in order to *be* in the first place, only the community is in a position to understand it, while as individuals, or virtual readers, we merely interpret it. The "message" of the "medium" of dramatic performance is thus that the relation between understanding and interpretation is *reversible*, that the apparently clear priority of understanding, in time or in individual experience, at some level becomes problematic. It must be emphasized that this point is not so abstract as it might initially appear. The very idea or belief that there is a reason for drama as drama, including performance—and could drama persist in the absence of such a belief?—implies that performance is more than *merely* interpretation of the work. That performance *is* interpretation emerges in the discrimination from cinema and opera; but what we mean by drama, if we mean anything at all, requires that performance, at the same time, also be something more fundamental in the work's constitution. What we need now is as systematic a description as possible of that "something more fundamental"; that it is there to be described is evident from experience and intuition.

The first step in clarifying matters is to specify what we mean by understanding and interpretation. I use the terms in only a slightly broader sense than that of E. D. Hirsch. Understanding is the mental activity by which we initially come to grips with a text, before we make any attempt whatever to communicate what we think; the attempt at communication, on the other hand, especially in verbal form, indeed any attempt to give specific, communicable shape to our understanding, even for ourselves alone, constitutes interpretation. "Understanding is silent, interpretation extremely garrulous,"[17] as Hirsch puts it. As soon as our silence is broken, even vis-à-vis ourselves, interpretation, in the sense I am using, begins.

The performance of a play is thus evidently an interpretation. And while this application of the term expands its reference beyond the limits Hirsch carefully observes, since practically any performance seeks to communicate the work's "significance" as well as its "meaning," still the distinction between understanding and interpretation corresponds quite exactly to the characteristic internal division in a dramatic spectator's experience. By the time we begin to formulate separate judgments of the work and the performance, we have of course already begun to interpret the work ourselves. But we carry out the initial separation between the objects of those judgments (the separation that characterizes drama, as discriminated from cinema) only by distinguishing, or thinking we distinguish, an area of silence in the midst of the insistent sensory impressions of the performance, an area within which the perfor-

[17]Hirsch, p. 135.

mance, as a performance, *says* nothing, but simply *is,* as the present means of our confronting the work; a silence that we associate with the silence of understanding, by contrast with the obviously interpretive gesturing of the stage; a silence which (as Hirsch would argue) is also always there in the process of reading, but which in the theater is thrown much more sharply into relief.

In what sense, however, can we then also *reverse* this application of the distinction between understanding and interpreting? Is it not enough to say that performance, as interpretation, can deepen or alter our understanding of the work? Such a statement would not violate the terms in which I have formulated the distinction. When we find an interpretation so persuasive that we concede the wrongness or incompleteness of our previous understanding of the work, then in effect we are confronting the work itself as if for the first time; our understanding of the interpretation combines with our newly silent relation to the work in a single movement of understanding. But it does not follow that the functions are reversed, that we can now classify our original understanding as an interpretation. And how is the situation any different in drama? When the replaying of a scene in Pirandello awakens in me a clear consciousness of my condition in the theater, when Vladimir's carrot becomes the occasion for a sudden awareness of the miracle of communication, when the not-thereness of the Professor's knife impresses me as a truth beyond words, are these mute mental events really anything other than developments in my understanding of the respective texts?

If we argue strictly from the dramatic spectator's point of view, as it were from within his or her experience, we find that the situation is, after all, fundamentally different from that of the reader of a persuasive interpretation. Meanings of the types that I have argued are revealed only in performance, once again, are in a strong sense simply *not there* for the reader, whereas when our understanding of a work is deepened or altered by an interpretation, we immediately concede that the meanings revealed to us are meanings that have been there all along. In fact, the perception of these new meanings must already have been an obscure part of even our earlier understanding of the text, our original silent encounter with it; otherwise the interpretation could not possibly convince us that they belong to the text. And while the reader of a drama might imagine or infer the existence of meanings arising, for example, from the meeting of words and actual things on the stage (as we have inferred such meanings in the foregoing discussion), these meanings, for that reader (as for the author and reader of this book), are the *result* of a definite nonsilent interpretive process (a process not dissimilar, incidentally, to the process of creative visualization by which a director might plan a performance). For the reader, therefore, these meanings cannot be imagined as belonging to the mute experience of understanding that we take to be the original object or kernel of the interpretive endeavor. For the reader, words and things never *actually* meet, the carrot is not *a* carrot, the knife, even with the adjective "invisible," is simply there, the replayed scene is only a pattern of similarities and explicit references between pieces of text; at least all this is the case until one consciously, nonsilently, quasi-verbally dissociates oneself from one's situation as a reader. For the reader, it is not even clear that these theatrical meanings, in Hirsch's terminology, belong to the sphere of "meaning" at all, rather than to that of "significance," which is the object of a formulative process already one step beyond interpretation strictly defined. But for the spectator in the theater they are unquestionably meanings, the immediately experienced objects of understanding, and indeed meanings proper to the *work*, not merely to the performance, since they are not affected by exactly how the carrot is handled or the knife wielded or the scene replayed.[18]

Perhaps an analogy will clarify the difference here. The answer to a riddle is certainly part of the intention of the riddle's author. But solving a riddle is different from understanding it. That is, the answer does not belong, as a meaning, to the text of the riddle considered as an immediate object of understanding; for it requires, in order to be arrived at, a definite amount of independent, systematic thought on the reader's part, involving the manipulation of relations between features of the text and facts wholly outside the text. The same applies, from the reader's point of view, to what I have called theatrical meanings, whereas from the spectator's point of view, these same meanings *are* immediate objects of understanding.

I contend, moreover, that this difference is more than an abstract quibble, that it is significant *for* the dramatic spectator, even if he or she is not specifically conscious of its significance. Let us recall, first,

[18]I am not talking here about the same type of meanings as Ubersfeld, p. 33. The meanings I have in mind are entirely decipherable from the text alone, but are still absent for the reader. Indeed, it could be argued that these meanings are *necessarily* absent for a reader, that they belong to something more like that "poetry for the senses" of which Artaud says, "this physical and concrete language . . . is not truly theatrical except insofar as the thoughts it expresses escape from all articulated language" (Antonin Artaud, *Oeuvres complètes*, 7 vols. [Paris, 1956–69], 4:45).

that the distinction between understanding and interpreting is more than just a way of talking about drama; it is, if our discriminations are at all valid, a part of what we mean by drama, hence part of the experience of even a relatively naïve dramatic spectator. Even the naïve spectator, in other words, to some extent occupies the role of a virtual reader of the text; and this relation to the text as virtual reader is, for him or her, the locus of an understanding of the work, as opposed to the interpretation represented by the performance. It follows that if the spectator now also understands the work at a site *outside* that locus—that is, if, in the theater, a meaning now appears that is proper to the work, but which the spectator (*as* a virtual reader) knows is *not* available to the mere reader as a meaning— then this experience will constitute a definite event, a clear contour in the overall experience of drama, a part of what that spectator now means by drama.

And if we agree, in addition, that the distinction between understanding and interpretation replicates the (equally questionable) distinction between experienced immediacy and the verbal or quasi-verbal mediation of experience in self-consciousness, then we can describe what happens to the spectator in the theater as a *reversal* of functions. In the first instance, the known or (by virtual reading) inferred text represents the work, as a potential object of immediate experience, while the performance offers itself as the result of other people's systematic interpretive thinking about the work. But the experience of directly understanding, in the theater, meanings of the work that are not there for the reader, throws into relief the *merely* verbal quality of the text; now it is the performance that represents the work, while the known or inferred text appears as an attempt to come to grips verbally with the meaning and significance of what happens in the theater, hence as an interpretation of that happening—in the same way, incidentally, that the riddle, once solved, takes on the character of a verbal interpreting of its answer. I do not mean to say that at some point in every dramatic performance the reversal in question simply occurs once and for all. Such an assertion would imply that performance is revealed, once and for all, as the true form of the work, while the text, correspondingly, is reduced once and for all to the status of an interpretation; and these conditions are clearly not what we mean by drama. My point, rather, is that *both* manifestations of the relation between understanding and interpretation remain in effect for the dramatic spectator, and that the quality of reversal that connects them—or, if one prefers, the quality of paradox—is a striking feature of the spectator's situation with respect to the form.

In any event, crude as this analysis may be, I do not think it can be convicted of stretching the experience of the theater on a Procrustean bed of abstraction. If we agree that a dramatic performance *is* an interpretation, and yet, *as* an interpretation, is somehow also something more central to the existence of the work, then we face a situation in which paradox is inescapable anyway. My argument merely attempts to develop the structure of this vaguely felt paradox in a reasonably clear hermeneutic terminology.

7.

But is the terminology, in itself, sound? Can the distinction between understanding and interpretation be maintained as neatly as I have assumed? Strictly for the purposes of drama, where this distinction is represented, albeit reversibly, by the clear separation between text and performance, the answer is yes. But in order to discuss the *significance* of dramatic form (our stake in it), we must deal with the question in a more general context. And here problems arise. Where exactly, after all, does understanding stop and interpretation begin? Is thought as such not verbally conditioned? Can any mental activity, for instance understanding, actually be "silent"? Is the act of reading not itself already a translation or paraphrase of its text, thus already an interpretation? Hirsch, in distinguishing between understanding and interpretation, stresses "the fact that two different interpretations are not necessarily disparate," that they may refer to the same construction of meaning.[19] But it is equally true that the same interpretation may sometimes reasonably be taken to refer to different constructions of meaning, that two scholars, for example, may agree completely about the correctness of a given interpretive formulation, yet discover, on further discussion, that they disagree seriously about the meaning of the text. Is there then any warrant for the belief that identical constructions of meaning exist in the first place, that anything actually exists, any preinterpretive "understanding," to which an interpretation might refer?

Hirsch's answer to these objections is that the final object of understanding is the author's meaning, which is there even if identical

[19]Hirsch, p. 130.

constructions of meaning cannot be shown conclusively to exist. And his now decades-old criticism of Gadamer, especially of the doctrine that "all understanding is explication," remains persuasive.[20] But even if we put aside for a moment the suspicion that "authorial intention," when we begin to attach theoretical pretensions to the term, turns out a mere conceptual device employed *for the sake* of maintaining an otherwise untenable distinction between understanding and interpretation, even if we suppose that authorial intention exists in a manner that enables it to be distinguished clearly from its expression, there is still reason for serious discomfort with Hirsch's thinking, because of its implications concerning the general character of our world. If understanding is not in some way a truly creative or productive activity, if it is only a response to the author's meaning, and if interpretation properly only serves understanding, then the idea of an intellectual hierarchy is practically forced upon us, in which the creator or "original" thinker occupies a higher place than the interpreter, in which an invidious distinction is drawn between those minds whose thought is worth thinking about and those that are only fit for elucidating the thoughts of others. Such an idea, despite more than half a century's "great books" propaganda, is unacceptable. The intellectual disciplines would all wither and die, in less than half a century, if intellectuals did not have a sense of *participating* productively in the life and growth of their objects of study, and participating on a level not substantially different from that of the "great" figures they talk about. Longinus says that the encounter with true greatness fills us with personal pride, indeed vainglory (*megalauchia*), as if we ourselves were the creators of what we hear.[21] And it is this feeling, raised to the level of philosophical conviction, that spurs on a Gadamer or a Heidegger in the effort to produce a more integrated picture of human intellectual endeavor; it is this conviction that gives rise, for example, to the idea of "hermeneutic conversation," as opposed to the idea of elucidation of a given static meaning, or to the assertion that a text speaks "for us" only when it is "brought to speech" by our interpretation.[22]

The positions represented, for our purposes, by Hirsch and Gadamer, are thus both justified, while remaining irreconcilable. Gadamer at least takes up the struggle with our indispensable but

[20]Gadamer, p. 336; Hirsch, pp. 245–64, esp. p. 253.
[21]"Longinus," *On the Sublime*, 7:2, in *Aristotle, The Poetics; "Longinus," On the Sublime; Demetrius, On Style*, Loeb Classical Library (Cambridge, Mass., 1965), p. 138.
[22]Gadamer, pp. 365, 375.

inevitably vague sense of direct participation in tradition, our sense of the sweep and totality of human intellectual existence, of human-kind as the "seat" of "memory," as itself the ceaselessly creative source of whatever order human beings perceive in this otherwise "distracted globe." As Hirsch points out, however, there are logical difficulties in Gadamer's argument, difficulties that reflect not faulty thought so much as an *illegitimate point of view*. What Gadamer says may be true; indeed, for the sake of our sense of purpose in existence, it has to be true that understanding is at bottom indistinguishable from interpretation as a central component of the ceaseless intellectual activity by which human order is ever generated anew. But this truth is not legitimately available to the individual thinker. As soon as we attempt to think such a truth as individuals, we find ourselves drawing conclusions that in practice lead not to order but to chaos, not to memory but to distraction. Ultimately, as Hirsch argues, we find ourselves flirting with chains of inference that would permit us to attach any meaning to any text. Something much more like Hirsch's position on the determinacy of meaning, the separation between understanding and interpretation, and related matters, is therefore necessary precisely in order for us to *carry out adequately* that vast world-ordering work which is envisioned behind Gadamer's thinking. That Gadamer requires of us a point of view we cannot actually occupy, is perhaps clearer, or less hedged about, in the work of his predecessor Heidegger, in the latter's occasional attempts to persuade his readers or hearers that they are doing something other than merely understanding him, a persuasion that is itself inescapably mediated, for the individual recipient, by exactly the sort of understanding or construction it seeks to abjure.[23]

But then, since we cannot jump over our own shadow, since we cannot hope to think or know except as individuals, how can we hope to salvage *in* intellectual tradition, on some ground firmer than that of vague feeling, the vital truth that Gadamer may perhaps be accused of squandering? The answer I propose to this question is *ceremony*, in the sense of a limited communal action that shadows forth an action or truth whose proper domain is humanity as a whole, or a whole culture, and that so establishes that larger action or truth in reality, as an experience, but without requiring that the individual pretend to occupy with respect to it the godlike point of

[23]For example, see Martin Heidegger, *Einführung in die Metaphysik*, 2d ed. (Tübingen, 1958), pp. 16, 23, on what is meant by "asking" a philosophical question. The analysis is reasonable enough, but the attempt actually to reshape the relation between speaker and audience is self-defeating.

view of theoretical knowledge. And my main point, in turn, is that modern drama aims typically at the production of ceremony in this sense.

Whether or not it can be demonstrated as a logical or empirical truth, the strict distinction between understanding and interpretation must be maintained in practice for the sake of the integrity and legitimacy of individual intellectual endeavor. In fact, I think it can be argued that this distinction is involved in the very structure of our individual existence, as a manifestation or model of the distinction between what we have in common with others and what separates us from others. Without an understanding of other people as subjects, or at least the firm belief that we understand them—something not far from what Herder or Schleiermacher means by "divination"—no sort of communicative relation among individuals is possible.[24] But such understanding must be "silent." As soon as we give specific shape to it, we must acknowledge that the shape is contributed by us, and is not an essential characteristic of the person we are thinking about; otherwise we fail to respect his or her individuality, and *he* or *she* is not what we have understood. We must seek, and we may claim, as great a degree as possible of validity for the interpretive act relative to another person; but if we confuse interpretation with understanding, in this extended sense, then we deny the other person *his* or *her* identity—as we might correspondingly deny a text *its*, or its author's meaning—and we are then not dealing, as individuals, with "others" in the first place. (The parallel between this argument and the argument earlier on the needful simultaneity and distinguishability of the two cubist moves in Strindberg, or of the expressionistic and mimetic tendencies in Ibsen, suggests the possibility of a fundamental theoretical relation between drama and communicative ethics as such.)

A hermeneutics of the type Gadamer proposes thus tends ultimately toward a violation of the limits beyond which our very experience as individuals in contact or discussion with each other becomes impossible. But Gadamer's endeavor is not pointless; for those otherwise salutary limits also prevent us from *making sense* in

[24]Johann Gottfried Herder, "Vom Erkennen und Empfinden der menschlichen Seele: Bemerkungen und Träume," in *Herders Sämmtliche Werke*, ed. Bernhard Suphan, 33 vols. (Berlin, 1877–1913), 8:208. As far as I know, Schleiermacher does not use the word "Divination," but "the divinatory" ("das Divinatorische," "das divinatorische Verfahren") is a central concept in his hermeneutics. See F. D. E. Schleiermacher, *Hermeneutik und Kritik*, ed. Manfred Frank (Frankfurt/Main, 1977), e.g., pp. 325, 327, 338, 340.

general of our existence and experience as individuals. Can the limits in question, therefore, be circumvented without being violated? One solution to this dilemma is what I contend is the ceremonial character of our paradoxical experience in the modern theater. On the one hand, the distinction between understanding and interpretation is not violated; that distinction, in a strict, practically visible form, is part of what we mean by drama. But on the other hand, its reversal, the awakening of each mental activity in the locus of the other, is also part of what we mean by drama. In the significantly collective or communal setting of the theater, our individualized condition is affirmed; yet at the same time, for a while, it is also ceremonially superseded or circumvented, in order to reveal our existence at the level of the human race as a whole, at that level where understanding and interpretation *are* interchangeable, where the tradition of interpretation of a cultural phenomenon *is* the phenomenon itself, as an object of understanding, the level of existence in relation to which our individual thinking, judging, questioning, discussing, formulating, do after all make sense as participation in the total human work of meaning. A dramatic performance, unlike the showing of a film, is ceremony in the sense of a shadowing forth, almost a direct experience, of the huge historical action, at once an understanding and an interpreting, by which humankind at once creates and comprehends itself and its world, the action by which humankind, in the form of memory or ordering consciousness as such, "holds a seat / In this distracted globe."

It will be apparent that equivalent arguments could be carried out in other philosophical terminologies. But the terminology of hermeneutics has the advantage of suggesting a relation to the general scheme of literary or poetic types, a relation I have attempted to describe by calling drama the church of literature. In any case, terminology need not be an issue. The importance of the paradoxical or internally tense experience of the theater, from which we began, emerges in part precisely from the readiness with which it takes its place in different terminological contexts. The argument of Chapter 1, on the internal tension of communicative ethics in Ibsen and Strindberg, might serve as an example—as might also my own more historical and psychological argument, in *Modern Drama and German Classicism*, that modern drama owes much to eighteenth-century German techniques that aim at making of the theater a huge, generalized projection of the spectator's internally tense self-consciousness. But again, many further possibilities exist.

8.

It must be borne in mind that the quality of ceremony, in the sense just described, does not belong to drama as an institution. Here the discrimination from opera is critical; for an opera exercises its ceremonial character simply by being an opera. The musical shaping of the text already shifts the quality of performance (what we mean by performance) from interpretation toward realization. But merely *being* a drama is not enough. The specifically dramatic reversal of understanding and interpretation must be achieved positively by the particular work; and the examples we have discussed up to now perhaps give the impression that what is required for this purpose is merely a bag of philosophical stage tricks. Let us therefore examine a couple of works in which the ceremonial quality is not superficially apparent. I am thinking of Bertolt Brecht's "Lehrstücke," his "teaching pieces."

To say that these plays are didactic is to understate the case considerably. In *Die Rundköpfe und die Spitzköpfe*, for example, the play's lesson, exactly formulated, is presented at the very beginning as a lesson the author himself has learned from experience; and the plot, as complex and interesting a parody of *Measure for Measure* as it may be, does focus single-mindedly on that lesson. In the somewhat earlier plays that Brecht actually called "Lehrstücke," *Die Maßnahme*, *Die Ausnahme und die Regel*, and *Das Badener Lehrstück vom Einverständnis*, the lesson material is divided among a number of different formulations in each text; but that the work exists for the sake of a definite lesson, formulated in the text by an interested author, and that the performance therefore has the character of interpretation, is in each case obvious.

What must disturb the spectator is the question of why there has to be a performance in the first place, why such definitely formulable ideas require theatrical interpretation, if indeed they do at all. This question is in fact strongly *suggested* to the spectator: in *Die Maßnahme* by the Agitators' own acting out of their story, where narration would suffice for communicating with the Control Chorus; in *Die Ausnahme und die Regel* by the curious request, in prologue and epilogue, that the spectators find "inexplicable" what they see, which, strictly speaking, cannot happen with respect to a written text except by nonunderstanding; and in *Das Badener Lehrstück* by the obvious question of precisely how the photographs or the clown act contribute to either the substance or the force of the argument that the text claims to be. In the last case, the idea of a reversal of functions is immediately obvious, since the showing of photographs and the clown act are conventional communicative gestures that *can* be interpreted in any number of ways, but *are* interpreted in one particular way by the text.

But is more than just the idea of reversal present in this didactic theater? In *Die Maßnahme* and *Das Badener Lehrstück*, it seems to me that precisely the absence of any sufficient reason for the interpretive act of performance makes clear to us that *our* participation in the unnecessary, unjustified theatrical event, as spectators, is an instance of what the texts themselves call "Einverständnis"—which etymologically suggests "understanding," but means specifically a silent or unresisting understanding, understanding that does not require to be justified, *acquiescence*. It might be argued, alternatively, that performance here represents practice—as distinguished from theory in a way in which it cannot be distinguished by the mere reader, for whom the distinction itself remains theoretical—and that learning in practice, in order to "change the world," is what the plays require of us. But precisely the bracketing of the theoretical distinction makes this argument useless as a *reason* for theatrical performance. In practice, as we sit there, our participation is not so much a positive act as an "Einverständnis," an acquiescence as arbitrary as that demanded of the Young Comrade or the three Mechanics. Or to put it more exactly, the text *interprets* the theatrical situation as such an "Einverständnis" on our part, and the reversal of functions is thus complete; the experience of understanding in the theater (which is also the object of understanding, what we must learn to do) is interpreted in a particular way by the text.

The case of *Die Ausnahme und die Regel*, while equally simple, is different—which supports my general argument by implying that the common element, the reversal of functions, is of prime importance. The prologue and the epilogue, again, insist that we find the play's action "inexplicable, if still usual," or "incomprehensible, if still normal," or especially, "unnatural." But for Brecht, the advocate of theatrical alienation, these qualities already belong to the play's action *in its theatrical performance;* the normal mimetic or "culinary" quality of the theater is rendered incomprehensible by alienation techniques that themselves bear toward dramatic tradition a relation of unnaturalness, which in turn encourages our recognition of the unnatural or inexplicable in the ordinary social reality depicted. And it follows that the performance, as an immediate object of understanding, is interpreted by the text—or by the alienated spectator, the virtual reader—as an image, *in* its theatrical strangeness, of social actuality. The performance in the first instance interprets the didactic text; but the work as a whole avows its intention to place us in a position to interpret reality, which we accomplish, here and now, precisely by taking the *performance* as an object of interpretation. Our interpretive alienation from the performance mirrors or anticipates (is interpreted as) that interpretive alienation from social reality to which the didactic text repeatedly gives direct expression. The text thus stands in an interpretive relation to the whole performance situation, including the auditorium.

I use Brecht as an example here to broaden the base of the argument. The notion of ceremony, especially, must not be taken too narrowly. In Brecht's case, the large human action shadowed forth by the circumvention of our individuality in the theater is not a quasi-religious conception of culture, but the communist revolution, understood, in Brecht's manner, as an unending task of human world-modification. I claim, however, that the notion of ceremony, as it emerges in the discrimination of drama from other types, applies as well here as in the case of less socially engaged works. Moreover, the collision of words and actual things plays no special role in Brechtian ceremony; thus, again, the *range* of possibilities included in what we are talking about becomes apparent. And in Brecht, finally, we have seen how the reversal of functions, between understanding and interpretation, is involved in the work as a whole, not merely effected at a particular point as a kind of trick. I think it is apparent that the same can be argued for the works of Pirandello, Ionesco, and Beckett mentioned earlier, that the particular moments we have looked at merely bring the whole character of each work into especially clear focus.

But the argument must also not be taken *too* broadly. If the ceremonial quality of modern drama is in itself only a potential that must be realized anew by each work, then we ought to be able to find works that do not realize it. Of course this type of strictly negative point cannot be argued conclusively; but yet another play that calls itself a "Lehrstück," Max Frisch's *Biedermann und die Brandstifter*, is an instructive example. Frisch calls his play "Ein Lehrstück ohne Lehre," "a didactic piece with no teaching," and the description seems to me to be accurate. The work, in both its aspects, but especially as performance, is calculated to thwart any attempt at consistent interpretation; the audience, by being a mere passive audience (not only by the fact that the Dr. phil. joins them in the auditorium), are implicated in the "stupidity" that passes itself off as "fate," implicated in such a way that any attempt they make at interpretation becomes an instance of that stupidity. The simple and elegant intellectual architecture of Brecht's plays is gone, and we are left in a state of interpretive vertigo, where the distinction between understanding and interpretation is not established and then reversed, but simply bent out of shape. The text does in a sense interpret the situation in the theater, but in such a way that precisely its adequacy as an interpretation, if it has any, entails the inadequacy of any attempt by us to understand or develop it. We might perhaps even find in this vertigo a theatrical version of what Hirsch objects to in Gadamer, an objection, if my argument holds, that must be involved in any reasonable justification of dramatic form. Perhaps this observation is unfair to Frisch. But observations of this type are made practically unavoidable by the present argument as a whole, observations that involve taking an entirely specific stand, at last, on the question of what we mean by drama.

I have spoken primarily of modern drama, and have not opened the question of ceremony in the history of the form. Can a direct line be followed into the twentieth century from the more obviously ceremonial dramatic genres of the past? In my own opinion, the answer to this question is yes; and I do not deny the presence in my argument, for example, of Nietzsche's thought on the ancient metaphysical ceremony of tragedy. But an attempt to *base* the main points in this chapter on an historical discussion would have produced an unmanageable number of variables and an impenetrable terminology—since different ages require different discriminations. The historical argument becomes possible only after we have developed a clear sense for the ceremonial aspect of modern drama, a sense not only for what we *mean* by drama, but also for what *we* mean by drama.

9.

Two small matters remain. First, although I have insisted that drama is a literary type, the discriminations and boundary effects I have discussed are strictly *theatrical*, involving not other forms of literature but other forms of theater, namely cinema and opera. This difficulty has in part already been dealt with, in the discussion of the relation between cinema and narrative, which can be employed to translate the boundary effects we have talked about into boundary effects, and a discrimination, between narrative and drama. Cinema, as soon as it is established culturally as a form, turns out to have an interesting boundary with literary narrative; and this boundary then brings into focus qualities or contours in narrative that permit a type of discrimination from drama which is not compromised by the ontological defectiveness of the dramatic text. The case of opera, in history, probably has to do more with the boundary of the literary as such, vis-à-vis the musical. But perhaps boundary effects with the type of lyric poetry also operate here, considering that lyric has a tradition of public performance much more recent than, say, that of epic, and considering that the idea of interpretation in a sense close to paraphrase (as it were, an intellectual performance that aspires to *be* the poem, to realize it, not merely to build on it) is strongly associated with modern lyric.

There is of course a logical circle in this reasoning. For literary discriminations to be mediated by theatrical discriminations, it must be true that boundary effects between the literary as such and the theatrical as such are already a possibility. And this possibility in turn—the existence of an area where it is impossible to distinguish definitively between the literary and the theatrical—is equivalent, if my argument holds, to the existence of the genre of drama. That is to say, the existence of drama must be presupposed in order to discern the particular contours by which we satisfy ourselves about the existence of drama as a literary type in the modern period. But this logical circle does not invalidate the argument in the form in which I have made it, in response to the question of what we mean by drama. I think it is undeniable that we do mean something by "drama," and the question is not whether drama exists, but rather *how* we mean what we mean by it, what kind of stake we have in it, and especially whether our meaning is immediately productive in our own literary situation. I claim that this last question—which would probably have to be answered in the negative, for example, with respect to the genres of "epic" or "Arthurian romance"—is what my argument responds to.

These considerations lead us to the second matter that still needs clearing up, the situation of Ibsen and Strindberg with respect to this chapter's theoretical categories. What is meant by drama in a period late enough for the ontological gulf separating dramatic from nondramatic literary forms, but too early for the idea of the cinematic? *The Great Highway* is certainly a kind of ceremony, and involves a reversal of functions in that the text (the ethics of maximum commitment to the quest for the self) interprets our situation in the auditorium (side by side, facing in the same direction) as a model of perfected human community. Even in late Ibsen this kind of argument can be made. In *When We Dead Awaken*, for example, Rubek's artistic development interprets by negation our decision—represented by our sitting in the theater—to retain mimetic convention and resist the development of sensibility that "experience of life" apparently requires of us. But these arguments say nothing about the place of Ibsen or Strindberg in dramatic history. The reversal of functions between understanding and interpretation would not be part of what *we* mean by drama (with the benefit of a discrimination from cinema) if we did not expect to find some version of it in practically all drama, not just that of our own time.

What must disturb us in Ibsen and Strindberg, I think, is the combination of a sharp and productive focus upon dramatic style, in its historical dimension, with a curious lack of the sort of self-conscious theatricality, or theatrical self-consciousness, that we learn to expect, say, in a Brecht or a Pirandello. Stylistic history is clearly a factor in Ibsen and Strindberg, but the specifically theatrical is apparently not assigned a central role in that history. The theater of readers is a theater in which the spectator's experience is not substantially different from what the experience of reading the text would be if our reading were carried out in the full communal spirit that that theater promotes and prefigures. Specifically theatrical meanings in the sense of this chapter, meanings that can *never* be there for a reader, do not figure in these plays.

If these basic perceptions are agreed upon, then the historical position of the early modern Scandinavians emerges, with some clarity, as one characterized by the *absence* of sufficiently distinct boundary effects to delineate drama as a particular type. Ibsen and Strindberg do not exploit the established communicative potential of drama (which in a strong sense is not available to them for exploiting anyway), but rather they are concerned with communication, or the ground of communication, *as such*, in the most general possible sense. This is not to say that their endeavor is without precedent, or that it has no anchor in dramatic tradition. I think it is fairly clear that their model is the success of German Classicism at creating an apparently new national literature, an apparently new ground of communication, practically from scratch, in the form of drama. Nor would it be true to say that the absence of exclusively theatrical meanings makes Ibsen's and Strindberg's works less properly drama than, say, the works of Beckett or Ionesco. Drama, for Ibsen and Strindberg, is still the church of literature. The difference is that it is a prophetic church, a church directed at the future. The virtual reader, in this theater of readers, is not a reader understood to be excluded from certain significant present experiences, but rather a more than merely individual reader of the future, who will no longer *require* his or her present situation as the spectator in a theater.

Or to put it differently, the drama of Ibsen and Strindberg envisages a future for literary communication, but, in the absence or obscurity of the requisite boundary effects, cannot envisage a future *for drama*. And it is a measure of the complexity of dramatic tradition that Ibsen and Strindberg then themselves become permanent seminal figures in a modern drama that frees itself from their difficulty. The early modern or premodern period, in general, is of major significance in understanding modern drama as a whole, and we will discuss another aspect of it in the next chapter.

CHAPTER THREE

Nestroy and Schnitzler:
The Three Societies of Comedy and
the Idea of a Textless Theater

Given the operation of certain boundary effects, the tension between virtual reader and actual spectator in the theater turns out to
be artistically useful in modern drama. But in premodern drama the
same tension is a vexing problem, and in Ibsen and Strindberg it is
accepted as such, interpreted as the inevitable tension between an
achieved community of the future and a communicatively inadequate present. We can understand the relation between the opposed
aspects of this tension a bit better by looking at premodern drama in
Vienna.

1.

The ontological defectiveness I have spoken of earlier is only one
symptom of a more generally problematic quality of the dramatic
text. We might inquire, for example, into the relation between the
dramatic text and the physically real action that it can be considered
as describing or prescribing or standing for, or merely getting in the
way of. The written text of a ballet or mime lays before us, mainly,
the question of whether it makes any sense for us to be *reading* it in
the first place. And stage directions, if we once yield to the tempta-
tion of worrying about them, can become an obsession. Robert Frost
versifies them together with the dialogue. In Bernard Shaw they
yank themselves free and become "prefaces," in such a way, I think,
that the quality of essay and that of stage direction still infect each

93

other. In Friedrich Dürrenmatt's *Die Physiker* there is an instance that the play's theme tempts us to classify as insane.

But even dramatic dialogue, in its quality as actual or potential speaking, can question its own quality as text when it contrives to give the impression of being *nothing but talk*, nothing but those familiar colloquial gestures whose unique expressiveness vanishes in the very moment of their happening. Obviously this impression can never be created by a dramatic text alone; it depends, always, on the situation of a particular audience in a particular theater. Gerhart Hauptmann's dialect plays—which record phonetically the most minute differences of region, class, and social pretension—are an instructive negative example. We recognize that an actor not already familiar with the dialect could never learn it from the written speeches, no matter how accurate their phonetics, whereas the actor who does know the dialect from experience, and does understand the character's social situation, needs no word-by-word phonetic respelling. Precisely in its extreme faithfulness to mere talk, the play thus detaches itself from our hearing or speaking it and becomes *mere* text in the crudest sense, a scribal system. It is even possible that this quality belongs to the interpretable meaning of those dialect plays, at least in the case of *Und Pippa tanzt!* where Wann reads the play's action, and more than just its action, in a book.

To achieve the complete *suppression* of the text (which is perhaps a form of Artaud's goal for the theater) a vehicle is needed, a special relation between theater and audience, in which the play as text can be dissolved; and such a situation is not common, perhaps not even possible. But the comic theater of nineteenth-century Vienna, especially the theater of Johann Nestroy, appears at least to approach the condition of textlessness. For Nestroy's are also dialect plays, employing a wide range of Viennese and other Austrian linguistic physiognomies, plus those of some foreigners; but their attitude toward dialect has nothing of Hauptmann's scribal fussiness. In *Weder Lorbeerbaum noch Bettelstab* the poet Leicht says, "Bis zum Lorbeer versteig' ich mich nicht. G'fallen sollen meine Sachen, unterhalten, lachen sollen d'Leut."[1] Diction and spelling make it clear that the first sentence must be spoken in a manner relatively free of dialect signs; but the form "G'fallen" signals that the speaker then deliberately drops into a more vulgar Viennese. It *signals* this change

[1]Johann Nestroy, *Sämtliche Werke*, ed. Fritz Brukner and Otto Rommel, 15 vols. (Vienna, 1924–30; rpt. 1973), 3:355–56. Further references by vol. number and page in parentheses.

of level; it does not reproduce it phonetically. The "ll" in both "gefallen" and "sollen," for example, is heard only as a semivowel in the words as Leicht now pronounces them. The written text is thus specific enough to show the actor his task, while still acknowledging it as *his* task (not the text's), in the theater.

More important, however, are the character and situation of Nestroy's audience. For a large proportion of the city's reasonably well-educated inhabitants, Viennese dialect was in the nineteenth century, and is still today, a manipulable artistic device. It is the means by which one consciously insists on one's identity as a Viennese and an Austrian, not (for example) a German.[2] This is not to say that the average Viennese is capable of speaking an entirely dialect-free German, or even that there is such a thing as dialect-free German. But average Viennese *are* in some degree capable of adjusting the shape and saturation and level of their dialect to suit either their whims or their circumstances (as Leicht does in insisting on his works' popular appeal). And they do so not in the spirit of distanced imitation, not in quotation marks—as a Londoner might joke in Cockney, or as a New Yorker might parody Brooklynese—but simply to express themselves and mark out precisely their present relation to others. (The sudden shift to a lower dialect level, depending on the situation, can be anything from a sign of affection to an insult.) The Viennese have perhaps no "natural" way of speaking at all, and have therefore an exceptionally clear sense of *all* speaking, even the most casual, as deliberate artifice.

This aspect of Viennese linguistic life, taken together with the city's political self-consciousness and its tradition of actual theaters, provides Nestroy with his needful artistic vehicle. The one apparently irreducible difference between our own actual daily talk and language as spoken on the stage is that the latter is strictly artificial, put on for the occasion by the people speaking it. Precisely this difference, however, becomes minimal in Nestroy's theater, where stage-language is similar to actual Viennese talk *even* in the matter of its artificiality. Here, therefore, if anywhere, the play as text can be entirely supplanted by the play as talk, as performance; and I will argue that this tendency of the text to vanish is crucial in Nestroy's

[2]Peter Wehle, *Sprechen Sie Wienerisch?* (Vienna, 1980), appears to be enjoying excellent sales *in Vienna*. This book, which includes not only a dictionary of Viennese dialect words, but also detailed (if disarmingly witty) instruction on how to keep one's dialect authentic (in such matters as the use of the rounded "a"), is thus purchased and read by people whom we might have expected to dismiss it as an unnecessary codification of what they do "naturally" anyway.

dramatic strategy. I do not intend to leave this proposition in a state of aesthetic seminudity; I will not try to evoke or pin down the atmosphere, the flavor, the *je ne sais quoi* of Viennese theatrical experience, which is undoubtedly lost in any form of translation.[3] I am talking about artistic strategy in a sense that I think can be held fast quite adequately in critical discussion.

2.

The various excessively complicated attempts that have been made to divide Nestroy's work into categories are, I think, the response to a justified puzzlement about the social significance and social mission of that work.[4] Shall we leave Nestroy in chaos, dismiss him as a theatrical opportunist and occasional satirist who directed his wit at whatever targets were not sufficiently protected by the bumbling of Austrian censorship, and who otherwise simply wrote what he thought people would pay to see?[5] This will not do. Nestroy's satirical and critical treatment not only of specific social phenomena, but also of the subtleties of social psychology, is far too earnest and complex to be regarded as anything but the expression of a profound and cohesive social *vision*. His career ought to make sense; there ought to be a governing idea to explain the relation, for instance, between such apparently harmless works as *Lumpazivagabundus, Der Talisman, Einen Jux will er sich machen, Häuptling Abendwind*, and such apparently more aggressive works as *Weder Lorbeerbaum noch Bettelstab, Der Zerrissene, Der Unbedeutende, Freiheit in Krähwinkel*, the Wagner parodies.

But where shall we seek that governing idea? What, for instance, does Nestroy advocate? A revolutionary uprising of the lower classes? A movement toward representative government? Monarchy with increased constitutional safeguards? Economic reform? Simple

---

[3]Max Knight and Joseph Fabry perform some minor miracles of translation in their Johann Nestroy, *Three Comedies* (New York, 1967); but there is no conceivable way of transplanting elsewhere the whole cultural and linguistic element that Nestroy's plays need in order to live as what they in truth are.

[4]See the classifications in Brukner and Rommel's edition (*Sämtliche Werke*), and in Franz H. Mautner, *Nestroy* (Heidelberg, 1974).

[5]Mautner, p. 112, comes close to taking this way out when he says, "Gewiß war Nestroy, der Theaterdichter, so sehr von der Leidenschaft für 'Theater' besessen, sein Schreiben trotz seiner geistigen und ästhetischen Ziele so sehr vom Streben nach 'Erfolg' auf der Bühne beherrscht, daß er sacrificia intellectus beging, die durch nichts, auch nicht durch die Gesetze der Komödie, zu 'rechtfertigen' sind."

freedom, especially in cultural and artistic matters? Wherever we turn, Nestroy's acid psychology causes us discomfort, his recognition that social injustice or malproportion is never entirely separable from the mentality of even those who suffer under it, hence his inability to resist satirizing even what he appears to be in favor of, even what he unquestionably *is* in favor of. And why, in such plays as *Der Zerrissene* and *Freiheit in Krähwinkel*, does he allow an obviously serious initial question to be obscured by the conventional mechanisms of farce? We *can* say, at various points, that he advocates a particular idea or attitude or activity or concrete institutional change; but such advocacy is never sufficient to make real sense of either the particular work or the career as a whole. There is always a level of farcical or satirical awareness that undermines the apparent message. Must we, therefore, see Nestroy simply as a cynic or nihilist? Must we recognize, in his earnest social concern and even in his good humor, nothing but the self-mocking surface of Luciferian despair? This idea is in the first place merely an admission of critical defeat; and in the second place, we recall that even the devil is an object of satire in Nestroy.

The Nestroy problem is thus a literary problem, involving the question of how certain texts come into existence, what sort of social or personal intiative is represented by them. But my point is that this problem is insoluble in strictly literary terms, that there is no answer to the question except by way of an idea of the theater that tends to crowd those texts, *as* readable texts, out of existence, an idea of the theater as *nothing but* social or colloquial dynamics. When we discuss the social significance of comedy (or other poetic types), we ordinarily distinguish two societies: the fictional society, as represented by the action and personages of the work; and the real society of which the fiction is an image. We begin by defining the latter in terms of the work's scope of reference: does the fiction refer to a particular society, a particular type of society, or human society as such? We then identify the aspects or features of the real society on which the fiction focuses, and with what sort of judgment; and we draw a conclusion about what the work is aiming at. This analysis, crude as it is, applies even to very subtle ideological criticism, at least to the extent that such criticism does not normally pay attention to the third society of comedy, the immediate society, the actual social group, including both players and spectators, that is present in the theater at the performance. We are accustomed to think of this actual social group as a mere vehicle, having no function in the work's meaning except to transmit and receive. In the case of

Nestroy, however, I contend that the social unit consisting of the people in the theater is an indispensable communicative and symbolic device that delimits the work's meaning at precisely those points where the written text, taken by itself, fails to.

This third society is often the focus of songs, such as Johann's in *Zu ebener Erde und erster Stock:* "Da finden d'Leut' dran a Vergnüg'n, / Ich, offen g'sagt, nit, ich müßt's lüg'n" (Nestroy, *Werke,* 6:79–81), "In such things people find pleasure, but frankly I'd be a liar if I said that I did." Nestroy the singer (who the audience of course knows is the work's author) expresses contempt for the way people waste their time at card games ("Spiel"), and concludes by addressing the spectators:

> Ich kenn' nur ein einziges Spiel, was mich g'freut,
> Nämlich das Spiel, was Ihrem Vergnügen geweiht.
> Wenn man da reüssiert, spielt man g'wiß nicht umsunst,
> 's winkt einem hoher G'winn und der ist Ihre Gunst.
> Das läßt sich mit Gold nit aufwieg'n,
> Daran find' ich 's größte Vergnüg'n.
>
> [8:141]

I find only one kind of playing really enjoyable, the playing that is devoted to *your* pleasure. When we succeed here, we are definitely not playing for nothing; we are beckoned onward by the genuine profit which is your favor toward us, and which is worth more than gold. In such playing I find the greatest pleasure.

But can we take this polite compliment at face value? The mere association of "Theater spielen" with "Karten spielen" reminds us that our time in the theater may easily be regarded as time wasted. The pointed references to gold and profit remind us that whereas in card playing we can at least hope to win, the money we have spent on the theater is gone forever, some of it into the pockets of the person addressing us. And when it is Johann, whom we have watched obsequiously flattering Goldfuchs while in truth exploiting him, who now obsequiously flatters *us,* the suggested analogy is obvious. In the scene immediately preceding, Johann had said to Goldfuchs's daughter Emilie:

Drum seit der Preisgebung Ihres Geheimnisses müssen Sie ja nicht mehr glauben, Sie sei'n meine gebietende Frau! Jetzt bin ich der Herr! Übrigens das nur zur Privatnotiz. Sie zahlen mir jetzt das doppelte Honorar und ich leite untertänigst bereitwilligst Dero Intrige. [6:76–77]

Therefore, now that your secret is in my hands, you need no longer believe yourself in a position to give me orders. Now I am the master! But this is just between the two of us. You will now pay me double the usual, and I, with uncomplaining submissiveness, will conduct the intrigue for your ladyship.

Again the analogy is uncomfortable; for Nestroy, the author and chief actor, is also "conducting" *our* intrigue, the intrigue being staged for our amusement. Who, in *this* case, is "Der Herr"? Are the actors our obliging servants, or are we merely their dupes? The situation in the immediate society of the theater thus echoes uncomfortably the structure of society in the fiction, the society of capitalist exploiters, with time and money to waste, who are in turn exploited by those whom they hire to display and make pleasurable their power. It is thus made plain to us that the real society of which the fiction is an image is a society in which we *continue to participate* even while enjoying the detached view of it (in this case, as it were, geometrically detached, with upper and lower stages) that the theatrical situation affords us.

In *Weder Lorbeerbaum noch Bettelstab*, the poet Leicht spells out exactly what he requires of an audience: "I make no presumptuous claims to the laurel. My stuff is meant to give pleasure, to entertain, to make people laugh—and, for me, to make money, so that I can laugh too, that's the whole purpose" (3:355–56). But how, in the theater, are we to receive *this* play? Simple entertainment, as required of us by Leicht, is out of the question; for the content of the play, and specifically this speech, obliges us to *think* about entertainment as an aesthetic category. We are forced into a paradoxical situation that echoes the paradox experienced by Leicht himself in the fiction: his desire not to have his work taken too seriously causes him to take his work too seriously to ignore the pretentious criticism that results from people's taking his work too seriously. Or we think of *Der Zerrissene*, which shares with *Einen Jux will er sich machen* the special dramaturgical complexity of having its farcical plot deliberately initiated by the main character in response to social and cultural ennui. The boundary between the fictional society (hence also our real society) and the immediate social unit in the theater (where farce is the conventional shape of *our* response to ennui, ennui being what makes us go to the farcical theater) thus becomes uncomfortably permeable. And this feeling is reinforced by the last stanza of Lips-Nestroy's song in act 2, scene 11 of *Der Zerrissene*, where the "dramatic artist" admonishes himself:

Doch halt—glaubst denn, Dalk, daß das wen int'ressiert,
Ob ein Unrecht dich kränkt oder sonst was tuschiert?
's is Simi, 's wird auf'zog'n, jetzt renn' auf die Szen',
"O Jegerl, mein' Trudl, die is gar so schön,
Und i g'fall' ihr, ich bin ein kreuzlustiger Bur!"
: Sich so zu verstell'n, na, da g'hört was dazur. :

[12:297]

But wait, you fool, do you think anyone's interested if you've been
done wrong or if something's bothering you? It's seven, curtain time,
get onto the stage! "O jiminy, my Trudi is so pretty, and she likes me,
I'm a real happy guy." (This kind of make-believe takes some nerve.)

Clearly the *actor* addresses us here directly, not the character, which
means that the process of "make-believe" moves in the wrong direction, since it is the character Lips, not the actor, who has just had to
swallow painful insults or "Tusche." Again, the boundaries that
divide fiction from theater from social reality are confused.

Finally, in *Freiheit in Krähwinkel*, Frau Pemperl asks her husband
where he is off to, and receives the answer, "A bisserl Revolution
anschau'n" (5:179). He is going to "take in" the revolution, do a little
revolution watching. But we in the theater are engaged in exactly
the activity these words describe; we are being *amused* by the spectacle of revolution. We as an audience, the third society of comedy, are
again maneuvered into a situation of uncomfortable inner tension.
The play is at base unquestionably sympathetic to the revolution of
1848 in Vienna, which at the time of the premiere, 1 July 1848, was
showing only the first signs of its ugly petering out. But precisely to
the extent that we share that sympathy, we must recognize that our
actual situation in the theater, our willingness to think of revolution
in terms of the antics of an Ultra, alias Fürst Knutikof Sybiritschefsky
Tyrannsky Absolutski (5:172),[6] is in a strong sense politically irre-
sponsible. The attitude of a theater audience is always, in the nature
of things, "A bisserl anschau'n," an indolent and uninvolved and
relatively self-satisfied looking on. Our condition as spectators is
thoroughly paradoxical, in a manner already suggested by Ultra's
name, which marks him as an "extreme" revolutionary yet also
reminds us of the royalist reactionaries in French parliamentary history. To experience even the possibility of revolution we must posi-

[6]This name suggests the word "Knute," "knout," which is a standard symbol of
absolutist repression, and manages to balance between the connotations "Siberia"
and "Sybarite."

tion ourselves beyond or outside ("ultra") our actual society; but this attitude makes us onlookers, prevents our sufficiently committed participation in the revolutionary movement, and so helps preserve the old order. Ultra not only pretends to be, but in a sense *is* Prince Absolutski. Precisely by being outside, we also find ourselves inside, in complicity with the social order we criticize.

This argument perhaps does not apply universally or objectively in history. But it does represent what Nestroy sees as a typical political dynamics in nineteenth-century Europe, where *ennui* is a basic social ill; and it does apply strictly to the psychological situation of a theater audience. Our very coming to the theater is already a significant social act with worrisome consequences. Indeed, it seems to me that Nestroy's theater compels us, the audience, in the expectations we bring with us, to accept responsibility even for the standard mechanism of farce or "Posse." In *Der Zerrissene* and *Einen Jux will er sich machen*, where the farcical plot arises directly from a character's response to culturally conditioned ennui, the parallel with *our* reasons for being in the theater is especially clear. Without the character's ennui there would be no plot; without our ennui, our having nothing better to do, there would be no audience. The quality of farce reminds us that by going to the theater we participate willingly in a social act that compromises our critical perspective, especially our perspective on the quality of ennui. It has been suggested that the farcical quality of Nestroy's work interferes with the development of the serious social and political issues he touches. My point is that we are meant to perceive this interference and to attribute it to *ourselves*, as we sit in the theater; we recognize that our acceptance of the social conventions that regulate, here in the theater, our relation to each other and to the actors, is what really interferes with the tendency toward radical social criticism.

And if we look back now at our original problem, the problem of reconciling the cynical aspect of Nestroy's social vision with the constructive aspect, we find that this philosophical tension is exactly analogous to the tension we experience as an audience, between critical objectivity and willing participation with respect to our society. Only the *triple* society of comedy produces this effect: the real society of mid-nineteenth-century Europe, especially Austria, which, as *depicted* in the fictional society, is an object of satire, while at the same time, as *represented* by the immediate social unit in the theater, it commands our positive involvement. And if we agree further that the conventions of farce already make us aware of our involvement in the same society that is subjected to satire, then even the apparently most harmless plays fit the pattern. Especially interesting is the case of *Der Talisman*, where the critical and the farcical as it were tread on each other's toes. Redheaded people in fact were made fun of in Nestroy's time; but society, then as now, especially the multinational society that was mismanaged by the government in Vienna, was beset by much more dangerous and damaging forms of prejudice—against Jews, Czechs, Balkanites, not to mention social or economic groupings. The choice of the injustice experienced by redheads as a target for the play's ostentatious attack on prejudice ("Vorurteil") reduces that attack to a farce, which, precisely in its emptiness, holds up a mirror to the self-critical posturing, the self-righteous "liberalism" of certain Europeans, and of the present actors and audience (the third society) in particular. It is in this complicated structure, appropriately, that the tension between criticism and participation is thematized, in Titus's monologue of act 1, scene 7 (10:393–94); and it is here that the notion of "eine traurige Posse," "a sad farce," is suggested (10:455). Or we think of *Häuptling Abendwind*, in which a cannibal chieftain's son returns home from Europe, having become a professional hairdresser, and narrowly escapes being eaten incognito at his father's peace-feast with an old enemy. As in *Der Talisman*, the satire on European civilization is turned back against the audience precisely by the farcical triumph of European values at the end; we are presented to ourselves as *requiring* the type of resolution we receive.

3.

The self-questioning of satire in Nestroy has the effect of highlighting the separation between virtual reader and actual spectator. If we understand that merely by being in the theater we are exposed to the play's satirical attack, it follows that our situation as spectators is clearly delimited in our self-awareness, clearly distinguished from the part of us that affirms the satire, a part of us that is thus set off as being *not* entirely in the theater but in a situation more like that of a reader. To understand fully the position here, we must go further into the background of the tension in Nestroy's thought and in his theater.

Täuschung ist die feine, aber starke Kette, die durch alle Glieder der Gesellschaft sich zieht. [15:682]

Täuschung ist ein großes Wort, sie hält
Zusammen das Dingsda, die Welt,
Drum hat man auch keine Wahl auf Erden,
Als täuschen oder getäuscht zu werden;
Wer glaubt, daß es ein Drittes gäbe,
Der täuscht sich selbst, so wahr ich lebe.

[15:682]

Illusion is the delicate but strong chain that connects all members and sections of society.
    Illusion is an important concept; it holds together the thingum, the world. We have no choice on earth but either to delude or to be deluded. Whoever believes that there is a third possibility is deluding himself, as surely as I am alive.

We might have expected the word "betrügen" (deceive) rather than "täuschen" (delude), in these aphorisms. In fact the word does occur in the context of the first; but the actual emphasis is on "Täuschung," illusion, and we can understand why by referring to a monologue sketch entitled "Dumm is g'scheit."[7] It is stupid to be intelligent, argues Nestroy, and it is intelligent to be stupid, because the intelligent person inevitably becomes aware of facts and truths that make his or her contented participation in society impossible. Illusion is the chain that holds the human world together, for too much clear intelligence, too accurate a perception of the way things really are, too well-developed a critical or satirical sense, necessarily excludes us from society; and a society of such excluded, overintelligent (but Nestroy insists, not really intelligent) individuals would be no society, no "world," at all. Delude or be deluded: there is no third possibility. If we decline to participate actively in the illusion-creating and illusion-preserving processes of society, if, for example, we imagine that satire is the strict opposite of illusion, then we are even more deluded than those whose (unquestioned) stupidity we satirize.

    For Nestroy, however (as for Nietzsche in "Vom Nutzen und Nachtheil"), it is precisely this extremely passive and uncontrolled form of delusion, this stupid overintelligence, that characterizes mid-nineteenth-century Europe, an ostentatiously self-critical but socially impotent Europe, repeatedly dabbling in revolution but achieving nothing of consequence. Satire is necessary, for the in-

---

[7]Johann Nestroy, *Gesammelte Werke*, ed. Otto Rommel, 6 vols. (Vienna, 1948–49; rpt. 1962), 6:582–83.

justices and absurdities of the social order are too obvious and immediate to be passed over in silence. But on the other hand, the practice of criticizing or satirizing presupposes a conventionally given place *within* the social order (a place such as the theater) from which to broadcast our message. We are torn, "zerrissen," like Lips, between an intelligence that destroys all satisfaction in social involvement and an inevitable social involvement that clouds and confuses our intelligence.[8] And this situation is permanent. Nestroy welcomes the revolution of 1848—to do so is part of his own acceptance of social involvement and responsibility—but it is plain from *Freiheit in Krähwinkel* that he does not expect a fundamental change in society. Human intelligence, by nature, is not capable of detaching itself from its conditions sufficiently to create a new social order, any more than Nestroy's theater is capable of resisting its nature as farce. The evil spirit Lumpazivagabundus, whose business is to make a mockery of all supposed human self-reform, is by any reasonable standard victorious in the two plays where he appears; his defeat, the theatrical triumph of reason and virtue, is mere "Täuschung," thus part of what holds the old *un*reformed world together. (As in *Häuptling Abendwind*, the "happy" ending is itself the final satirical barb directed at us.)

But then why does Nestroy write? Why create in the theater a replica (reader versus spectator) of the tension that our social and historical condition already compels us to experience anyway? Ennui as "Zerrissenheit," the passing of our life without direction or accomplishment ("Denn sehn Sie, Sie leb'n, doch warum, wissen S' nicht" [2:172]), implies ennui as boredom, "Langeweile"; and I contend that Nestroy's central artistic purpose, throughout his career, is set forth in his aphorism on this subject: "Das Interregnum der Langeweile aufheben und den Geist wieder auf den Thron setzen" (15:697), "To terminate the interregnum of boredom and restore wit (or spirit) to the throne." For it turns out that the paradoxical structure of our ennui, the tension between irreconcilable opposites, is also the fundamental structure of *wit* or "Geist"—which, for Nestroy, is nothing but the enjoyable playing with just such opposites.[9] To replace ennui by wit requires not that ennui be sup-

---

[8]Nestroy's manuscripts themselves offer a practical instance of the ambiguous advocacy of illusion. The first of the two aphorisms quoted earlier on illusion was first written down by Nestroy, then *erased*—as being itself too intelligent, too free of illusion?

[9]See Mautner, pp. 91–99, for infinitely detailed examples of the oppositional, antithetical, paradoxical quality of Nestroy's wit.

pressed or resisted (which is impossible anyway), but simply that its nature be redirected, its structure affirmed and energized, turned into action rather than passivity. Ennui must *become* wit, but without ceasing to be ennui, just as the depressingly constant and typical stupidity of existence is realized as a pointedly paradoxical wit in Nestroy's songs.

But this transformation of ennui can actually happen only in the third society of comedy, the model social group in the theater. If ennui and wit are to become identical, then either our large real society must become fundamentally witty, which is difficult to imagine, or else the theater—where wit is at home, where we make the choice for deluding over being deluded, where we assent willingly to delusion—must be thoroughly infected with ennui. This last is Nestroy's strategy. His theater entraps us in an exact replica of the paradox that besets us in real life, in a situation uncomfortably analogous to our general historical misery, but a situation which we now, in the theater of farce, experience as a field for spirited, witty invention, for "Geist." In the theater, for a few moments, the revolution actually arrives; we are now in a position to exploit and enjoy, not seriously but spiritedly, the selfsame paradox (of detachment and involvement, reader and spectator, intelligence and stupidity) that elsewhere engenders our mere anguish. The theater is prophetic, not in what it says but in the character of the temporary social group that constitutes it, a group whose self-critical awareness is deluded—yet in being deluded is also sharpened—by wit, by a cheerfully corrosive intellectual perversity that prevents all pretensions to self-betterment as well as all melancholy resignation. The theater is prophetic, in the sense that its small social unit must become a model for society at large, if society is to survive the ennui of the nineteenth century.

This social vision, to the extent that it is one, cannot be adequately set forth as doctrine, for the inevitable solemnity of doctrine would violate just that infinite paradoxicality of wit which must be encouraged. As I have said, the Nestroy problem can never be *solved*, but can only be *dealt with*, in the theater of wit; Ultra, as a figure of farce, is perhaps a true revolutionary after all. What must be encouraged, moreover, is wit not merely as a form of thought or speech, but as a cohesive social force, of which we can therefore experience the foretaste only in an actual social situation, such as that of the theater. The community-forming "chain" of illusion cannot hold permanently. Inevitably ennui takes hold of us: the state of seeing through illusion and recognizing what is fundamentally wrong with the social order, yet also perpetuating that wrong in the very act of recognizing it; the state, therefore, of living without a reason for living; a state characterized simultaneously by anguished self-division and deadly boredom. But there is no way to counteract ennui directly. Knowledge, once known, cannot be abandoned in favor of illusion; ennui itself becomes an object of knowledge and so nourishes and feeds on itself. Only the affirmative realization of ennui as wit can renew our communal life; only in the form of wit can ennui, which we do undeniably have in common, become a source of community. What offended Nestroy most about Wagner, I think, was the latter's solemn proclamation of an art of the future. Precisely the future of human community, in a decidedly more livable form than that represented by Bayreuth, was the territory claimed, if not proclaimed, by Nestroy himself, whenever the curtain rose and permitted the assembled human elements to fuse yet again into that crucial third society of comedy.

4.

What will Nestroy's revolutionary or postrevolutionary society look like? Exactly how will the restoration of wit as a principal communal force be manifest in social institutions and social life? That this question is unanswerable is fairly obvious; but we need to grasp exactly why it is unanswerable. The problem lies in the phrase "look like." As soon as we observe society with the sort of objectivity and seriousness that will enable us to say what it "looks like," we find ourselves violating the very principle of wit by which society must be renewed. Society after the revolution will not look different from society now—at least not to the extent that we understand its "look" in terms of the kind of "looking" that is characteristic of our present historical situation. But still, society will *be* fundamentally different, in a manner of which the theater gives us a foretaste. Nestroy, as I have argued, compels us to recognize that our experience in the theater, under analysis, *looks exactly like* our corrupt experience in the corrupt real society to which we belong outside the theater. Yet at the same time we also recognize that our experience in the theater *is* different. The theater thus becomes an exact model of the new society, which *is* different, but in a manner not judgeable by what it looks like.

This is not to say that there will not be discussible institutional changes in a society at last governed by wit. Changes are obviously

necessary. But our present corrupt perspective is such that by con-
fining our attention to needful changes in detail, we *prevent* the
fundamental change without which all temporary institutional initiatives must prove futile. Nestroy's theater is not nihilistic or direc-
tionless, but unfocused; more exactly, it is repeatedly *de*focused by
its own farcical wit. It would not be recognizable as a revolutionary
theater in the first place—we could not take even the first step
toward experiencing it as such a theater—if it did not make the
gesture of focusing upon specific social abuses. But its relentless wit
always carries it a step beyond that gesture, into a questioning or
mocking of its own social viewpoint, which throws open, in the
theater, an uncommitted space in which wit itself can begin to operate as the motor of revolution.

Nestroy's, then, is a revolutionary theater that operates by creating for its audience a model of the radically developable difference
between how things look and how they are. But we must not lose
sight of the limitations of the reasoning by which we arrive at this
idea. The argument moves in a universe entirely separate from the
universe it attempts to describe; it is inescapably a *literary* argument.
It begins with the recognition of certain conceptually unresolvable
anomalies in a body of text, and proceeds to the conclusion that a
nonconceptual resolution must be postulated, a resolution indistinguishable from the immediate experience of an audience in the
theater. In other words, the argument is about texts, but it ends by
asserting that its texts, *as* text, are utterly superseded—in a sense
made nonexistent—by their own meaning.

The tension between virtual reader and actual spectator does
function in Nestroy, in the relation between our critical or satiric
perspective and our continued participation, even as an audience, in
the object of satire. But my point is that this tension now exists for
the sole purpose of being transformed into the active and fruitful
internal tension of wit—in the same way, perhaps, that a top with
painted figures on it exists for the sole purpose of becoming that
miraculously self-balancing object (if it is still an "object" at all, not
rather a pure action) on which the figures, the text, are no longer
legible. And the idea of a reversible interpretive relation between
text and performance requires similar modification. What happens
in Nestroy's theater must, it is true, undergo a kind of interpretation
to be realized as social change; yet precisely the text, with its perverse undermining of its own gestures of advocacy, refuses to provide interpretation of the sort needed.

The literary anomalies in Nestroy are crucial in indicating the line of thought I have taken, and one further anomaly will perhaps make the case clearer still. Frequently in the songs, and sometimes in dialogue, Nestroy encourages in us a complicated awareness of our actual situation in the theater. Why does he never thematize this awareness and develop it as the structural center of an entire play? Why does he not go further toward making the theater a fully self-conscious institution? Certain late plays, such as *Theaterg'schichten* and *Umsonst,* make gestures in this direction; but as in the case of the political farces, the comic intrigue and the resolution of the love and money plots shift attention away from whatever deeper issues might seem about to arise.

The theater play, the play about play-acting, represents a definite logical possibility for Nestroy, but a possibility that he in the end *avoids* developing. For a fully developed theater play, in the manner, say, of Pirandello, or of Hugo von Hofmannsthal's *Ariadne auf Naxos,* tends toward symbolic closure, toward the erection of the theater as itself an adequate symbol of truth, not the eternally inadequate gateway to revolution that it must be for Nestroy. The completion of the theater as a symbol does not obscure the relation between performance and text but rather articulates it, brings it into focus, whereas for Nestroy—if my argument holds—the play-as-text must in a sense simply cease to exist. Closure or codification in any form would mean the death of this revolutionary theater, which has no goal whatever except to propagate the ever self-dissolving intellectual kinesis of wit. That Nestroy is capable of radical theatrical experimentation is evident, for example, from such works as *Das Haus der Temperamente* with its vision of human polyphony on a four-part stage. That he sketches the ironies of theater-within-theater, but never fully develops them, therefore shows a significant restraint on his part, which I think is explained by my argument. We, the audience, must become conscious of the theater as theater, especially of the structural analogies between our experience there and our corrupt social experience in general. But if our consciousness is *focused* on the theater, then the theater no longer opens directly upon that as yet nonexistent, as yet hardly conceivable world where it is meant actually to operate.

In the terminology I suggested earlier, Nestroy's theater must become a theater of pure or mere talk, of sheer dialectical kinesis, for which the dramatic text is literally a mere pretext, now utterly superseded by the actual theatrical event, no more present in the theater than the needful hot pitch of its manufacture is present in the sound of a trumpet. But the theater of sheer talk is not achievable by self-reflexive theatrical irony; its very nature excludes the efficacy of *any* self-consciously artistic device. It was simply *there* for Nestroy, waiting to be exploited, in the peculiarly Viennese relationship between staged language and the talk of everyday life, in the natural artificiality and artificial naturalness of Viennese dialect.

Nestroy's awareness of the advantage he thus enjoys is shown not only by his use of dialect in general but also by occasional specific touches. In *Liebesgeschichten und Heiratssachen*, for example, one of his most harmless and most popular farces, Marchese Vincelli intercepts and reads aloud on the stage a letter supposedly written in thick dialect. Much to the delight of the audience, he has to spell out the word "Pfirtigott" (= "behüte dich Gott," "God keep you") before he understands it (11:441). But an obvious problem arises here. Can this sort of dialect—as Vincelli scornfully but (we must assume) accurately reproduces it—actually be contained or determined or dictated by the *document* (the letter, the text) he is looking at? "'s is 's G'scheiteste," he reads; but no one, no matter how he or she speaks, *writes* "Es ist das Gescheiteste" in that form. Or even supposing it is written thus, how can Vincelli—who is not himself a speaker on that dialect level, who does not even know the dialect—read it *as* dialect? The point is that Vincelli is reading a text (the letter) that does not exist (because it cannot exist) in the form in which he reads it; and the parallel with the relation between the performance and the text of the play we are watching is plain. The written text, as I have argued, is meant to have its very existence discredited, to be crowded out of existence, by the immediate theatrical event.

In Nestroy, then, we have at least the approach to a purely theatrical drama, drama entirely lacking a literary component. Yet the theoretical questions remain. Does it make sense to talk about the disappearance or virtual nonexistence of the dramatic text, when precisely that text is the sole basis of our argument? Does it make sense to concentrate on the question of what happens in the theater, when the essentially literary nature of the argument excludes evidence about what actually *has* happened in the theater we are talking about? We have noted that the relation between virtual reader and actual spectator still operates in Nestroy. Does this not contradict the argument's conclusion? I think I have shown how a reading of Nestroy at least *raises* these questions. Doubtless other types of play, and particular plays, are a good deal more obviously nonliterary than Nestroy's, simply by possessing no philosophical or social dimension whatever. But in such cases—say, run-of-the-mill musical comedy for Broadway—we shall probably not speak of "drama" to begin with; the philosophical or social dimension is part of what we mean by drama, if we want to mean anything at all. Again, therefore, Nestroy is theoretically crucial. Before pursuing the issues suggested by his work, however, let us turn to another Viennese comic playwright.

5.

Arthur Schnitzler, like his friend Hugo von Hofmannsthal, was not a Viennese dramatist in quite the same sense as Nestroy. He was not as deeply involved in Viennese theatrical life; many of his premieres took place in Germany. The Viennese theater—or rather the whole Viennese theatrical and linguistic situation—was not there for him or for Hofmannsthal in quite the same way, did not serve them as simply and directly, as for Nestroy. In Hofmannsthal's case, especially, we observe not the exploitation of an existing theater, but rather a constant striving to create that institution anew.[10] There are still definite signs of kinship between Hofmannsthal and Nestroy; in *Der Rosenkavalier* and *Der Schwierige*, for example, Hofmannsthal creates forms of Viennese dialect that never really existed in history, forms, therefore, that precisely by being artificial *are* Viennese in almost exactly the sense Nestroy had exploited. But Hofmannsthal's kinship with Nestroy, for our purposes now, is not as significant as Schnitzler's.

For Schnitzler, despite lacking Nestroy's advantages, attempts to establish something very like Nestroy's theater of sheer talk—except that he goes about it, so to speak, the other way around. Especially the "cycle" of one-act plays entitled *Anatol* shows this tendency. The technique of having a single group of fictional characters appear in a number of different works is not as simple as its use in some relatively trivial forms might lead us to assume. The figures Anatol and Max, first of all, do not admit of being analyzed down to the level of Todorov's "ideal proper nouns."[11] They have an existence *prior* to the particular work in which we are observing them, namely in the other works of the cycle, which are prior precisely by being "other" (not now in the process of unfolding), regardless of the occasional

---

[10]See my *Hugo von Hofmannsthal: The Theaters of Consciousness* (Cambridge, 1988), esp. p. 350, on the seven distinct conceptions of the theater developed by Hofmannsthal at various times.

[11]Tzvetan Todorov, "The Grammar of Narrative," in his *The Poetics of Prose*, trans. R. Howard (Ithaca, 1977; orig. 1971), p. 110.

hints at chronological relations; they are limited by valid predicates that are not fully derivable from the action and dialogue now before us. Nor is the situation the same as when figures from history or from the works of another author (in parody or otherwise) are used in a literary fiction. In cases of this sort, the new text acknowledges an obligation to make those old figures new; the predicates such figures bring with them, as a rule, are used as the mere scaffolding within which to erect an entirely new *kind* of predication. The traditional character of a Julius Caesar or a Don Juan or a Faust must be retained in sufficient detail to justify the name, but must also be derived from a new matrix of thought, feeling, motivation, language—in roughly the same way that a new scientific theory must rederive the same basic phenomena as its predecessor and so in a sense make new phenomena of them.[12] But serial characters such as Anatol and Max must *not* be made new; rather, they must be placed in new situations (even in new genres—Schnitzler planned both a novella and an operetta on Anatol) in which precisely their *old*, predictable character asserts itself interestingly.

And yet, Anatol and Max also do not have the same status as the traditional or typical figures of, say, Italian comedy. For we know, and cannot deny the knowledge, that they are the imaginative creation of the author whose work we are watching, whatever affinities they may have with figures in other conversation comedies. So Anatol and Max are, to an extent, "ideal proper nouns" after all, names uttered by an authorial consciousness strictly distinct from our own, names that therefore refer only by undergoing predication; whereas the "typical" figure, by definition, is always already loaded down with predicates that belong to *our* consciousness. The situation thus involves a profound paradox. We understand that Anatol and Max possess an existence, an identity, prior to the operation of the work with which we are now engaged; but we also understand that their prior identity is fundamentally literary, that it depends on the receptive analysis of texts more or less continuous with the text now being presented. The whole problematics of "character" in literature is brought home to us, the question of whether (or in what way or to what extent) the receptive process by which we perceive and recognize a fictional character can be said to give that character existence or identity as a person.

Anatol and Max, again, have an existence prior to the literary text

---

[12]Lessing suggests an argument of essentially this shape in no. 91 of the *Hamburgische Dramaturgie*.

now being enacted for us, in the sense that this text is a single one-act sketch; but they also have the quality of strictly fictional characters whom this same text, considered as belonging to the whole of *Anatol*, engenders. I maintain that this paradox forms the center of Schnitzler's dramaturgy, at least in the early plays, and that its main function is to awaken our sense for the corresponding paradox in our own relation to language, for the quality of being at once both "real" and "literary," which infects even our own personal identity. This thought, after all, is present in practically all of the witty points scored by Max, who demonstrates repeatedly that the supposed ineffable uniqueness of Anatol's personal experience can easily be reduced to typical and predictable patterns of response, to something very like literary clichés. We think also of Freud in this connection, or of the vogue enjoyed in Vienna, a few years after *Anatol*, by Ernst Mach's argument that personal identity is an illusion, a constantly changing patchwork of self-imaginings or self-fictionalizing acts.[13] Personal identity, even one's own personal identity, is indistinguishable in kind from literary fiction.

This point in turn establishes the similarity of Schnitzler's theater to that theater of sheer talk which Nestroy had distilled from the less thoroughly self-conscious atmosphere of an earlier Vienna. If the literary is indistinguishable from the real, the supposedly immediate, in our experience of our own personal identity, then it follows that precisely in our detached recognition of its literary quality, we experience the dramatic dialogue of works like *Anatol* as nothing but talk, in the sense of nothing but what our actual everyday talk *really* is. If in Nestroy the literary component of drama is crowded *out* of the theater, in Schnitzler it is invited *into* the theater and permitted to infect every aspect and element of the theatrical experience, to achieve a ubiquity which in the end prevents its being distinguished or articulated *as* the literary. Once we develop a sense for the indifference of the literary and the nonliterary that is suggested by Ana-

---

[13]Mach's own formulations do require some interpreting to be transformed into the literary terminology I use to characterize Schnitzler's thought, but not a great deal of interpreting. The ego, says Mach, is "only an ideal unit in the economy of thought, not a real unit." Even the content of this limited ego-unit does not *belong* to the individual, since, "with the exception of trivial and valueless personal memories, it survives—in *other* people—even the individual's death." Significant ego-contents, in fact, "Bewußtseinsinhalte von allgemeiner Bedeutung," are the domain and the task of such activities as art and research, of people who are interested in "understanding the structure of elements (feelings)" as such, not in *who* experiences these structures. The references are to Ernst Mach, *Die Analyse der Empfindungen* (1885), reproduced in Gotthart Wunberg, ed., *Die Wiener Moderne: Literatur, Kunst und Musik zwischen 1890 und 1910* (Stuttgart, 1981), pp. 141–42.

tol's and Max's quality as serial characters, once we understand that by having his experience constantly brought down to the level of literary topoi, Anatol becomes not less real, or less genuinely human, but more so, then we must also begin to recognize the quality of literary cliché, of textually transmitted configuration, even in the particular features and mannerisms and inflections of the actors before us. The interpretive tension between text and performance begins to disappear. Even our knowledge of the possibility of differing performances is swept along in this experience of the literary character of reality; for the performance of the same text by different people in different ways now itself becomes a symbol for the various performances, in real life, of the essentially literary patterns that in truth make up our identity.

In Nestroy the text of the play, or indeed written language in general, represents a social danger, not because the truth about how society must be reformed is ineffable, but for exactly the opposite reason, because it is so *easy* to understand and formulate that truth—as Nestroy himself does in his remark on deposing boredom in favor of wit. The trouble is that the very act of formulating operates, in society, against the *implementation* of the truth it holds fast, since holding fast is precisely the operation that wit refuses to carry out on thought or ideas. As long as the text of the play is present for us, it remains possible for that text to be interpreted (and interpreted correctly) as a complex but intelligible formulation of just the sort that must be avoided. Therefore the text must be crowded out of existence by the immediate communal play of wit in the theater, in the third society of comedy. In Nestroy, the theater of sheer talk thus arises from the text's being *nowhere* with respect to our situation as an audience, whereas in Schnitzler essentially the same theater is a result of the text's being *everywhere*, a result of the indistinguishability of the text's written quality from what the play teaches us to recognize as the "written" quality of everything that happens to us, including what actually happens as we sit and watch. Schnitzler's text, in other words, does not detach itself as the strict object of an interpretive process (on either our part or the actors') from which it is different in kind. And paradoxically, this implies that the actual situation in the theater is as indispensable for Schnitzler as for Nestroy, since the "written" quality of the receptive process, for a reader, is merely a presupposition, not a meaning. Again the theater of sheer talk appears to prevail; and again, therefore, we shall have to ask whether, in general, that theater can really exist, whether it is even a theoretical possibility.

6.

The preceding argument about Schnitzler can be supported by more than just the serial quality of *Anatol* and a sense for the content of Max's wit. The idea of *mood* is also relevant, in the sense of a unity that manages to obscure the boundary between the individual's inner state and his or her surroundings. Not only is Anatol himself characterized as a connoisseur of mood, but mood also obviously describes the expectations of the audience. We do not come to this particular theater, to the performance of short sketches like the *Anatol* plays—"Plaudereien," said the publisher S. Fischer[14]—for the sake of either high edification or an exercise of the tragic depths of our nature. Mood—as Anatol understands it, as a momentary resonance between the internal and external aspects of our experience—is what we are seeking here.

The notion of mood, however, is not without its complications. A certain resonance between outward and inward aspects must be present in *all* our experience; contact between the outward and the inward is what we mean by experience in the first place. Therefore Anatol is philosophically justified (and we, as an audience, are justified correspondingly) in the attempt to capture and sustain and understand particular nuances of mood. Such an attempt belongs inevitably to the quest for an intuition of the nature of our experience in general. But mood considered as *an* experience, an articulated unit of experience somehow distinguished from the incomprehensible whole, presupposes on our part the act of detached critical consciousness by which it is distinguished as one particular mood; and this movement of consciousness is inescapably a *disruption* of the mood's presumed unity. The act of conscious detachment that disrupts our mood is thus part of the very definition of "mood" as a particular type of experience. Mood and its opposite—call it self-consciousness or detachment or alienation—not only imply each other, but are mutually indwelling *as* experiences. Alienation is experienced only as the disruption of a sense of mood that must still somehow persist in the experience of its disruption; and mood is experienced only as the obscuring of a boundary (between inner and outer) that must still be there in order to be obscured.

Hence the necessary relation between Anatol and Max. (Our

---

[14]According to Schnitzler's own notes, quoted in Arthur Schnitzler, *Anatol*, ed. Ernst L. Offermanns, Komedia, no. 6 (Berlin, 1964), p. 153.

sense here of a strictly necessary relation, a symbiosis, is also favored by the serial form, which enables Max's absence in two of the playlets to assume the *quality* of an absence, a perceptible void, hence a kind of inevitable presence after all. Even when absent, Max is still there, for us, in the sense that our knowledge of the series permits us to recognize that he is not there.) Anatol, precisely as a connoisseur of moods, requires Max as a *representative* of detached rationality, of the *other*, in order to define and articulate for himself the aspect of experience that especially interests him; and Max requires Anatol for exactly the same reason. To focus upon one or the other aspect of my experience, I require another individual who is disposed to take up the opposite aspect as a kind of role that enables me to set out the boundaries of my own vision. Only in the process of contact between individuals, only in company, can the analysis of one's own individual experience be carried out; in strict isolation, in the individual's solitary self-examining, the mutual indwelling of aspects of the self must be realized as constant instantaneous transformation, hence mere confusion. And the possibility of successful self-analysis, in turn, is itself an integral component of individual experience, the component I have called detachment or alienation. It follows, strictly speaking, that individual experience does not even *happen* except in company, in society. (Compare the argument, from Chapter 1, on the superimposition of levels in *The Great Highway*.) The relation between Anatol and Max thus elucidates the relation between Anatol and each of his women, or more generally the relation between Anatol the seeker of himself and Anatol the lover, the seeker of others. For the disillusionments to which Anatol is subjected by women are now revealed as belonging to the original if concealed *intent* of his love, as the necessary movements of alienation by which the special mood of each affair is shaped, articulated, brought into focus, made *an* experience in which the mysterious totality of experience ("mood" in the general philosophical sense) is for a moment legibly replicated.

This relation between the individual and the interpersonal, in turn, fits with the relation between the personal and the literary; and the whole pattern can be understood as manifesting Anatol's own main characteristic, his constant need to examine the state of his own feelings. Self-examination, as Anatol practices it, reduces drastically the experienced difference between one's own self and other people. The inner distance of self-examination presents the self to itself as both an ever deepening (personal) mystery and a repeatedly exploded (literary) fiction, which is exactly how other

people—Anatol's women, or Anatol himself to Max—present themselves. And the basic requirement for dealing effectively with other
people is the same as that for maintaining the self as an object of
philosophically fruitful examination: preservation of the balance between mystery and fiction, between helpless fragmentation and the
illusion of complete control—preservation of the same type of balance that sustains communicative ethics in Ibsen and Strindberg and
conditions the characteristic dramatic sundering of understanding
from interpretation as discussed in Chapter 2. Anatol's failure to ask
Cora the crucial question, in "Die Frage an das Schicksal," is the
same type of act as his resistance to Max's pat formulations about
himself. It is not merely a passive acceptance of delusion; it is a
maintaining of balance, against the threatening one-sided illusion of
formulable knowledge of the self. And in "Weihnachtseinkäufe,"
where Max does not appear, Anatol must play out both sides of the
Anatol-Max relation, thus revealing that relation's correspondence
with internal experience. Namely, Anatol persuades himself that
precisely the experience of literary melancholy generates moments
of happiness in his relation to the "sweet girl."[15] And in doing so, he
also operates in the interpersonal realm, by providing Gabriele with
a formulable dramatic role by which to balance *her* internal situation.

The structure of *Anatol* has three main components: the paradox
of a self-examination that repeatedly creates the very riddle it struggles to solve; the interpenetration of individual and collective existence (self-directed and other-directed, autotropic and allotropic);
and the equivalence of the personal and the literary. This pattern is
sustained precisely by its *not* assuming the quality of a detachable
literary "meaning," however, since the individual playlet is developed only far enough to illuminate momentarily a single aspect of it.
In "Episode," for example, Anatol's amusing discomfiture, the reduction of his remembered experience to a mere literary posturing,
entails as a result, paradoxically, that that experience *had* been strictly personal, incommunicable, shared not even by Bianca. And his
situation now, as he leaves the stage without a word, has the same
paradoxical quality, for his lonely anguish is a recognition of precisely the commonness, the mere literariness of his experience—
both the remembered experience and the present inevitable disillusion. In "Denksteine," by a similar paradox, the gem that represents
for Emilie the one amatory experience entirely un-overshadowed by

15Arthur Schnitzler, *Die Dramatischen Werke*, 2 vols. (Frankfurt/Main, 1962), 1:46.
Further references by vol. number and page in parentheses.

her relation with Anatol serves apparently to cement that relation, whereas the gem whose associations are strictly common (in
every sense, including the economic and the moral) causes a rupture.

Even "Abschiedssouper" and "Anatols Hochzeitsmorgen," the
most superficially comic episodes, belong to the pattern, and belong
to it in a manner that requires precisely their comic use of accident.
Both scenes have in common with "Agonie" the emphasis upon
Anatol's inability to terminate an affair, which in turn reflects his
experience of the nondifferentiation of internal from external relations. Anatol can no more break his connection with Annie or Else
or Ilona than he can break his connection with himself. But on
the other hand, the breaking of connections with the self is a movement that belongs to the very nature of life, especially life in the
radically self-examining, thus self-separating form in which Anatol
lives it. And since these contradictory imperatives, self-adhesion
and self-separation, tend to cancel each other out, neither of them
can ever actually be satisfied without the intervention of external
accidents.[16] Again, individual existence, even in its strictly internal
organization, requires an "other," an accidental outside—as also
represented by Max—in order to happen. In particular, the imperative of separation (which is in truth the internal imperative of self-
alienation) requires the comic trappings of "Abschiedssouper" and
"Hochzeitsmorgen"—or the uncomic accident of monetary value in
"Denksteine." Where those trappings are absent, in "Agonie," the
imperative is unfulfilled.

Once again, however, the whole pattern, the basic structure of
meaning in *Anatol*, is known to the spectator only in a relatively
distant manner, via a knowledge of the cycle as a whole, and is not
clearly derivable as a meaning from the playlet actually in progress.
That is, the spectator's situation is structurally comparable with
Anatol's relation to mood, the combination of a large philosophical
awareness with an unabated exposure to the incomplete and accidental quality of the present moment. Even my situation *as* a spectator confirms this tendency toward identification with Anatol, who

---

[16]In the terminology of Chapter 1, Anatol's is a life lived for the self as subject, fully
exposed to the paradoxes, the opposed imperatives, of temporality. "I'm going
now—but I am staying just the same," says the Cook in *The Ghost Sonata*, and comes
very close to describing the action of "Agonie." Resonances of this sort will suggest
themselves repeatedly, and do have a bearing on our theoretical concerns—in this
case, the relation between the theater of readers and the textless theater—although
they cannot all be traced in detail here.

is incessantly a spectator with respect to himself. Precisely by adopting the detached attitude of, say, a Max, I find myself further entangled in Anatol's mode of experience. And this situation, in turn, is reflected back at me by the mutual dependence of Anatol and Max within the fiction; as Anatol and Max need each other in order to be just themselves, so also my own participation in the one point of view inescapably engenders my participation in the other. My watching the play is thus realized as an internal process in the consciousness of an individual who is, indifferently, Anatol or myself; and this boundary blurring of individual identity is itself practically a definition of mood as an experience, hence a further confirmation of my anatolized state.

Now from the point of view of a reader, this situation is not exceptional; that the experience of reading should be realized as an experience of world or life that oversteps the limits of the reader's actual accustomed individuality is practically an axiom in the theory of the reading of fiction from, say, Henry James to Percy Lubbock to Wolfgang Iser. But from the point of view of a theater audience, this identification of the spectator with the character Anatol represents an invasion of the theatrical by the literary, or of the collective by the individual. In the social situation of the theater, where we are ordinarily only virtual readers, for whom the text is a distant object of interpretation more than a vehicle of experience, we now find ourselves entangled in an intensely individual experience very like that of the actual solitary reader of fiction. And if we consider that the theater (at least in such works as *Anatol*) also carries out an invasion of the private by the public, that members of a theater audience find themselves eavesdroppers, for whom a piece of world that is normally concealed has been thrown open, then it follows that in *Anatol* the invasion of the collective (theatrical) by the individual (literary) is balanced against an invasion of the individual (private) by the collective (public), hence that the interpenetration of individual and collective, in the work's governing pattern, is repeated and reinforced on the level of the audience's actual situation. The invasion of the private by the public, however, repeats on a different scale the infection of personal experience by literary structures in Max's diagnoses of Anatol. In *both* of the opposed invading movements, therefore, the invading force is literary in nature. The work's whole mechanism is flooded with literariness, and the result, as I have suggested, is an approach to the theater of sheer talk, in which the literary is no longer separated and circumscribed as such.

7.

But the theater of sheer talk, if it ever exists at all, requires special circumstances that are beyond the control of any particular author. And if the happy combination of linguistic and historical circumstances that supports Nestroy's theater no longer obtains for Schnitzler, then what takes its place? Let us approach this question by way of some other of Schnitzler's early works.

Reigen, the play that occasioned Schnitzler's brush with censorship, has a good deal in common with *Anatol*. Personal identity is a major concern for all the characters in *Reigen*, including the Prostitute, who insists on the uniqueness of her name and of her sentimentally tinged soliciting technique. The complicated relation of personal identity to the self-examining process of self-consciousness is exposed repeatedly; and as in *Anatol*, the very idea of personal identity is called into question, since it is the striving for identity that leads repeatedly to the sex act, which, especially in the stylized form in which it is shown us (or rather, not shown us), represents the opposite of identity or individual uniqueness. The invasion of the individual by the communal, by what we have strictly in common, is thus prominent in *Reigen*; but the opposite aspect of the *Anatol* pattern appears to be missing. Anatol himself embodies the invasion of the collective by the individual. By recognizing that despite his inevitable disillusion, Anatol's exploration and delectation of the experience of mood is philosophically justified, and that the situation of being a spectator in the theater involves me in an exercise of identification with Anatol, I am led to experience the play, even in the theater, as an intimate personal exercise not unlike the reading of fiction. Max, the detached miniature audience, is in this sense only a foil by which Anatol's quality as the focus of our experience is given the force of a dramatic revelation. But there is no such focus in *Reigen*. The circular structure, as a diagram of society, in fact compels us to acknowledge that our position is entirely outside the fiction; the detachable pattern of meaning, which in *Anatol* is kept out of our reach as spectators, is here handed to us in a geometrically exact form.

And yet, our situation as detached spectators is compromised in *Reigen* by the cloaking of the sex act in darkness; for we understand that this excision of a crucial element in the play's action is made necessary by a system of convention in which we ourselves, *as* spectators, participate. Thus the pretense that we observe in the characters, the insistence upon an identity that is shown to be illusory by its repeated culmination in the leveling sex act, is shown to be *our* pretense as well, belonging to our state as spectators. Our sparing ourselves a direct view of the human action that submerges our presumed individuality in perfect commonness must be interpreted, by analogy with the fiction, as *our* struggle for personal identity; and it follows that our whole situation as spectators, our adoption of a perspective detached from the hopeless pretense of the characters, is part of that struggle, is *our* pretense after all. The parallel is very strong here. Precisely by attempting to use the sex act as a confirmation of personal identity, the play's characters *make* that act (which would otherwise express only a physical need) into a discrediting or undermining of personal identity. And we, correspondingly, precisely by participating in a refusal to view the act by which our unique individuality is threatened, *make* that act into a perfectly uniform, stylized darkness, more thoroughly devoid of personal uniqueness than it ever is in reality.

The play's strategy, in other words, is to offer us a position as detached spectators, and then to attack that position by suggesting that the act of being a spectator itself involves us in the hopeless dynamics of pretense and illusion that we see played out before us. But this does not mean that *Reigen* is merely negative or cynical, merely an attack on its audience. The ending, in fact, is curiously conciliatory, for the Count and the Prostitute are evidently the two least deluded human individuals who appear. It is never clear whether the airs the Prostitute gives herself (her name, her choosiness about clients) are delusions produced by a need for identity, or merely her stock-in-trade; her pretense hovers *between* the deluded and the deliberate, giving her character an attractive element of irony that is lacking in the others, giving her something approaching the detachment that we by rights ought to enjoy as spectators. And it is the Count who, upon being told that he had in fact carried out his intention of copulating with the Prostitute, expresses *disappointment*, and so shows some understanding of the problematic relation between identity and the sex act (Schnitzler, *Dramatische Werke*, 1:390).

There is yet a further subtlety in the last scene, which is the only scene where copulation does not occur. Although the Count accepts the Prostitute's word about what had happened the night before, it is by no means certain that she is telling the truth; business considerations would prompt her to say what she does anyway. That is, we are presented in the last scene with a sex act about which we cannot say whether or not it has occurred. This is interesting, because precisely the question of whether or not, and when, a particular copulation has occurred, is crucial in the structure of the society *Reigen* satirizes; the validity of marriage and the legitimacy of children are decided by this question, as are therefore also the belonging of individuals to social classes and the transfer of property. Thus the satirical shape of *Reigen*, the reduction of hierarchy to circularity, is reinforced by the recognition that the hierarchy-determining question of whether the sex act has been performed by particular individuals is *not* strictly decidable. Its answer, since the act is as a rule performed in private, depends on what one or two individuals say (for whatever reasons) and on what they remember. Even the sex act—which appears to represent reality, by contrast with the slippery self-compromising of consciousness in quest of identity—is as entirely soluble in the fermenting and mixing of consciousness, as dependent for its effective existence upon memory, self-dramatization, self-persuasion, persuasion by others, as any other "reality." Again, our situation in the theater offers us a model of this general state of affairs. For the one thing that happens in the fiction that does not *actually* happen on stage, the one thing that must be supplied by our imagination, by the operation of consciousness, is the (supposedly "real") sex act; otherwise the characters do nothing but talk to one another, which is exactly what the actors do. Stage and audience together thus enact the truth that whenever a particular event becomes important to us *as* being real, its reality is automatically compromised by consciousness, by our conscious insistence upon it or clinging to it. Consciousness is by nature *doubt* (in the etymological sense that includes doubleness, duplicity, self-division), which undermines the real in the very act of focusing upon it.

We began, however, by noticing the sympathetic mood with which *Reigen* ends, which suggests that consciousness may be regarded not only as a failure to grasp reality, but also as a conquest or indeed a *creating* of the real. Even the reality of the sex act, which, considered as a generative act, determines our birth and so strictly limits our existence in space and time, is dissolved by consciousness. And if we understand reality as the domain of the collective, as that which we have strictly in common, then the operation of consciousness as doubt, as individual consciousness, becomes an invasion of the collective by the individual, so that we find ourselves thinking along the same lines as with *Anatol*. The questioning of personal identity has two faces: considered as the reduction of personal experience to a mere pretense that masks literary patterns, it defeats individual consciousness; but considered as the recognition, by way of "mood," of the indifference of internal and external, individual and collective, it represents a philosophical achievement of consciousness, the establishment of individual consciousness as the focus of a kind of power.[17]

This interpretation of *Reigen* is validated not only by the parallel with *Anatol*, but also by a consideration of the idea of death. Death is never spoken of explicitly in *Reigen*, except (as we might expect) by the Count in the last scene (1:386). But the idea of death, the breath of mortality, is always present, as the ultimate motive behind the characters' quest for permanence in personal identity; and the idea of a helpless and futile dance immediately suggests the motif of the dance of death, the great circular dance of life which Death himself names "Reigen" in Hofmannsthal. With regard to the idea of death, however, the two most disturbing features of the play, its futile circularity and its constant return to the sex act, assume positive significance; for circularity in the sense of permanence and the sex act as the act of generation both represent *adequate* responses to mortality. Somehow the futile operation of consciousness which, precisely by struggling, fails in its struggle for permanent personal identity, is still a kind of victory over death, still humanity's holding of its own against mortality. Our "condition," as Schiller has it, is realized as our "deed."[18] As in Nestroy, where the same corrosive wit that shows our existence to be hopeless is also itself the hope of regeneration, so in Schnitzler the very signature of our despair becomes a vehicle of human affirmation.

But what use to us, as individuals or as a society, are the positive aspects of *Reigen*? In what sense are they positive *for us*? It is easy enough to say what the play teaches. We must learn to make of our consciousness a constantly world-dissolving and world-creating *act*, not merely a condition. We must not merely *be* conscious, but *practice* our consciousness as a kind of art, like the Prostitute; we must find the point of balance between being deluded and deliberately engendering delusion ("täuschen oder getäuscht werden," says

[17]This argument partially redeems an implied promise in my *Modern Drama and German Classicism* (Ithaca, 1979), p. 314, where I left unexplained the place assigned Schnitzler in a taxonomy of modern drama. The other component of that placing, the idea of low or minimum "saturation," follows from the manner (discussed later) in which Schnitzler's plays direct us out of their theater.

[18]See the twenty-fifth letter of *Über die ästhetische Erziehung des Menschen*, or the related point in *Über das Erhabene*, on how "nature" itself becomes our "own action." *Schillers Sämtliche Werke*, Säkular-Ausgabe, 16 vols. (Stuttgart, 1904), 12:102, 266.

Nestroy), in order that the positive potential of our conscious state be realized. But that point is not yet available to us in the theater, where we are still *mere* spectators; the teaching is an abstract teaching, a mere textual meaning for the virtual reader in us. The actors on the stage, *as* actors, perhaps represent for us the possibility of a fulfillment of that teaching, since their acting is a deliberate putting-on of consciousness; and it is they who enact human dominion over the natural by putting the sex act before us without actually copulating. But we, as audience, are still excluded from the stage, which in its circularity presents itself to us as a closed object; and it is our situation as spectators, the voyeuristic combination of desire with retreat or concealment, that draws the cloak of darkness over the sex act. We are implicated in the structure and content of the theatrical event, but only negatively; we are offered no Anatol here, no focus for the reconstitution of a philosophically fruitful consciousness.

Our experience in this theater is comparable to reading, but not in the same way as with *Anatol;* it is not the experience of the reader's expandable identity, but the experience of reading as *futility,* as the falsest possible relation to truth. Consciousness as our own creative practice is required of us, but is also prevented, for the time being, by this theater's symbolic closure. The play's teaching does not beckon, anatolically, as an experience, but is simply imposed on us as a task, a maximally difficult task, that must be carried out *elsewhere.* The play *Reigen* thus as it were turns us out of the theater, presents its meaning in such a way that it becomes true only when we have turned our backs on it, only when we have left the theater and so left behind our relation to the truth as text. The result is still, in a sense, a theater of sheer talk, except that this textless theater is now a *deferred* theater, a theater made both strictly necessary and, as yet, strictly absent by our actual situation as spectators. The text—in the form of a closed meaning that we receive as virtual readers—is clearly a factor here. But its function is that of the enemy, the negative, the thing we must turn our backs on; its presence for us operates like the shadowy presence of death in the play's fiction.

And if we now reconsider *Anatol,* we find that the difference is not so great as it might appear. We do, it is true, put on a kind of reconstituted individual consciousness in the theater of *Anatol;* but if the serial quality of that work has anything like the importance I have suggested, then deferral operates there as well. For our identification with Anatol, our philosophical exploration of mood, of the resonance between self and world, of the solubility of world in an activated consciousness, is influenced by that serial quality and so includes our recollection that the personality Anatol possesses an existence outside the playlet we happen to be watching, outside the theater we happen to be sitting in. The procedure is gentler than in *Reigen*, but the result is the same. We are invited into Anatol's personality, only to recognize, then, that we have as it were contracted to continue playing our consciousness with the same philosophical irony after the performance is over, in the strictly textless theater, the deferred theater, beyond the exit-doors. We must now *make good* on our supposed experiential understanding of the indifference of the literary and the real. The quality of the playlets as episodes, and of Anatol's as an endlessly episodic existence, is thus crucial. We never experience our relation to *Anatol*, or to Anatol, as being fully there, any more than Anatol is ever fully there with respect to himself.

8.

If in Nestroy—or more specifically in the social and theatrical Vienna exploited by Nestroy—the textless theater comes close to being a reality, in Schnitzler it is an object of anticipation. Schnitzler's theater is a theater on the brink of textlessness; precisely the absence of a theater that might contain the whole of either *Anatol* or *Reigen* is an integral part of the theatrical experience these plays aim at, the experience of a loss or literarization of personal identity, the experience of our personal identity as itself always an object of anticipation, never either entirely in existence or entirely excluded from existence. In Nestroy's theater the personal identity of the spectator is confirmed as the identity of a speaker of Viennese German, a language whose very essence is conscious wit. In Schnitzler this theater has been lost, and is known to have been lost; our personal identity now awaits us outside the theater, when we leave it, as an object of ethical resolve, something like Anatol's inconspicuous resolve in maintaining himself as himself vis-à-vis Max, an identity that is strictly fictive or literary, yet real precisely in this literary quality, in its being put on as a role like the Prostitute's, in its impenetrably ironic conformity to the literariness of the real in general.

It happens that there is a single early play of Schnitzler's in which all the main ideas of the present discussion are brought together in one sharp focus. We are perhaps at first inclined to dismiss *Der grüne Kakadu* as a simple tour de force of theater-within-theater. When we know that the characters in the fiction are play-acting, then their actions, for us, have the quality not of play, but of *reality,* since the actors on the stage—as actors, in *our* reality, our real situation in the theater—are in fact play-acting. And when "reality" then enters the fiction, in the actual events of Bastille Day or Henri's murder of Cadignan, the quality of this "reality" as *mere* play-acting, mere fiction, is therefore correspondingly emphasized for us, by contrast. The trouble with the decadent aristocrats in the fiction, however, the prime symptom of their decadence, is precisely their insistence on having reality itself staged for them, on treating the historical reality that will soon destroy them as if it were mere play-acting. For them, as for us, there is a strong correlation between an event's realness and their dismissal of it as mere play-acting; or at least an analogy is thus suggested between the two groups of spectators, which produces, once again, an attack upon us as an audience. We are protected from those events that ought to be most "real" in the fiction by a structural insistence on their artificiality, an insistence that is understood as a result of our own spectatorial attitude, like the obscuring of the sex act in *Reigen.*

Our situation as an audience is thus revealed as the symptom of at least a tendency toward the type of decadence represented by the French aristocrats in the fiction. And this suggestion of decadence, Austrian decadence, a decadence affecting the actual people in the theater, is also contained in the play's title, *Der grüne Kakadu,* in the common jocular association of "Kaka," "feces," with the abbreviation "k. k." by which Habsburg government agencies were designated "kaiserlich königlich." The last words of the play, shouted by the revolutionary philosopher Grasset, set the seal on the accusation directed against us: "Laßt sie für heute—laßt sie.—Sie werden uns nicht entgehen" (*Werke,* 1:552), "Let them go for now—let them go.—They will not escape us." Just as the aristocrats, who are now fleeing from their tavern-turned-theater, will not long escape the nascent revolution, so also we, it is suggested, who are about to leave *our* theater, will not long escape the consequences of the decadent tendency in ourselves, the consequences of our willingness to play games with the uncertain boundary between artificial and real, and of our failure therefore to come to grips with reality. Indeed, Grasset's very last words, taken in isolation, could mean "*You* will not escape us," and would thus be a direct challenge hurled at us— with a kind of triumphant contempt in the use of the normally respectful "Sie."

But our situation in our theater is also significantly different from

that of the French aristocrats in their tavern, for we, in the anonymity of the darkened auditorium, are not *exposed* to the accusation
leveled against us in the same way. When Séverine applauds Henri's
long speech, Rollin admonishes her, "Was tun Sie, Marquise? Im
Augenblick, wo Sie Bravo! rufen, machen Sie das alles wieder zum
Theater—und das angenehme Gruseln ist vorbei" (1:548), "What are
you doing, marquise? The moment you cry 'Bravo,' you make the
whole thing into mere theater again—and our pleasurable terror is
gone." Even those of us who are not readers of Aristotle understand
that the combination of terror or fear with pleasure is part of what *we*
are seeking in the theater; but it is also clear that the pleasurable fear
experienced by Rollin and his company is heightened by a real fear,
a real exposure to danger that is *lacking* in our situation. In certain
respects, the theater as we experience it, here and now, suffers by
comparison with "theater" as experienced by the decadent French
aristocracy of the fiction. Once the idea of decadence arises, it becomes apparent that our attitude as spectators is in a sense more
decadent, more deluded, more self-centered, less in contact with
reality, than that of Prospère's customers.

What, we are compelled to ask, are *we* doing in the theater? And
the answer, in Schnitzler as in Nestroy, involves the idea of ennui.
Like the clientele of the Green Cockatoo, we are attempting for a few
moments to freshen up an emotionally jaded existence. And we do
so, like those spectators on the stage, in part by permitting ourselves
to be accused and attacked for the same decadent tendency that
brought us here. But for us this accusation is literarily mediated. We
are affected by it only as virtual readers, only by inferring and understanding and interpreting the text of the play being performed,
whereas for the doomed fictional aristocrats there is no such mediation. The accusation against them includes a real threat. The play
they are watching, unlike our play, is textless, a theater of sheer
serious talk, an unrepeatable theater, and in this respect *superior* to
our theater, more gripping, a greater intensification of the emotional
life. Schnitzler's theater, in general, hovers on the brink of textlessness; and in *Der grüne Kakadu* we have a glimpse of what lies
beyond that brink.

But is Prospère's theater really itself the theater anticipated by our
situation? The trouble is that the patrons of the Green Cockatoo
have no use for a textless theater. They are seeking exactly the opposite of what such a theater by rights offers them; they seek as-
surance that the reality that imperils them is *merely* literary, has
merely the quality of a dramatic text. "Mich beruhigt das sehr," says

François. "Solange das Gesindel zu Späßen aufgelegt ist, kommt's doch nicht zu was Ernstem" (1:533), "I am comforted by it. As long as the mob is in the mood for playing jokes, nothing serious will happen." The only exceptions are the poet Rollin and the nobleman who turns out to be an admirer of Rollin's work, the Duke of Cadignan. Thus it appears, paradoxically, that precisely a literary or artistic sensibility is required to appreciate the textless theater for what it is.

Cadignan—twenty-four years old and already full of regret for a lost youth (1:534)—is an especially significant figure. It is he who understands that in a textless theater the acting is no longer transitive, no longer an acting *of* something, but has become absolute, an end in itself.

> Aber ich muß sagen, wär' ich nicht der Herzog von Cadignan, so möcht' ich gern ein solcher Komödiant—ein solcher . . . Es ist doch die schönste Art, sich über die Welt lustig zu machen; einer, der uns vorspielen kann, was er will, ist doch mehr als wir alle. [1:536]

> But I have to admit, if I were not the Duke of Cadignan I would like to be that sort of comedian—that sort . . . It's the nicest way of having fun at the world's expense; someone who can act out for us whatever he wants is more than all of us.

Nor is it illogical, then, that Cadignan should be the one, in his aristocratic company, who has the clearest perception of reality, of what is really happening in France and on the streets of Paris. For the textless theater, if there is such a thing, must in its fully developed form be indistinguishable from reality; otherwise the distinction defines precisely a fictional text that that theater interprets. And the combination of "having fun at the world's expense" with a clear comprehension of the world's real seriousness, this combination of absolute artificiality (play-acting as such, not as imitation) with absolute reality (play-acting as indistinguishably involved in the historically real), is then repeated in Cadignan's death, the most strictly real event in the fiction (in the sense of being most irrevocable, least affected by consciousness), but also the event which, precisely for this reason, is from *our* point of view the plainest instance of strict play-acting, involving the largest gap between what happens in the fiction and what actually happens on the stage (like the sex act in *Reigen*).

Prospère's participatory theater thus moves in the direction sug-

gested by our own theater's inadequacy, by the decadent tendency
that our own situation as mere spectators reflects and encourages;
but in the end it overshoots the mark represented by Cadignan's
finely balanced ironic mastery of his condition as belonging to a
decadent class. It is not so much that the Green Cockatoo (considered as an approach to textless theater) is itself faulty, as that the
expectations of the people connected with it, both actors and audience, inevitably thwart its aim. The aristocrats who patronize it do
so for the sole purpose of convincing themselves that the reality it
offers is merely literary, a fictional text from which the actuality of
their lives is clearly distinguishable. Nor can they, strictly speaking,
expect anything different; for the very idea of having "expectations"
from a theater involves us in a world of literary conventions and
patterns. And the one maximally adequate spectator, Cadignan,
who comes closest to avoiding the trap of literary expectation, is
destroyed by the theater itself, in the person of the master actor
Henri, who, like the aristocrats, engages in the futile attempt to
desubstantialize reality (his love life) by making a dramatic text of it.

Where, then, shall we find the textless theater we require, the
theater in which our situation as an audience will not expose us to
the charge of decadence, of empty spectatorial presumption? Does
that theater exist only in the relation of our being on the brink of it?
Even this possibility is excluded in *Der grüne Kakadu*, where we are
shown that what lies beyond the brink, the Green Cockatoo itself, is
still not the theater we are looking for. Like *Reigen*, therefore, *Der
grüne Kakadu* drives us *out* of its theater; and the reality we enter
when we leave the theater, as in *Reigen* and *Anatol*—or for that
matter, *A Dream Play*—represents the beginning of the play's actual
meaning. The words that follow us through the exit-doors, Grasset's
implied "You will not escape us," are in this sense *encouraging*. Yet
exactly how can our own everyday reality be regarded as a textless
theater?

9.

Let us go back to *Anatol* and the idea of the merging of the personal and the literary. If it is true that our personal life, our experience of
reality, does not in the end belong to us at all, but is composed
entirely of literary patterns, clichés that belong primarily to written
tradition and are gathered together only by a temporary historical
accident into the configuration we experience as "our" life—it being
understood that this configuration can change from day to day, from

moment to moment, without our knowing it—then the idea of "facing reality," the opposite of decadence for both the audience of *Der grüne Kakadu* and the customers of the Green Cockatoo, becomes deeply problematic. For it follows that the distinction between "reality" and whatever fictions or delusions or pretensions are opposed to it is itself a literary or artificial distinction. To "face reality," therefore, is to succumb naïvely to a literary illusion, to privilege blindly a particular literary distinction that is in truth no different from any other such distinction, no less artificial. Exactly this situation is allegorized in the Green Cockatoo, where the French aristocracy do face reality, do encounter the people who will destroy them, and precisely in doing so, succeed only in confusing their grasp of their condition.

There is no such thing as facing reality, in the sense of achieving a direct understanding of the supposedly objective conditions of our existence. But it is possible to distinguish between higher and lower degrees in the *mastery* of our condition. And the belief in a reality that can be faced represents a low degree; for degrees of mastery are measured only by the depth of our literary sensibility and critical acumen, by our capacity not for belief but for irony. Therefore Rollin and especially Cadignan possess a better command of their political and social situation than any of the other characters—a better command even than that of such republicans as Prospère. Hence also the special status of the impenetrably ironic Prostitute and the philosophical Count in *Reigen*. It is interesting, moreover, that in *Der grüne Kakadu*, as in *Reigen*, one of the characters is a poet, and that in both cases the poet, while representing a certain approach to what I have called mastery, is surpassed in this respect by other characters, Rollin by Cadignan, the Poet in *Reigen* by the Count and the Prostitute. Even the type of literary sensibility represented by a professional poet, in other words, is unbalanced by comparison with the perfection of irony that Schnitzler's plays require of us. The poet, after all, is what he is only by attempting to captivate his audience, to enmesh their lives in an orderly textual meaning, whereas *Der grüne Kakadu* and *Reigen* aim at a meaning that is to be found only after we have left all possibility of text behind—as Cadignan, incidentally has left Rollin's actual text behind while still retaining its "sense" (1:535). Even *Anatol* fits this pattern, for in one of the earliest sketches, "Das Abenteuer seines Lebens," Max (who is to become the foil, we recall, for a philosophically more central Anatol) is introduced as a poet.[19]

---

[19]*Anatol*, ed. Offermanns, pp. 118–19. Was *Anatol*, at first, to have been the same

The rainy or snowy or foggy or balmy or noisy streets into which we are expelled by *Anatol* or *Reigen* or *Der grüne Kakadu*, therefore, are not "reality" in the sense of the ordinary distinction from an imaginary world of the theater. Rather, if we have understood the play adequately, then the theater follows us out into the street—"Sie werden uns nicht entgehen," says Grasset—and only there finally *becomes* the textless theater that it in truth is. The artistic endeavor is focused on our condition *after* the play (or *between* plays, in the case of *Anatol*), a condition that must now lose the quality of "reality" for us and find us aroused to a state of ironic literary sensibility by which our whole world is transformed into the textless theater that the play has only managed to gesture at from a distance. Like Nestroy's, Schnitzler's plays manifest in performance a kind of struggle against their own quality as literature, which is signaled by their treatment of the characters whose business is literary, namely Biebitz, Rollin, the poet Max. And like Schnitzler's, Nestroy's textless theater must eventually become indistinguishable from reality; its theatrical exercise is pointless except as the genesis of an actual social restoration of wit, a reestablishment of wit as the governing principle in "real" social dynamics and institutions.

Thus the gap between what I have termed premodern and modern drama is narrowed. The ultimate historical aim of the textless theater is now seen to be similar to that of modern drama as hermeneutic ceremony: the establishment or reestablishment of human dominion with respect to human destiny, the understanding of the world and of history as a huge work of art. Both Nestroy's vision of a restoration of wit and Schnitzler's idea of an ironic mastery of our condition are examples of just the sort of practical goal that is implied by the ceremonial reversal of the relation between understanding and interpretation as discussed in the preceding chapter. And the idea of a communication that is constituted by nothing but a repeated creating of its own ground, in Ibsen and Strindberg, belongs here as well.

10.

The discussion of Nestroy and Schnitzler helps us understand better what modern drama is directed *against*, what cultural lack or

---

type of play as *Reigen* or *Der grüne Kakadu*? Did the developing serial quality of the work make unnecessary Max's being a poet?

imbalance it responds to, its role in a literary universe. For it is apparent that the textless theater (whether achieved or deferred) is a model of *readerless literature,* of literature that is never "received" but only repeatedly created, hence a significant counterforce against what not only Nestroy and Schnitzler, but Nietzsche as well, in "Vom Nutzen und Nachteil der Historie," see as a major cultural evil in late nineteenth-century Europe: the passive or *readerly* attitude toward society and history, toward practically every aspect of our existence.[20] This attitude is favored by philosophical Hegelianism, by the development of what come to be known as the "human sciences," by the mass culture of "movements" rather than achievements, by the growth of government bureaucracies (here especially we think of Austria) to the point where they become quasi-organic, self-moving, entirely unaccountable. Life has become something that is meant not to be lived but to be understood. It has become, we fear, too complex and self-complicating to be enacted adequately by the individual; it requires, rather, to be reflected with quantitatively maximal completeness by the conglomerate mind of an ideally anonymous, utterly receptive reader. This is the atmosphere in which Nestroy suggests harnessing for society the apparently destructive or negative power of wit, the atmosphere in which Schnitzler suggests developing, as a new ironic mastery, the writerly rather than the readerly aspect of the indifference of the personal and the literary. This is the atmosphere that cries out for a theater of readers, where reading becomes an ethically responsible, world-shaping act, or for a modern ceremonial drama in which history becomes nothing but the repeated human focusing of concern and effort in an otherwise "distracted globe."

I do not insist that modern drama is entirely engendered or determined or explained by this movement of historical challenge and response. But I do claim that this aspect of the historical situation is the one that most deeply engages drama *as a genre.* The readerly attitude toward human history and achievement is represented concretely, in literary life, by the institution of the anonymous reader, the entirely undetermined reader of mass-produced books, the soli-

---

[20]The word "readerly," in modern critical parlance, is marked by its use to translate Roland Barthes's "lisible," which is an aspect of how I mean it to be understood here. Cf. Barthes, *S/Z* (Paris, 1970), p. 10: "Our literature is marked by the implacable separation that the literary institution maintains between the text's manufacturer and its user, between its proprietor and its client, its author and its reader." The textless theater clearly merits a place in Barthes's category of the writerly, "le scriptible" (p. 11).

tary reader who can be anyone at all, whose status as the reader of a particular text is not necessarily affected by any social structure whatever. Without this institution, it would not be possible for me to carry out the practice of reading—in defiance of hermeneutic theory—*as if* it were a strictly passive or receptive process, *as if* who I am, the social determinations of my existence, did not matter. And without the establishment of this habit, this "as if," in my reading, without my willingness to practice reading as a genuflection before the text, it would never occur to me—at least not in a relatively secularized age, not without a belief in omniscient Providence—to regard the large book of history, helplessly, as a kind of self-contained and inexorably self-developing organism.

But I have already pointed out that the idea of the anonymous reader is equivalent to the idea of the ontological integrity of the text or of the literary work, the idea, ultimately, of the poem or novel or story as an organically perfect, therefore inviolable and unalterable entity, as the vestige of a naturally integrated human state which deserves our nostalgic reverence. Of course most written texts, in referring to specific real objects and demanding to be used in specific real ways, demonstrably fail to possess this sort of integrity. Therefore the whole structure of ideas that produces the idea of history as organism depends on the selection of certain types of text to *represent* the object of strictly anonymous reading: for instance, the supposedly self-grounding systematic philosophical text, in the manner of Hegel; but above all the poetic or literary text, which is assumed to have a distinguishable level of meaning beyond all mere reference. Thus the idea of "literature" is employed, perversely, in the service of an intellectual attitude that contributes to the collapse of literature considered as *practice,* as the constant collective activity of human self-definition.[21]

[21]This argument must not be taken as part of the now popular repudiation of New Criticism. There is a great deal more historical responsibility and subtlety in New Critical writing than is generally recognized. And the organic model of ontological integrity in the literary text, in turn, manages to infect the writing of some thinkers, such as Paul de Man, who oppose it programmatically. See Chapter 2, n. 8. Nor do I mean to exempt myself from these complexities. There is a debate on de Man that involves two important concepts in this book. Rodolphe Gasché, "Deconstruction as Criticism," *Glyph* 6 (1979), 207, is worried by de Man's apparent facile claim "that it is precisely [the] self-reflexivity of the literary text that preserves it from metaphysics"; but later, in "'Setzung' und 'Übersetzung': Notes on Paul de Man," *Diacritics* 11, no. 4 (Winter 1981), 57, he credits the de Man of *Allegories of Reading* with an overcoming of this problem by the "concept of act," a "poetics of 'act.'" Suzanne Gearhart, however, "Philosophy *before* Literature: Deconstruction, Historicity, and the Work of Paul de Man," *Diacritics* 13, no. 4 (Winter 1983), 80, is not as impressed by the notion

And it follows now that the existence of drama as a literary type—despite the apparent gulf between the defective (drama) and the integrated (poetic literature)—is sufficient to collapse the whole counterliterary structure of nineteenth-century hyperhistoricism. Drama is the church of literature; and at this historical juncture, the business of drama is to assert itself as a literary type despite its defectiveness as text, thus to undermine the whole idea of an ontological integrity in literary texts, hence the idea of such integrity in any text, hence the idea of the anonymous reader, hence the whole idea of history as system.[22] In the case of modern drama, the problem of ontological defectiveness, of a separation rather than a boundary between drama and other literary types, is circumvented by the boundary effects discussed in Chapter 2. But in the premodern drama we are now considering, that problem must be met head-on; and this necessity helps explain the otherwise troublesome fact that in Ibsen and Strindberg, specifically theatrical meanings are absent, that no substantial difference is established between the reading of the text and the experience in the theater. Our experience in that "theater of readers" must be *forced* into the immediate vicinity of the literary, must foreshadow directly a reformed type of reading, a reading no longer anonymous or solitary, but carried out as a form of ethical resolve within a community whose dynamics determines

---

of act, and makes a good case for taking de Man's "theory of literature" as "a theory of self-reflexivity" after all. The trouble with this controversy, from my point of view, is that it overloads a terminology to which I can see no alternative. When I speak of the literary as a happening of "maximal" self-reflexivity in language, and argue that there is a corresponding relation between the dramatic and the literary, I am not talking absolutes or attempting to establish criteria for definitions. I am assuming that we do in practice *mean* something by "the literary" or "the dramatic," and that self-reflexivity is a useful lever for analyzing our practice; and I intend it to be understood that the act of self-reflection necessarily infects its own object in such a way that the "maximal" can never in any sense be a determinate entity, but is always a kind of wager or speculation. The case of the notion of act or action or activity or activeness is trickier. When I speak of a literary activation of history, or of our relation to history, I refer to what I think is a more or less demonstrable ideal (or dream) in literary tradition. But I do also get into the business of speaking of inaugural acts, with respect to both signification and genre; and the discussion conducted by Gasché and Gearhart raises the question of whether I have not, by this route, returned in effect to a more pretentious and less defensible version of the notion of self-reflexivity. I have tried to keep a focus on the relatively manageable ideas of boundary and boundary effect; but I expect that my formulations have consequences and presuppositions that I have not accounted for.

[22]I claim that there is no conflict here with my argument in *Modern Drama and German Classicism*, pp. 254–64, on Hegel's role in the transmission and dissemination of an eighteenth-century German poetics of drama, in keeping open the "question" of drama as a genre (p. 261). It is simply a question of different uses of Hegel in the history of thought.

constantly and specifically who we are, a reading constituted by our turning unceasingly toward the self, in the sense of "the one" we want to be, rather than by our simply presupposing the amorphous receptacle-self of reading in an age of ennui. Precisely by insisting on a theater of readers, that drama thus plays its historical role *as drama*.

But what of Nestroy and Schnitzler? Is the textless theater, even the deferred textless theater, a literary type in the first place? Is it a historically valid dramatic initiative, or merely drama's capitulation to literarily difficult conditions? Let us return first to Nestroy. It must be conceded, namely, that the situation of the audience in the theater, even of the Viennese audience for whom Nestroy was writing, is inescapably passive. It is not *our* wit that is operating in the theater, and indeed not even immediately the wit of the people on the stage. Especially the musical interludes in the farce—a feature of Nestroy's work we have not yet accounted for—remind us of the *repeatability* of the performance, hence of the quality of the play's verbal wit as a written text.[23] (Here the discussion of opera in Chapter 2 is relevant; music inevitably moves performance in the direction of the text's realization, not its interpretation, hence stresses repeatability, not difference, in the performance.) Yet repeatability is a quality that comes close to being the direct antithesis of wit, and where does this leave our sense of the theatrical event as preparation for a social order in which precisely wit must be the principal shaping force?

In fact, the experience of the inevitable degeneration of wit into text, into the stasis or repeatability of writing, not only is unavoidable in Nestroy's dramatics (which approaches textlessness by trying to crowd the text out of existence, not by not having a text), but also belongs centrally even to the renewed social order that that dramatics foreshadows. A social order governed by wit, the full realization of textless theater, is an order that can exist only by being torn down incessantly, only by being denied its own ever threatening quality as order (in the sense of stasis), only by being interminably deferred. Wit, in the sense of the sheer dialectical kinesis that Nestroy has in

[23]That there was much room for improvisation in the acting style of the time, and in Nestroy's own style, does not change matters, but merely *throws into relief* the quality of the play as text. For Nestroy, in fact, improvisation served both to circumvent government censorship and to emphasize the work's radical politics. (See, e.g., W. E. Yates, *Nestroy: Satire and Parody in Viennese Popular Comedy* [Cambridge, 1972], pp. 150–52.) It is precisely improvisation that calls the attention of the audience to the political *object* of censorship, the text.

mind, cannot palpably exist except as the breaking up of some repeatable static order of text, which it thus requires as its own vital
element. Not some final victory over the text, but rather the *process*
of crowding the text out of existence, the text that wit itself inevitably becomes, is the prophetic vision in Nestroy. The theatrical exercise represents its hypothetical renewed society not only as an
achievement (our own participation, as both "zerrissen" and Viennese, in the witty invention), but also as a frustratingly interminable
struggle (against the evanescence of wit in the inescapable medium
of writing). And this second element *authenticates* the vision, makes
it a more exact model of what it foreshadows, in the very act of
compromising it, for the achievement and the struggle are in truth
identical. Or to be a bit more precise, we might refine our terminology by saying that it is not actually "the text" that is crowded out
of existence in Nestroy, but rather the *identity* of the text, in the
sense that such an identity is needed to support the idea of ontological integrity that poisons literature as practice.

And in Schnitzler, finally, the literary is itself an operative category. The ubiquity of the literary, the merging of the literary and the
personal—to the extent that this idea assumes the quality of experienced truth for us—evidently entails a dismantling of the identity
and ontological integrity of the literary text, since we will now lack
any specific sense of where the literary is located. It is the ability to
distinguish the merely real from the supposed integrity of the literary
that provides us with a place where we can be anonymous readers
of the sort that the audience in the Green Cockatoo wish to be—
even though that particular audience then immediately confuses the
distinction.

But *does* the idea of an existence swamped by the literary have
"the quality of experienced truth for us"? Do we really fail to escape
from the revolution when we leave our theater seats? In what sense,
if any, has our existence become wholly literary, wholly "written"?
The inescapability of the literary implies that the distinction between
reality and literary fiction is itself a literary fiction, an illusion. But it
follows further from the same premise that this distinction is unavoidable, that we cannot pretend to dispense with it; for to avoid
distinguishing between the literary and the real would be to escape
from the domain of literary illusion, which we began by admitting is
impossible. As in Nestroy, therefore, even the inadequacy of our
situation in the theater becomes an enactment of truth; even the
dark anonymity within us, where we retreat in order to be virtual
readers of the play as a philosophical text, is an integral component

of the new ironic mastery that the play envisages for us. For that anonymity is no longer merely presupposed by us; but rather, in being represented by the actual dark anonymity of the auditorium—which the play specifically attacks us for occupying—it is now given us as a histrionically manipulable role. The artificiality, the quality as conscious contrivance, of the whole theatrical situation, is thus mobilized to open for us the possibility of recognizing our part in that situation as a theatrical *playing* of the inescapable distinction of the real from the literary, comparable to the Prostitute's playing of personal identity as a role. We still distinguish the literary, we still experience the tension between actual spectator and virtual reader, but with an irony that now realizes that tension as the adumbration of its own hypothetical supersedure.

CHAPTER FOUR

The Church Militant:
Audience and Spectator
in *Rhinocéros*

Premodern drama, at least in the Scandinavian and Viennese examples we have considered, has in the broad sense a political function, which depends strongly on its quality as actual theater, not the mere possibility of theatrical realization. And yet, at the same time, the exercise of this function, which has to do with texts and their uses, involves indispensably the assertion of drama's place in the literary realm. Not surprisingly, therefore, the argument supports its own initial premise, my assumption that the most crucial questions about drama engage its operation as a literary type. This combination of factors, moreover—drama's political function, its theatrical actuality, and its place in the scheme of literary types—is not unique to the works we have looked at. It occurs obviously, for example, in Brecht's "epic theater." In this chapter, I try to show that the general political question of fascism also marks an intersection of literary with theatrical issues.

1.

The tension discussed in the preceding chapter, between drama as a cultural-political project and the established order in which any particular play inevitably participates as a piece of writing, not only produces the tendency toward a textless theater, but is also, I think, already pregnant with the idea of an "absurd" drama. Strictly speaking, this idea is probably meaningless. It is difficult to see how the absurd, in any form, can actually play a part in our experience, since

137

the organization of experience implied by our sense of our own identity must necessarily include a set of relations—whether or not we take the trouble to analyze them—in which each element of experience takes its place; otherwise we should have no basis for distinguishing a particular element of experience to begin with. In the sentence "That is absurd," the very syntax undermines the meaning of the predicate as a concept. But the notion of "absurd drama" nevertheless has an interesting background and consequences.

Perhaps the general difficulty in the idea of the absurd is a mere terminological paradox. But in the particular case of an *intentional* object, like a drama, it is unquestionably real. As soon as we take cognizance of such an object, as soon as we attend to it and think about it—even if we find it stupid or self-contradictory or pointless—we have already necessarily *made some sense* of it, in relation to a pattern of actual or conceivable intentions. We may fail to see any thematic reason for the appearance of Pozzo and Lucky in *Waiting for Godot*. But our understanding of the quality of the object, as a play or as a work of literature, always leads us at least one step further: perhaps Pozzo and Lucky are there precisely for the purpose of having *no* relation to the rest, and so disrupting what might otherwise be the logic of the relation between Vladimir and Estragon. And any such conclusion makes sense of the work, makes it something other than absurd—as does also, for example, the paradoxical perception that most of the speeches in *La Cantatrice chauve* are there purely in order to exhibit their needlessness, their replaceability by practically any other speeches one might imagine. The Satirical Poet in Goethe's *Faust* desires to write a piece that "no one would want to hear"; only that sort of work, a work we would reject without paying it any attention whatever, could be strictly absurd.

These problems, including the general philosophical question of experience, are developed in Ionesco's *Victimes du devoir*, which is, so to speak, a play that despairs of being absurd. Choubert and Nicolas both theorize about the possibility of a radically new form of drama, a form that will be absurd in the sense of having no relation whatever to any accepted ideas, and it is precisely his commitment to this idea that *prevents* Nicolas from writing. "One must write," says the Policeman; and Nicolas responds, "No point. We have Ionesco, and Ionesco is enough!"[1] Our attention is thus called (by

---

[1] Eugène Ionesco, *Théâtre I* (Paris, 1954), p. 231. References to this volume, as well as to *Théâtre II* (Paris, 1958) and *Théâtre III* (Paris, 1963), are by vol. number and page in parentheses.

the author's name) to the writtenness of the play we are watching, hence to its inescapable belonging in tradition, its inescapable making sense to us, its quality, literally, of what Choubert had earlier dismissed as "detective theater" (1:186). Even the death of the Policeman (the death of "théâtre policier" personified) does not help matters, for the other characters are then compelled to make sense of that death by continuing the inquiry; even the Lady, who has as yet done nothing but (absurdly) be there, joins in the closing chorus. In a final twist, moreover, precisely a dissolution of identity, the process by which Nicolas had hoped to arrive at a strictly nontraditional theater (1:226), is the process (his becoming the Policeman) by which he himself now makes sense of this play's action.

Nevertheless, if the idea of the absurd arises as a movement of opposition to the orderly writtenness of texts, and if it thus represents (in the sense of Chapter 3) an undertaking on behalf of literature as a whole, then the genre of drama is still uniquely suitable as the vehicle of this undertaking. For in the domain of experience, the Absurd is a perfected instance of the radically Other, a notion that figures not only in drama's upholding, as a form, the theoretically untenable distinction between understanding and interpretation, but also in the ethical dimension of the stylistic development in drama that leads to cubism. The idea, in Ibsen and Strindberg, of a communication aimed primarily at preserving the otherness of others, at avoiding the assimilative quality of nineteenth-century solitary reading, involves two radically opposed moves that make it paradoxical in exactly the same way as the idea of an identifiable experience of the absurd. Or we recall that the situation of virtual reader and actual spectator entails a kind of semiotically absurd double vision with respect to the things and people on the stage. These things and people are evidently signs, by being on the stage; and as signs they represent (for the virtual reader) elements of the textual signified. But by being actual things, not *our* response to the inferred text, they also stand in a definite relation of otherness to the very sign-relations they establish. It is as if the two sides of Saussure's sheet of paper were somehow ripped apart. Theater, says Ubersfeld—and I think that she means what I mean by "drama"—is "l'art même du paradoxe."

More crucial, however, with regard to the possibility of the absurd, is the reduced effectiveness, in drama, of *language* in the sense of that universal syntagmatic element which inevitably knits together into some form of order any piece of prose or verse narrative. It may be true that the overarching syntactic order of a piece of

narrative can be disrupted violently, either within the language itself, or by such extralinguistic devices as pictures or odd typograph-
ical structures. But precisely in its being available to be violated or
disrupted, the basic linguistic order of narrative—from which even
strictly nonlinguistic relations receive their contour and significance
as nonlinguistic—is still *there*. The quasi-syntactic order that knits a
drama together, by contrast, always first needs to be *constructed* (in
either the imagination or a performance) from disparate elements,
from an order of language or discourse and an order (of real things
and events) understood to be different from language—which difference is represented in the written text by the disjointness of two
discourses, dialogue and stage directions, which manage somehow
to work together without syntactic continuity. (It must be borne in
mind that I am talking about *generic presuppositions* here, not facts or
truths. Narrative can of course also operate with multiple disjoint
discourses, which then challenge the reader to imagine a single
larger discourse in which their disjointness is reduced. But no such
extraordinary discursive creativity is required of us by the disjointness of dialogue and stage directions, which we simply accept.)

The possibility of disorder, hence ultimately of absurdity, therefore lies nearer at hand in drama, in our routine acceptance of disparity or defect. We might ask, for example, what a narrative version
of *La Cantatrice chauve* would look like, whether the complicated
questions raised by such a text would not utterly obscure what we
recognize, in the play, as a kind of simplicity. It is true that several of
Ionesco's plays, including *Rhinocéros*, are developed from actual
prose stories, and I deal with this fact later on. For the time being, let
it suffice to note that the grouping together, under the rubric "absurd," of the plays of Ionesco and Beckett on one hand and the
stories of, say, Kafka on the other, is at least profoundly questionable. The *existence* of a syntax of relations among speeches and
events in Kafka—even if we find it difficult to reproduce that syntax
in experience—is always suggested by the singleness of the syntac-
tically organized medium.

Drama, then, is the proper home or domain of the absurd in
literature, assuming that literature contains such a place to begin
with. And in fact, if the argument on Nestroy and Schnitzler holds,
if drama can remain a literary type while still suggesting the desir-
ability, perhaps even the possibility, of a "textless" version of itself,
then drama in effect verges on being a reductio ad absurdum of
literature as such—which in this case does not mean a destruction
or cessation or rejection. This idea is not mere speculation. The

antifascist initiatives of Ionesco and Thomas Mann, I contend, give it an entirely concrete meaning.

2.

The idea of absurd drama, then, is not necessarily nonsense. But can the absurd be considered a significant historical project, either in drama or in literature as a whole? This question can be approached by way of the idea of dramatic style as an index of the self-reflexive intensity of our experience of time. The types of style discussed earlier in connection with Ibsen and Strindberg do not form a complete classification. But it seems to me that the structure of that little catalog, including the analogy with styles of painting, is significant for modern drama as a whole, in suggesting that dramatic style is a shaping or interpreting of our experience of time, and is never in this sense achieved except by way of a definite ethical resolve on the part of the audience. Even in cases that do not fit one of the types from perspective to cubism, this argument can be made. Brecht's "epic" style, for instance, teaches that it is an ethical lack on our part if we fail to experience time—*experience* it, not merely reflect upon it—as rational social self-analysis. Eliot's doubly parodistic style, which parodies earlier dramatic idioms to gain leverage for a distant, almost nostalgic parody of contemporary idiom, initiates an ethical and religious experience of time, the playing of our own time as a kind of venerable and sacred game, whose absolute significance we accept but avoid pretending to comprehend. Dramatic styles based mainly on various sorts of wit—say, in Shaw or Giraudoux or Cocteau—cannot remain *merely* witty in the environment of modern stylistic experimentation, but tend rather to show that ethical *advocacy* of wit which we find already in Nestroy.

Examples, however, cannot establish this type of point. Here again, the crucial question is what we mean by drama. If we agree that what we mean by drama includes an attempt to think the difficult thought of a strictly active or creative relation to history, then the idea of a collective shaping of theatrical time by ethical resolve is clearly indicated, and examples will not be hard to find. In the contrary case, it is difficult to see how any discussion of positive characteristics of style is possible in the first place. But the critical helplessness of this position does not necessarily prevent it from representing our *experience* of modern drama. In fact, the present argument itself implies that from a conscientiously disinterested point of view, a point of view unaffected by the insistence on a unified ethical dimension in the act of play-watching—and I concede that my own argument is as much an insistence as an insight—style ceases to be a question. "Style," if we still use the term, has lost its theoretical leverage; it now means whatever we want it to mean in this or that particular case, and is no longer the scene of the sort of tension or development that we observe, for instance, in Ibsen and Strindberg.

Yet style, in the sense of just such a scene, is the very life of the genre. With respect to a particular work, style is that level of determinateness that mediates between genre and interpretable meaning. Without a relatively cohesive stylistic scene, where significant moves can be made and significant events occur, without the possibility of stylistic tension and stylistic history, the work can still perhaps *belong* to the genre, but the genre can no longer *live* in the work. The question of our stake in the genre, of what we mean by it, can perhaps still be asked and answered; but the exercise has become academic. This is the situation of modern drama, once its stylistic scene has disintegrated into something that appears primarily as "diversity"; and it is this situation—or this apparent situation, if it is only a matter of ethically conditioned blindness in the audience—to which drama of the absurd responds.

The effect of the absurd is achieved precisely by the thwarting of all sense of a stylistic identity that might limit and order the work's meaning. The absurd, for reasons discussed earlier, is never fully achieved; but the approach to absurdity, in the relatively sympathetic medium of drama, opens the possibility of an antistyle, of a strict opposite to style, and so reopens the question of style *as a question*. Absurd drama unveils a stylistic scene for drama that is virtually unbounded and without internal order, hence not really a scene at all. If style, as the needful mediation between genre and meaning, is in decay, then the absurd explodes style altogether, in order to display the consequences of that state of affairs. Thus the *question* of style is raised, in a manner that requires a response at least as ambitious, at least as resistant to conclusive demonstration, as the response I have suggested with the idea of an ethically based shaping of theatrical time. The form of the response, however, is not as important for the life of the genre as simply that the question be raised; and this last is one main effect of the dramatic absurd.

Let us approach the matter from another direction. If we ask how absurd drama typifies or mirrors its time, the question appears to admit no answer except in the most general sense possible. This aspect of absurd drama is managed differently by Beckett and Ionesco. In *Waiting for Godot* and *Endgame,* satirical or topical references are practically absent, whereas in Ionesco a commentary upon at least general features of the time—bureaucracy, authority, various forms of pedantry and idolatry, and especially the learning and use and development of language—is maintained throughout. The effect, however, is ultimately the same. The satire in Ionesco serves to awaken our attentiveness to the question of the play as a mirror of the time, but is then itself dismembered by an insistent non sequitur and so loses the quality of constructive or even malicious satire. The play does not adopt any sort of firm critical stance vis-à-vis its time, but rather it simply *is* what it satirizes. It is the compoundedly absurd and thus self-confirming manifestation of an age whose absurdity is itself compounded by exactly that willingness to acknowledge its absurdity which we manifest by attending this theater. And in the sparser texture of Beckett, the mere quality of the play as a public spectacle is already sufficient to suggest a mirroring of the time on a level so general that our actual situation *in* the time offers us no perspective from which to measure the correspondence between original and image. There is simply no other way to comprehend our own attending to the work being performed—*our* own attending, in the theater, an attending that the spectator not only carries out individually, but also sees others carrying out. Either the play has no point at all—which is impossible *because* we attend to it—or its point is everything that we ourselves are in particular.

(Nor will it do to insist on the "universally human" in Beckett or Ionesco. The poignancy, the brutality, the fear, the primitive gropings of love or religious feeling—all this is evident and easily understood when it occurs in the fragmented action and dialogue. What is not universally human, and not easily understood, is that those human stirrings should be embedded in just *this* sort of fictional or antifictional context, that the acknowledgment of the universally human should be carried out in just *this* sort of theater, that a particular social or historical version of humanity—the version represented by us, the audience—should not only view itself, but expose itself publicly, in just *this* sort of ritual proceeding.)

Absurd drama, then, as represented by Beckett and Ionesco, offers itself not as *a* mirroring of its time but as *the* mirroring, as the very signature of the age. Or rather, it reveals as an absurdity the whole idea of an intelligible signature of our age, the whole idea that our own position in history can become an object of public knowledge. "Precisely in wishing to be 'of our own time' we are already

passé," says Ionesco.[2] Absurd drama thus invalidates the whole
Hegelian notion of a consciousness whose history is the increasing
perfection of its command over its own situation. To suggest that
absurd drama shows us our own age as one of existential despera-
tion, of confrontation with the absurdity of existence, is to talk nonsense. The supposition of valid structure contained in the very idea
of "showing" or "confronting" conflicts with the idea of what is
supposedly to be shown. What *is* shown is the absurd result of the
very *attempt* to take our own historical situation as an object of
seeing or showing. Thus the question of history is opened in a
manner that requires perhaps not exactly the formulations I have
suggested so far, but at least a thinking in that direction, toward a
sense of history as the material for artistic endeavor, for a kind of
ever re-begun sculpture. And in particular, absurd drama opens the
question of the historical operation, the stylistic scene, of drama
itself as a form.

The word "purpose" perhaps mocks itself in this context, but I
maintain nonetheless that the central purpose of absurd drama is
the opening or reopening or keeping open of questions that are
crucial both to the genre and to literature as a whole. This sense of
purpose appears at practically every point in the fabric of questions
we have worked out so far. If we agree, for example, that the absurd
is by definition the uninterpretable, and if we still recognize the
performance of an absurd work as a kind of interpretation, then we
are faced with a *too* obvious instance, a trivialized or travestied instance of interpretation's constituting its own object, as it were an
anti-instance which therefore, again, *opens* the fundamental questions discussed in Chapter 2. And the question of drama as both a
literary and a theatrical type is evidently engaged here as well.

3.

It will perhaps now be asked whether this idea of a purpose in
absurd drama can be documented, whether it can be shown to correspond to a personal sense of purpose for either Beckett or Ionesco.
And if the question is understood narrowly enough, the answer is
no. My aim, however, is not to "explain" as someone's personal
initiative what I contend is nothing of the kind anyway, but rather

---

[2]Eugène Ionesco, *Notes et contre-notes* (Paris, 1962), p. 191. Further references designated by *Ncn* plus page number in parentheses.

the dynamics of the genre. Even in a history of modern drama, it would not be necessary to demonstrate purpose behind what I have described as the effects of the absurd; for it is clear that the elements of which absurd drama is composed had been well established in over half a century's worth of especially French drama and literature, in Jarry and Apollinaire, in the dada and surrealist movements, in Cocteau or in Ghelderode, even in such politically or philosophically engaged work as that of Sartre and Camus. And in our enterprise here, which is concerned not with causes or reasons for what happens in modern drama, but with the question of what we mean by drama ("we," in a sense that seeks to exclude mere opinion, but can still include anyone and privileges no one, not even the authors who are discussed), the issue of authorial purpose or intent is still less relevant.

Having said this, I will now talk about Ionesco's critical and theoretical writings anyway; for there are, after all, definite points of contact with the present argument. In "Expérience du théâtre," the reasons Ionesco gives for his early uneasiness in the theater, indeed his dislike of it, are immediately translatable into the experience of the gap between virtual reader and actual spectator. "There on the stage there were, so to speak, two planes of reality: the concrete, material, impoverished, emptied, limited reality of those ordinary living people, moving and speaking up there, and the reality of imagination. The two face to face, neither reducible to the other" (*Ncn*, pp. 4–5). The method Ionesco claims to have found for dealing with this difficulty is a method we have discussed in detail: the attempt not to bridge the gap between reader and spectator, but to exploit it, indeed to enlarge it. "If the theater was only a deplorable coarsening of nuances, which made me uncomfortable, the trouble was that it was not enough of a coarsening. The excessively coarse was not coarse enough; the insufficiently subtle was too subtle" (*Ncn*, p. 12). And this argument (like ours in Chapter 2) is in part derived from an understanding of the essentially narrative quality of cinema (*Ncn*, p. 5).

Or we recall the jocular "pataphysical" self-interview concerning *Rhinocéros*. Ionesco begins by insisting, in a parody of Brecht, that all types of identification with a fictional hero are merely "bourgeois"— which turns out to mean that everybody in history, at least as far back as Abraham, is bourgeois. He then claims to have avoided this fault by turning his figures into rhinoceros, thus causing disgust in the spectators. "There is no more perfect separation than by disgust. Thus I could achieve the 'distancing' of the spectators from the spectacle. Disgust is a form of lucidity" (*Ncn*, p. 181). Of course one character in the play still manages to remain human, and Ionesco admits that this character invites the spectator's identification; but he wiggles out of the difficulty by boasting of a "synthesis" of bourgeois with antibourgeois drama (*Ncn*, p. 182). The trouble with this joke is that there is some truth in it. Ionesco himself points out frequently that his works provoke self-alienation in their audience, especially with regard to the customary use of language. The presence in *Rhinocéros* of a clear invitation to what we should probably call not "bourgeois" but "readerly" identification is therefore a real problem. It *opens* or *reopens* the problem of the spectator as reader, in the manner that I have suggested is characteristic of absurd drama. We will return to this problem later.

I do not claim that Ionesco proposes a theory of drama identical or even consonant with my argument here, or that the collection of concerns I call *the* theory of drama represents his intention in his plays. But his self-commentary, upon analysis, turns out to move in a discursive universe not nearly so far removed from our concerns as his antiacademic tirades might lead us to expect. For example, with reference to the image of Shakespeare's Richard II in prison, he says:

> What we have here are theatrical archetypes, the essence of theater, theatrical language. A language that is lost in our time, where allegories and schoolish exempla seem to supplant that image of living truth which must be rediscovered. Every language evolves. But evolution or self-renewal is not the same as self-abandonment or becoming something different; it is repeated self-rediscovery in every historical moment. One evolves in conformity with oneself. The language of the theater can never be anything but language of the theater. [*Ncn*, p. 19]

But this "essential" theatrical language is not simply there to be spoken; the "false" language that has supplanted it may not simply be ignored, but must be "disarticulated" before the original true language can be "rearticulated" (*Ncn*, p. 20). It turns out, in other words, that Ionesco is speaking of something very like what I have called "style," which exists only to the extent that it is insisted upon as a problem, as a question that requires decision and refuses to be dismissed by simply admitting everything. Ionesco continues, "Theater cannot be anything but theater, even if certain doctors of 'theatralogy' consider this self-identity false, which seems to me the most implausible and stupefying of paradoxes" (*Ncn*, p. 20). The trouble with those "doctors" is that their thought is tied to the project of *defining* theater, which means setting it equal to something else, as for example "idéologie, allégorie, politique, conférences, essais ou littérature." What Ionesco pleads for is an attentiveness to our presumably saying something *different* when we say "theater," an attentiveness to the question of what we mean by theater, what we mean by drama.

It may be objected that this manner of reading Ionesco's prose twists the texts out of shape, reads into them concepts and arguments that are not really there. My response is that we do not read these texts, and cannot read them, in a vacuum. If Ionesco were not himself the author of radically experimental plays, we could take his statement that "theater can never be anything but theater" in the simplest possible sense, to mean that drama does not need thinking about, that the theater, with its "archetypes," is an organically sound historical entity that can only be damaged by intellectual tampering. As things stand, however, in the light of Ionesco's own experimental tampering with the theater, the possibility of such a dismissive reading of his critical prose is *itself* a problem, which appears with special clarity in such passages as:

My plays have never meant anything else. But simply that man is not a social animal imprisoned in his time, but also, and especially, at all times, identical in essence, despite accidental historical differences. Universal man, I think, is not an instance of some abstract general humanity, but is real and concrete; man "in general" is truer, more real, than man limited to his epoch and thus mutilated. [*Ncn*, p. 60]

Either we read these assertions dismissively, to mean that Ionesco's plays never do anything but present examples of simple "essential" humanity, or else we focus on the negative point, the insistence that human beings are not fully determined by their historical situation. This second reading implies that history is something other than an objectively given system, which implies in turn what I have called the keeping open of history as a question, as the question of what we mean by history and what history becomes in our meaning it, history as that field for free activity without which our "meaning" anything is pointless. The problem is then complicated by the consideration that the first, apparently dismissive reading not only conflicts (at least in spirit) with the second, but also in a sense follows from it. For the second reading envisages the possibility of a field in which "meaning" *establishes* its own object, in which, therefore, the otherwise untenable definition of a human "essence"—or of the "essence," say, of drama—might become valid after all. By meaning anything at all, Ionesco's plays thus perhaps do mean what he says they do, and we find ourselves entangled yet again in the conceptual complexity that attends the notion of genre and its human function.

4.

This type of problem is also the problem of *Rhinocéros*, the problem of an absurd play that has, in the midst of its absurdity, an entirely transparent message. Despite Ionesco's emphatic rejection of "allegory" in the passages just quoted, it is obvious—even without the preface to the American school edition and the story of Denis de Rougemont at Nuremberg (*Ncn*, pp. 176–77)—that *Rhinocéros* is a political allegory referring to Nazism or, at its broadest, to European fascism. Ionesco himself protests that he is concerned with types of "collective hysteria" in general (*Ncn*, p. 177), or indeed with something as apparently harmless and therefore insidious as "what one might call the current of opinion," which, if not resisted by the individual, can become "a veritable mental mutation" (*Ncn*, p. 182). But in the mid-twentieth century, and especially in view of the play's premiere in Düsseldorf, these protests change nothing. The play refers specifically to the phenomenon of fascist hysteria, and if it suggests that the same phenomenon also occurs in less obvious and thus more dangerous forms, this does not make it any less allegorical.

What has happened, then, to the idea of absurd drama? The foregoing discussion of the absurd does apply reasonably well to some of Ionesco's earlier works, *La Cantatrice chauve*, *La Leçon*, *Jacques ou la soumission*, and *Les Chaises*. But already in the case of *Victimes du devoir*, we begin to have doubts about whether the work's meaning is perhaps too intelligible and cohesive, perhaps insufficiently dismembered by the apparent absurdities in style. I have suggested that this last play is a drama that is absurd only by its despairing of being absurd, and this point is supported by Ionesco's designation of it as a "pseudodrama," as well as by its association—which the idea of the absurd resists—with a work of narrative. And novellas also form the bases or first versions of *Amédée ou Comment s'en débarrasser*, *Tueur sans gages*, and *Le Piéton de l'air*, not to mention *Rhinocéros* itself. What has happened to the idea of absurd drama? What has happened even to the idea of literary "ambiguity" (*Ncn*, p. 61) in *Rhinocéros*, where we are clearly invited to identify with one character in his struggle against all the others?

One possible answer to this question suggests itself immediately. If theater as a form is "too coarse" ("trop gros"), says Ionesco, the way to deal with this fault is not to subtilize the theater, but to make it coarser still. And if the problem with absurd drama, as we noted at the outset, is that it can never be absurd enough, that it always inevitably makes too much sense, then the answer to this difficulty, by analogy, is to make *more* sense, to make a play like *Rhinocéros*, in which both the political allegory and the personal or human meaning could not be any plainer. Even the manner in which this paradox might operate is fairly clear. If we do identify with Bérenger, and if we do so because we recognize in him the heroic individual who maintains himself as an individual—*merely* an individual, on no abstract or ideological or logical basis other than his individuality—against the conformism of everyone else in his world, then it follows that we must carry out this identification strictly *as individuals*, which we cannot do in the theater. Identification with Bérenger, because the play's meaning is in this sense so plain, so unmistakable, *is* the "current of opinion" in the theater (since the other spectators cannot miss it), which we thus find ourselves conforming to rhinoceritically. This is the same type of bind in which Ionesco pictures himself in *L'Impromptu de l'Alma*, when he delivers a pedantic tirade against pedantry and unwittingly demonstrates that "ne pas être docteur, c'est encore être docteur!" (2:58).

We will go into this paradox later, but for the time being let us note that there is another aspect to the idea that making sense can itself become a form of absurdity. As in *Victimes du devoir*, where the problematics of the absurd, its unattainability, is also a central concern, so too Ionesco's own public career is specifically invoked in *Rhinocéros*, when Jean suggests that Bérenger go to an Ionesco play to receive "an excellent initiation into the artistic life of our time" (3:29). It seems to me that this is more than just a joke in the manner of Molière or Pirandello. For the name "Ionesco" refers to an actual series of theatrical events, plus their reputation, and so *signifies* stylistic absurdity in drama without having to demonstrate that such absurdity, in the strict sense, is possible. It is against this background that *Victimes du devoir* strives to be absurd, and fails; and it is here that *Rhinocéros*, precisely by making sense, is seen to be absurdly out of harmony with its public context, and so perhaps achieves absurdity by the back door.

This whole idea, however, that a work of art achieves its own nature only in its public context, only in relation to the established prejudices of its audience, not only appears to exclude, yet again, the possibility of the absurd, but also conflicts strongly with Ionesco's own—public!—insistence on the autonomy of the work of art: "The critic must not judge except by the particular applicable rules of artistic expression, by the work's own mythology, by penetrating into its universe" (2:57). Problems beget problems.

5.

Let us begin with a modification of theoretical concepts already familiar to us. Instead of virtual reader and actual spectator, let us now speak of spectator and audience, of the difference between the individual in the theater and the group in the theater. There is some risk of terminological confusion here, since spectator is to audience, roughly, as virtual reader is to actual spectator. But the distinction in its modified form is clearly dictated by the opposition of an individual and a group mentality in *Rhinocéros*, as well as by the question of the operation of public preconceptions.

In Peter Handke's *Publikumsbeschimpfung*, the people in the auditorium are addressed as follows: "Hier werden Sie nicht als Einzelmenschen behandelt. Sie sind hier nicht einzeln. Sie haben hier keine besonderen Kennzeichen. . . . Sie sind hier kein Individuum."[3] "Here you are not treated as individual people. You are not singular here. You have no special characteristics. Here you are not an individual." The immediate effect of these words, of course, is to call the spectator's attention precisely to his or her individuality, to that very quality, of "spectator," which is being questioned. (The formal German "Sie," like English "you," can be either singular or plural; and the establishment of a clear plural in Handke's first sentence thus creates in the last sentence a grammatical version of our questionable situation.) What Handke thus reminds us of, however, is a quality of theater in general, not only of this particular play: namely, that the theater does not treat us *as* individuals, that it requires of us not individual freedom or expression or action, but rather participation, a relinquishment of our individuality for the sake of the illusion or ritual or ceremony that is in progress. To put it more circumspectly, our situation in the theater at least involves, on

---

[3]Peter Handke, *Stücke 1* (Frankfurt/Main, 1972), p. 24.

our part, the *gesture* of divesting ourselves of individuality, in that we take our anonymous place, usually in the dark, among other people, whose otherness however is compromised by the conventional assumption that their experience will be identical with our own. The king of France, "le roi soleil," was perhaps nothing but a "spectator" in his theater; the rest of us, by being there, have already made the gesture of becoming a "Publikum," an audience.

I do not mean that drama addresses us only as an audience. In the dramatic theater we are addressed as both spectators and audience, both individuals and collective; and the tension between these two addresses has the effect that I have called a keeping open of questions, for it is clearly related to the tension between virtual reader and actual spectator, yet sufficiently different to articulate that tension. The spectator is addressed by what we can still think of as the implied text of the play—except that now we mean not the verbal text alone, but to an extent the gestural and visual and auditory "text" as well, depending on how much of what a particular spectator sees and hears that spectator recognizes as material for interpretive activity. For the spectator, in this sense, like the virtual reader, is defined, given an identity, by being invited to *interpret,* to exercise individual wit in organizing a suggested meaning. The distinction between these two interpreters, between the virtual reader and the spectator-as-individual, perhaps becomes a bit clearer if we note that for the latter, the strictly "theatrical meanings" discussed in Chapter 2 are no longer distinguishable as such, since they are not contrasted specifically with meanings available in reading.

The actual reader, however—or the virtual reader in the theater, who thinks strictly in terms of a verbal or literary text that determines the proceeding—is for his or her purposes the *only* interpreter of the text. The text, as far as the reader is concerned, is identical with his or her interpretation of it; interpretation is experienced simply as "understanding." It may be true, in the abstract, that neither understanding nor interpretation can happen except within some sort of community. But for the reader, that requisite community is not part of an immediate conscious experience; the effect of the communal interpretive standards that govern the reader's thought is precisely to support the individual interpretive act, to produce the feeling of *understanding* the text, of being alone with it. In the theater, on the other hand, the community of interpreters is actually present, or at least represented, and does belong inescapably to our conscious experience. To the extent that I do not maintain strictly my sense of identity as a virtual reader, to the extent that I am cognizant of other spectators as vessels of the same type of understanding (but not necessarily the *same* understanding) as my own, my understanding (now recognized as interpretation) is no longer simply *my own* natural way of apprehending the work, but is revealed as a ritual activity somehow engendered *by* the work, belonging more directly to the work than to any one of the assembled recipients; I have become, by the reflective awareness of myself in others, a mere cog in the large, complicated interpretive machine which is the audience.

A relatively minute shift in focus—from the virtual reader as contrasted with the actual spectator, to the spectator-as-individual as contrasted with the audience-as-group—thus produces a drastic change in our view of the shape of theatrical experience. In the case of the virtual reader, separation is of the essence, the maintenance in experience of a theoretically untenable separation between understanding and interpretation—for the sake, perhaps, of the persistence and ethical developability of our situation as particular individuals in contact with others. But in the case of the somewhat broader identity of spectator-as-individual, separation fails; for no sooner do we experience the condition of spectator in this sense than we also, automatically, find ourselves in the opposed condition of audience. Nor ought we to attempt either a structural determination of priority between these two focal points, or a psychological account of how the two of them can operate together. Virtual reader and spectator-as-individual, again, are forms of the experience of *identity*. A relation of priority would reduce at least one of them to the status of a mere self-image; and a psychological coordination of them would presuppose yet a third, more comprehensive form of identity for which they would be merely types of perception. What we are talking about here is the immediate ritual realization of identity as precisely a question or problem.

To look at the situation of spectator and audience a bit differently, it is true that for the reader, when one has been a reader long enough to reflect seriously on that condition, interpretation and its object (its text) begin to separate, and the belief in a direct understanding, prior to interpretation, collapses. But for the spectator in a theater, the immediate presence of *competing* interpretations brings about a detachment of interpretation from its object *in the very process of apprehending the object*. Even if I am not disturbed by the potentially competing interpretations of my fellow spectators, still *the performance itself* is inescapably such an interpretation. (This point does not conflict with the idea of a gestural or visual text for the spectator.

"Text," in any form, is *defined* here as the object of interpretation. The spectator-as-individual—even without becoming a kind of reader—still knows that the theatrical proceeding is intentional and artificial, and so must distinguish between what is open to be interpreted and what, in the acting or costumes or props or sets, is already someone else's interpretation of the same material—between, for example, Richard II's handing the crown to Bolingbroke and the way the actor does it.) My very recognition of the performance as a particular and inherently questionable interpretation of some text establishes a tension with my own supposed understanding; and this tension, this instantaneous questioning of the validity of my own individual point of view, reinforces the gesture of individual self-divestment that is implied by my being in the theater in the first place. Again, I automatically become "audience."

We can diagram the categories involved here if we distinguish four elements in the experience of a dramatic performance: (1) meanings belonging to the play as a literary text; (2) "theatrical meanings" in the sense of Chapter 2, which are not directly available to a reader; (3) the domain of interpretive latitude, as manifested especially by specific interpretive decisions on the part of the performers; (4) the event as sheer undigested experience, enveloping and controlling us, not appropriated by our understanding. The problem of identity then takes the form shown.

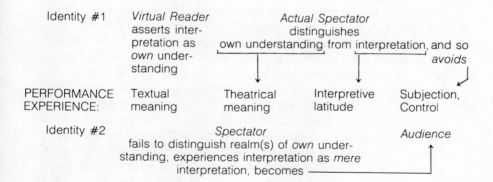

This diagram, however, is at best heuristic, and must be used carefully. For "performance" is not strictly the same thing from the two different points of view indicated.

Once again, then, drama in the theater addresses us as spectators, but also insists on the questionableness of our situation as spectators, as free individuals watching and understanding. *By* being addressed as spectators, that is, we become an audience. And the converse also holds. To the extent that the dramatic performance seeks (as it evidently does) to manipulate us, to enforce a *uniformity of response* in us, to the extent that we, the people in the auditorium, thus become as it were an *object* of interpretation, we are addressed as an audience. But precisely this initiative on the part of the performed work, since it has the quality of intention (an intention that Handke, for example, makes explicit, but that does not need to be recognized as any particular person's intention in order to have the quality), also necessarily presents itself to us as material for *our* interpretive endeavor, and so calls forth our sense of ourselves as spectators. *By* being addressed as an audience, therefore, we become spectators; and it follows that there is a *dialectical interchange* between the condition of spectator and that of audience. Each condition implies or generates the other.

This dialectic may be thought of as a dynamics of self-reflection. Interpretive thought, being by definition communicable or repeatable, necessarily opens onto the communal area of language; the act of personally appropriating a text or a meaning is always in truth a sacrifice of personal exclusivity, a cracking of the individual shell. The spectator in a theater, however, not only undergoes this necessary exposure to the communal, but is also compelled, by the performance and by the presence of other spectators, to reflect on it; thus the spectator loses what would otherwise be the blind self-confidence of the "understanding" reader, and becomes audience. But the audience, in its turn, is aware of itself—that is, the condition of being an audience enters our *experience*—only by way of a consciousness that turns out to be *individual* self-consciousness, since self-consciousness, as an experience, characterizes precisely and exclusively the individual; the subject and object of self-consciousness are the individual by definition. Individual self-consciousness, however, has no means of verifying directly its communal belonging; the audience therefore disintegrates into spectators by reflecting upon itself—which is why "audience" normally fails as an interpretive category. Alternatively, it is possible to think of this general dialectic in terms of power, as Handke thinks of it. The interpretive appropriation or control of the dramatic text is the assertion of power that defines the spectator, whereas the structure of the theater manifests an assertion of power that tends to transform the individual spectators into an audience by way of their presumed uniformity of response.

In any case, the theater thus reproduces in heightened form a basic dialectic of existence: that we are individuals *only* in relation to a community by which the very idea of individuality (the recognizable content of self-consciousness) is defined; but that we are aware of this community, in turn, only *as* individuals. I contend that it is the effect of drama *as a form*—or that at least, when it has happened, we recognize it as an effect of the form—to articulate this quality of our existence, to bring it to the fore, to offer it to us *as an experience*, to provide or create that magic space where the shape of our experience as a whole can be reflected *in* our experience. This type of argument was already made earlier. The reversibility of the relation between understanding and interpretation, the impossible necessity that understanding and interpretation be distinct, and that their distinctness be measured by the presence of a process of reflection that must itself end by recognizing them as indistinguishable, is a quality of our existence, but not ordinarily of our experience. The effect of the form of drama, as discussed in Chapter 2, is to open our experience to this difficult content, and thence to the still larger content represented by the idea of our historical being as the "seat" of memory. Or we think of *Anatol*, and the complications involved in making the general experience of "mood" into the content of a *particular* mood. But we are now interested in the application of this type of argument to the idea of the absurd.

6.

My argument on *Rhinocéros* begins with two assertions that appear strictly opposed. The symbol of the rhinoceros is *easily* interpretable, and absolutely *un*interpretable. In his American preface Ionesco tells us that the real subject of the play is the type of "collective malady" most recently represented by Nazism; that people turn into rhinoceros represents the process by which people turn into Nazis, which we could have understood without the author's help. But the symbol becomes uninterpretable as soon as we ask why, precisely, rhinoceros? Why not some other animal, or some other uncanny collective process? Ionesco also answers this question himself, but in a manner that insists on the *arbitrariness* of the symbol. He searched, he tells us, among representations of animals in his dictionary, until he was struck by "Le rhinocéros! Enfin, je tenais mon rêve, je voyais mon rêve se matérialiser, se concrétiser, devenir réalité, masse. Le rhinocéros! Mon rêve. . . ."⁴ *My* dream, insists Ionesco, and in accordance with the hermeneutic principle, "Individuum est ineffabile,"⁵ interpretation here comes to a halt, unless we undertake to reduce the *person* Ionesco to a mechanically explicable object. The symbol of the rhinoceros is thus both easily interpretable and absolutely uninterpretable. And even the role of Ionesco's own public statements in establishing this assertion—although it could be established firmly enough without them—will be accounted for in the argument that follows.

In the play's action, the symbol of the rhinoceros is presented mainly as being uninterpretable, as resisting all attempts to explain it. But it is also true, and a corollary of the unattainability of the absurd in pure form, that no object or event, however incomprehensible, is ever *strictly* uninterpretable. Merely by recognizing it as an object or event, we order the incomprehensible into our experience; we make an accommodation with it, thus understand it, and so are in a position to interpret it. Interpretation in this sense is necessarily reductive—since to understand any thing "in itself" is out of the question to begin with. Acts 1 and 2 dramatize this reductive process, in that the characters spend an inordinate amount of effort on questions we immediately recognize as trivial or irrelevant, with respect to both the rhinceros (one of them or two? do they have one horn or two?) and the plague of rhinoceritis (is it decision? sickness? imagination? political? reversible?). The trouble is that in the accommodation of subject and object that constitutes our understanding even of the incomprehensible, we have no way of controlling whether it is the object that is tailored to our way of looking at it, or whether it is *we* who change in accommodating ourselves to the object; and the spread of rhinoceritis suggests strongly the second possibility.

When understanding (given whatever our present condition happens to be) is strictly impossible, then it is necessarily *we* who change to accommodate the incomprehensible object that confronts us; we abandon our situation in a world where the object is unthinkable—indeed, we already *have* abandoned it, in that the object exists for us—and we *become* something new. We comprehend the incomprehensible only by becoming it. Thus a strict logical connec-

---

⁴*Le Figaro Littéraire*, 23 January 1960, p. 9.
⁵See Wilhelm Dilthey, *Gesammelte Schriften*, 19 vols., 6th ed. (Stuttgart and Göttingen, 1966–82), 1:29.

tion is suggested between the mere appearance of a rhinoceros (its presence in a situation where its presence is unthinkable) and the process of rhinocerization by which that event is accommodated. And this logical connection is nothing less than a mirror held up to the theater audience, who have already made the gesture of discarding their individuality. We, in the theater, as a group, like the characters in the fiction, are engaged in interpreting the uninterpretable. (Precisely our rejection of the characters' trivial attempts at interpretation proves this, since the judgment of someone else's interpretation is itself already an interpretive act. "We must always try to understand," says Dudard [3:93].) For all we know, therefore, the process of rhinocerization is under way here and now *in the auditorium*. It is not necessary that we, the spectators and performers, agree in our interpretation of the play, any more than it is necessary that the characters agree with one another in order to become rhinocerized. That we take part, together, in the act of interpreting, of coming to terms with the intractable object, that we thus allow our own existence to be reorganized by an object that otherwise does not fit into it, is sufficient.

Thus exactly the considerations that tend logically to exclude the absurd as a possibility are here themselves made to generate a kind of absurdity, a situation in which we see before us, and to an extent necessarily understand, a definite object, yet cannot be sure that just this seeing and understanding is not a kind of insanity. Just this type of process, the manner in which *we* are compelled to change, to forget who we are, to lose our identity, when confronted with an absolutely intractable object that refuses to be anything but what *it* is, had already been experienced by another Bérenger in *Tueur sans gages*. We recognize the hopeless inadequacy of the attempts by characters to understand the rhinoceros, to master it, to fit it into their world, and we therefore recognize that those attempts to understand are already equivalent to rhinoceritis, to a state of being mastered *by* the object. But even this recognition, let alone the more specific association with fascism, is itself already an attempt on *our* part to understand, and clearly an inadequate attempt (why rhinoceros? why not another animal?), which makes the analogy complete. The interpreting of rhinoceritis, again, *is* rhinoceritis; by interpreting, understanding, accommodating the rhinoceros, we become rhinoceros. The final tableau, with rhinoceros heads poking through the walls, is an allusion to exactly *our* situation, the situation of a theater audience who are enabled to see through the missing walls of rooms where a play's action takes place, which convention we are strongly reminded of in *Rhinocéros* by the use of the window-frame, the suggestion of a transparent wall, in acts 2 and 3.

By interpreting, the spectators become rhinoceros, which is to say, they become an *audience*, or rather their inevitable becoming an audience is realized graphically on the stage. Even by identifying with Bérenger, by interpreting his stance, say, as heroic human individuality, we become rhinoceros; for interpretation *is* rhinoceritis. The spread of rhinoceritis is an image, a mockery, of all the reductive interpretive procedures by which we come to grips with the play as individual spectators; the various human tensions that make up the plot are simplified reductively into the mere theme of "rhinoceros" before our very eyes. And this mockery, which is also present in the ridiculous interpretive attempts of individual characters, and in the reductio ad absurdum of individuality represented by Bérenger's situation at the end, reminds us that by interpreting as individuals, as spectators, we undermine our own individuality, become audience, community, rhinoceros.

The spread of rhinoceritis thus comes to stand for all the ways in which the theater addresses us as an audience. But at this point the other movement of the dialectic comes into play. For *by* being shown to us in the rhinoceros image, and so made into the content of a reflection on our part, our situation as an audience calls forth our situation as spectators, our individuality, since individuality *is* precisely the site of reflection. The community does not reflect upon itself except as individuals. For us, as for Bérenger, it is now also *too late* to become rhinoceros, since we are compelled to reflect upon our becoming rhinoceros. The "beauty" of being rhinoceros, by being presented to us (for example, by Daisy) in a form susceptible to questioning, escapes us after all.

The whole inherent spectator-audience dialectic of the theater is thus present in the closing tableau. By identifying as individuals with Bérenger we become rhinoceros; we do not become Bérenger, but rather we close in on him, as it were penetrating the walls of *his* individuality and so compromising our own, both directly and by analogy. But by having our situation as a rhinoceritic audience reflected back at us in the play's main image, we also inevitably do experience our reflective individuality after all, which in this theater means that we identify yet again with Bérenger, and the cycle repeats itself. The individuality of the spectator is thus in a sense constantly restored to us, but only as the groundless and ceaselessly threatened fiction that it in truth is, only as a *problem;* and in fact, it is perhaps only in this form that individuality as such can survive

against, say, Nazism, or even against the normal delusions of experience, against the automatic propaganda spoken by Jean, Dudard,
Botard. In the case of these figures, and even in Daisy's case, it is
clear that one's susceptibility to rhinoceritis is proportional precisely
to the strength of one's belief in one's own unproblematic individuality. It is Bérenger who *worries* about the appearance of a horn;
precisely the insecurity of his individual identity, his experience of
identity as a problem, is what preserves him as an individual. Thus
the circle of paradoxes continues on another level, and on into the
infinite. To the extent that we understand the value of experiencing
our individuality as a problem, in the theater of *Rhinocéros*, we have
identified with Bérenger yet again, which is in turn yet again the
onset of rhinoceritis, and so on.

There is, then, no escape for the audience in this theater, not even
in language, not even in our distanced perception of the characters'
entrapment in outworn and meaningless patterns of expression. For
the concepts on the basis of which we make this perception, the new
or at least newly defined concepts of "rhinoceros" and "rhinoceritis," are themselves, so to speak, instant clichés. They refer, in the
final analysis, to *everything* that happens, everything we do or even
think, in the theater. They can be used—because of the circle of
paradoxes in which they participate—to discredit anyone or anything at all, to dismiss any uncomfortable distinction, to defend any
convenient position, in exactly the manner that characterizes all
clichés. There is no escape for us; and again, precisely this merciless
focus upon problems that absolutely refuse to be solved is perhaps
the play's *response* to communal dangers like that represented by
fascism. Perhaps the antifascist interpretation of the play is strictly
accurate after all.

7.

Drama is the church of literature, and fascism is therefore an
essential, not an accidental concern of drama. For fascism, as soon as
it becomes even merely a possibility in politics, is also revealed as a
specifically *literary* disorder, which infects the very heart of literature
by way of the idea of uniformity of response that we touched on
earlier. Uniformity of response, I contend, is the heart of fascism,
but not merely in the sense of the behavior of a hysterical crowd like
the one Denis de Rougemont tells us about. There have been hysterical crowds throughout history, but fascism is a phenomenon

peculiar to this century. To ride in triumph through Persepolis, or even, in the opposite of triumph, to ride a tumbril through revolutionary Paris, might enable one to observe the effects of crowd hysteria. But although both Tamburlaine and the French Revolution produced a considerable quantity of atrocity, in neither case does it occur to us to speak of fascism. The envisaged uniformity of response that makes up the experience of fascism must transcend the crowd actually present, however large it may be, and multiply itself into the infinite. Fascism requires *everyone's* participation, and in its political form therefore had to wait for the age of mass societies and for at least the beginnings of instantaneous communication. For a fully developed fascism (that is, the German version) broadcast radio is especially important. We must be able to imagine that exactly what we feel is also felt, right now, by everyone, or at least by everyone whose heart responds to the accents of, say, the German or the Italian language. (The question of whether perfect uniformity of feeling or response ever *actually* happens is of course undecidable and irrelevant. Fascism feeds on the idea, the believed possibility, of such identity of feeling in huge numbers of individuals.)

But in its literary form, fascism begins with Aristotle. For it is Aristotle who first suggests the use of types of audience response to define types of literary work.[6] Thus the idea of a strictly universal uniformity of response is suggested, since the work can never—for any conceivable reader or hearer—be anything other than the type of work it is; if the work is in a significant sense constituted by our response to it, then the identity of the work (or of, say, a genre), which is taken as axiomatic, guarantees uniformity of response. The historical course of this idea, however, has not been smooth. This aspect of Aristotle's thought plays no significant role in actual Greek literature, and the influence of the *Poetics* in later European literature is not always based on an idea of aesthetic response or effect. But in the eighteenth century, for reasons having to do, as far as I can see, with the development of the culture of the printed book, the idea is strongly established that literature's *effect* on us is what defines and structures it. "Aesthetics" becomes a major intellectual discipline, so that the study of art becomes etymologically—and in post-Wolffian

---

[6]It is not necessary, in order to support this point, to show that Aristotle's own definition of tragedy in the *Poetics* is based on tragedy's effect. It is enough that Aristotle finds the effect of tragedy sufficiently predictable to attach *names* to it, such as fear, pity—perhaps catharsis, if the latter is not something more complicated than a direct aesthetic response. Eventually this naming does lead to the definition of types of work by types of response.

philosophy—the study of feeling or sensation, of mental passivity, of emotional or sensory response.[7] And both literature and the study of literature have suffered under the aesthetic preconception ever since.

I do not mean that Aristotle is a fascist, or responsible for fascism, any more than, say, Herder's notion of "Volk" or Hegel's conception of history is responsible for Nazism. As long as political fascism is not a possibility, ideas of aesthetic effect have a useful function in creative and critical debate. But when political fascism becomes a reality, literature as a whole suddenly finds itself implicated, by way of that aesthetic aspect of its thought which is also favored by the same modern cultural factors that make fascism possible to begin with, by the situation of masses of people whose hunger for a *participation* in history has been awakened, but who are still subject to the exclusion from historical *activity* which defines them, precisely, as masses. It is, moreover, specifically literature that is implicated, despite the broader customary reference of the concept of aesthetics. For only in the case of literature do we agree generally that the work, in all its purity, is universally distributable (in the medium of printed books), whereas in the case of painting or music or architecture it is felt that the full power of aesthetic response develops only when the individual is in direct contact with the "original" form of the work. Our sense of the situation of music, under the influence of modern audio technology, may be changing now. But in the first two-thirds of this century, the idea of an unlimitedly widespread or *universal* uniformity of response is associated most readily with literature.[8]

Fascism, then, is a concern of the church of literature, and *Rhinocéros*, accordingly, can be regarded as a strictly literary initiative. It is important, first of all, that the "spectators" who are implicated in the play's rhinoceritis are *not* virtual readers in the sense of Chapter 2. For if the virtual reader were addressed in this theater as he or she is elsewhere—even elsewhere in Ionesco, by the use of the invisible

---

[7]The term "aesthetics" was coined in Alexander Gottlieb Baumgarten's *Meditationes philosophicae de nonnullis ad poema pertinentibus* (1735), and of course thence caught on like wildfire.

[8]This view of the historical situation differs from that of Walter Benjamin, "Das Kunstwerk im Zeitalter seiner technischen Reproduzierbarkeit," but operates with basically the same categories. Literary fascism, in Benjamin's terminology, would be the attempt to retain the efficacy of "aura" (where "response" happens) even in a technologically infinitized ritual group. And in principle this impossible combination has been insisted upon for centuries in the idea of the "aesthetic" experience of reading printed books. See Benjamin, *Illuminationen* (Frankfurt/Main, 1977), pp. 136–69.

knife in *La Leçon* for example—that reader would not be implicated, would not become a rhinoceros. Being a virtual reader, we have seen, is equivalent to the experience of the reversibility of understanding and interpretation, hence to the experience of universal humankind's role as the shaper of history, not its victim, not a mere locus of potentially fascist response. It is true that the virtual reader is implicated, in *La Leçon,* in a kind of murder, in the ruthless subjugation of reality to language, in what we might also call the use of interpretive power or leverage to compel the object's accommodation; but he or she is not implicated in the opposed process, in the interpretive accommodation of the self to the object, which is rhinoceritis. What *Rhinocéros* demonstrates, however, is the precariousness of this state of being an interpretively active reader. All that is needed is that the focus of our situation change ever so slightly, that we fail to distinguish strictly between literary and theatrical meanings and instead simply take our meanings where we find them (as simple "spectators" in the sense of the spectator-audience distinction), that we cease to insist on a border between understanding and interpretation, so that the identity of the "work" is no longer a problem for us but becomes merely an image of our response to it. As soon as this seductively easy change occurs, an entirely new dynamics emerges, a potentially fascist dynamics, in the slippery dialectic of spectator and audience.

The theater of *Rhinocéros* is thus a theater of seduction, or rather a theater that opposes seduction by enacting it, presenting it for inspection. Despite Ionesco's personal opinions, this theater has exactly the same aim as Brecht's—the exposure and dismantling of an Aristotelian, aesthetic, "culinary" sense of literature—and differs only in approaching this aim by an exactly opposed strategic route. Our confrontation, as virtual readers, with the identity of the work as a *problem*, our knowledge of our own interpretive coresponsibility for that identity, for the work's working or operation in history, is separated by only one very short and seductively easy step from the entirely antiproblematic idea that the work's identity is represented simply and fully by our response to it—as if our responsibility were discharged in the mere process of responding. And this seduction, which is made possible in general by the historical force of the aesthetic component in literary thought, is what is enacted in the theater of *Rhinocéros*—in the whole theater, including the audience.

But seduction in this form is also antiseductive or antifascist, in that its dialectic constantly restores to us the reflective individuality, as "spectator," by which we might resist it, and constantly presents us with an image of such resistance in Bérenger. Or to look at the matter in terms of our earlier discussion of absurd drama, *Rhinocéros* clearly asserts its quality as the signature of our age. I say *our* age, not merely a general human condition, because of the specific reference to a political fascism that implicates literature and so makes the problem of the aesthetic into a matter of literary life or death; and I say *the* signature, not merely a satirical portrait of some aspect of the age, because the entrapment or rhinocerization of the audience insists that the phenomenon represented is too general to admit the existence of a perspective from which we might achieve a distanced view of it. Therefore our earlier argument can be applied here: that the idea of *the* signature of the age is itself already an absurdity, since in taking cognizance of it we find ourselves pretending to occupy precisely the distanced perspective that we began by knowing is impossible. We are thus compelled to think in the direction of an antiaesthetic conception of history, a history in which there is no signature of the age except insofar as we insist actively upon writing it ourselves.

We recall the point suggested by the idea of a textless theater, the argument that drama might be understood to operate as a reductio ad absurdum of the whole idea of literature. It is clear that *Rhinocéros* does operate in just this way, as long as literature includes an integral aesthetic component. More precisely, political history in the form of fascism has reduced all "aesthetically" conceived literature to an absurdity; and *Rhinocéros* exposes that absurdity. To the extent that we maintain the aesthetic attitude toward literature which is characteristic of our time, therefore, we are a people without literature. And the task of reestablishing the literary cannot be accomplished for us by anyone at all, or by any work at all; the metaesthetic restoration of literature obviously cannot be an event we merely respond to. It is a *task*, and a task we are *left alone* with. On the subject of *Rhinocéros*, Ionesco relates: "One of the major critics in New York complains that, having demolished a conformism and not replaced it with anything else, I leave him and the spectators in a void. That is precisely what I wanted to do. It is from this void that a free human must extract himself on his own, by his own strength, not by others' " (*Ncn*, p. 188). But this state of being left alone is also, from a literary point of view, the always imminently active state of the virtual reader, not the spectator or audience. Thus, in coming to grips with the play's relentless dialectic, we have already made at least a first step toward an active, nonaesthetic reconstitution of the literary after all.

8.

The relation between fascism and literature will perhaps become clearer if we trace it in another work, a work that not only is as different as possible, in other respects, from *Rhinocéros*, but was also written during the period when fascism was an actual growing political danger. I mean Thomas Mann's novella *Mario und der Zauberer*.

What catches our attention first in this story is the figure of the narrator, who shows himself, from the start, a master of the mildly narcissistic, semiphilosophical elegance of academic German prose, while at the same time he cannot prevent his own language from constantly getting the better of him. Already the subtitle disturbs us, "Ein tragisches Reiseerlebnis," "A Tragic Travel-Experience"—as if the idea of the tragic could be reconciled with the ideas of the new, the unexpected, the strictly accidental, that are suggested by the account of a summer's vacation travel.[9] And the first sentence worries us even more. "Die Erinnerung an Torre di Venere ist atmosphärisch unangenehm," "The memory of Torre di Venere is atmospherically unpleasant." What is meant here, obviously, is that the atmosphere in Torre di Venere, as the narrator remembers it, was unpleasant. But this is not exactly what the words say; and as we develop a sense for the narrator's style and its provenance, we soon recognize in general that the language he uses, which had been endowed with extreme analytic precision by Kant and Hegel and then tempered into essayistic toughness by Schopenhauer and Nietzsche, is here infected with what the narrator himself would probably consider (if he had the perspective) a suspiciously Mediterranean languidness and lability. Worse still, the recognition that we *know* what that first sentence and other such statements mean, even though they fail to say what they mean, is evidence that *our* relation to language is similarly infected. And worst of all, it turns out that precisely by conducting a valid criticism of the inadequacy of the narrator's stylistically revealed thinking, we ourselves fall into exactly the same faults that we criticize.

The narrator is obviously intelligent and educated, and repeatedly puts together long and conceptually intricate trains of thought. For just this reason, the instances of even a subtle looseness or confusion in his thought are striking. People go to Torre, rather than

[9]Thomas Mann, *Erzählungen*, "Stockholmer Gesamtausgabe" (n.p., 1958), p. 658. Further references by page number in parentheses.

Portoclemente, he says, because "it is more fashionable, and in addition cheaper, and the attractiveness of these qualities continues to prove itself while the qualities themselves have already ceased to obtain" (p. 659). Is Torre still more fashionable, or no longer fashionable? And what is the narrator himself doing there? We hear of "boats manned by children" (p. 659), and that "die Musik-kapellen . . . fallen einander wirr ins Wort" (p. 660)—which is an untranslatable absurdity, something like, "the various musical groups take the words out of each other's mouths." The narrator cites the existence of unresolved medical questions about whooping cough as a reason for not "taking it amiss" when his family is inconvenienced by a fellow hotel-guest's belief that this illness is "acoustically contagious" (p. 661)—as if medical science had any doubts on *that* score. Especially the idea of mixing or mixture lures the narrator into clichés that prove logically hopeless. It appeared, he tells us, that his conflicts with local and vacationing Italians "were not wholly unmixed accidents" (p. 667)—even though the very idea of chance or accident already implies the idea of an unruly mixture. His and his wife's feelings about Cipolla, he says, were of a "highly" or "extremely" mixed nature, "höchst gemischter Natur" (p. 695). Again, the reader has some cause to be embarrassed at merely knowing what the narrator means here, despite the semantically impossible combination of a superlative adverb with the concept "mixed."

Above all, however, the narrator's thought about Cipolla is embarrassing. "Cipolla" means "onion," which we cannot help thinking about since the text is liberally sprinkled with Italian words anyway. And how, then, are we meant to react to the phrase "der Choc mit diesem schrecklichen Cipolla" (p. 658)—"the shock with this terrifying onion"??—which occurs at a point in the text where we have not yet been told that Cipolla is a person? But we are bothered more by the narrator's supercilious attitude in explaining Cipolla's tricks. The hint of condescension in his reaction to the comment, "Parla benissimo" (p. 679), "He speaks well," about Cipolla, is barely noticeable. But when a French lady remarks, "Il boit beaucoup" (p. 685), "He drinks a lot," the narrator begins to get impatient: "Was that all that struck her? We couldn't make out how much in the picture the audience was at that point." Step by step he approaches, and prepares for, as for a climax, his own supposedly superior knowledge: "Anyway, Cipolla himself made sure that the character of his tricks lay beyond doubting for anyone with any knowledge at all; but he did so without ever uttering a name, a technical term" (p. 688). The narrator himself, also without naming names, now speaks of the "inscrutable paths from organism to organism" which, when we experience their effects, give us a sense of "the ambiguous-unclean and inexplicable character of the occult" (pp. 690–91). Then, finally, he says what he means: "Let me summarize: this self-confident cripple was the strongest hypnotist I have ever seen in my life" (p. 696). The climax arrives, and instantly becomes an anticlimax, for it is perfectly obvious that hypnotism does not even come close to "summarizing" Cipolla's tricks. The "arithmetic exercises" and the mind-reading would require (if we were to ask about them) either charlatanry, perhaps with shills, or a form of telepathy; and the narrator himself explains the dancing of the gentleman from Rome— who is facing *away* from Cipolla when he is made to obey— on philosophical-psychological grounds: "Not to will a particular thing and simply not to will, thus to do what is asked after all, are probably too close to each other for the idea of freedom to avoid being crowded out between them" (p. 702).

Cipolla probably is, among other things, a hypnotist. But the question of *the* true source of his power requires a more comprehensive answer, an answer that, upon reflection, does not appear difficult at all, and in fact is already suggested by the name, "onion," of an object that is composed proverbially of skin within skin—deception within deception, as in Boccaccio—leading to an empty center, a center that is not there. The central source of Cipolla's power is simply that there is no such source, that the center is empty, which means that Cipolla is *uninterpretable* in the same way as the rhinoceros. Therefore, in attempting to interpret him (as the narrator does), we accommodate ourselves. to him and give him power over us. Cipolla himself says practically this in his preface to the card trick with the gentleman from Rome:

> Freedom exists, and the will exists too; but freedom of the will does not exist, because a will that aims at its freedom thrusts into emptiness. You are free to draw a card or not to draw. But if you draw, you will draw the right one—all the more inevitably, the more independently you try to act. [P. 689]

If we play Cipolla's game, if we try to figure him out, to find an answer to a question that has no meaning, then we have *already* submitted to him, and whatever card we pull from the pack will be the one he wants.

The trouble with this answer, even if it is correct, is what it says about *us*, the reader. For even the idea of the empty center is an interpretation of Cipolla, a playing of Cipolla's game, and under even more humiliating circumstances than those of the actual fictional audience in Torre di Venere. From our point of view, as readers, Cipolla does not even "actually" do what he does; he is merely a figure in fiction, presumably with a certain symbolic value, but not characterized by the sort of immediate reality that might justify our inquiring into cause and effect with regard to what he "does." If we even *ask* how he accomplishes his feats—and the narrator's attitude compels us to ask this, since *by* reading and criticizing we are already playing the narrator's game—then, like the "cataleptic" young man (p. 697), we are going out of our way to be submissive. In the very process of recognizing the narrator's foolishness, we are ourselves implicated in it, just as we are implicated in his clichés by understanding them. After Cipolla is shot, the narrator says:

People called for a doctor, for the police. People stormed onto the stage. People threw themselves in a crowd upon Mario, to disarm him, to take from him the little stubby, metal, barely pistol-shaped mechanism that hung from his fingers and whose almost nonexistent barrel had guided destiny in such a strange and unexpected direction. [P. 711]

"People," he says repeatedly—in German, "man"—and so dissociates himself from the crowd, just as we dissociate ourselves critically from him. But if he merely watched that scene from a distance, how does he know exactly what the little pistol looked like? Dissociation in both cases, for us as for the narrator, is a transparent pretense.

Here, therefore, as in *Rhinocéros*, we have a reductio ad absurdum of the literary as such. We are free to read or not to read, but if we read at all, if we draw a card, then we carry out thereby the move of unworthy submission, we act like Cipolla's audience. As in *Rhinocéros*, moreover, it is by way of its aesthetic aspect that the literary is rendered absurd. For the trap we fall into, by adopting a critical attitude toward the narrator in *Mario*, is that of needing to use "reality" as a basis for our criticism; it is the trap of treating fictional events as if they were an actual present reality we had to come to grips with. And this critical habit of treating fiction as reality is in turn unmasked, by the association with fascism, as a form of belief in, or indeed of positive servile insistence upon, a universal uniformity of response—since reality is by definition that which is there in exactly the same way for everyone, that which requires no specific creative activity on our part in order to be there. The ridiculous first sentence of the novella thus finally becomes *for us* the literal truth. The story, insofar as we ask of it the sort of question that ought to be asked only of reality, insofar as we thus treat it as if it were our "memory," *is*, to say the least, "atmospherically unpleasant" for us, as the experience of participation in a fascist communal movement, an unpleasantness we must now recognize is characteristic of our aesthetically oriented reading of practically any story. The only conceivable solution to this problem, it appears, the only way out of the trap, might be something like the readerless literature we arrive at by extrapolation from Nestroy and Schnitzler, or something like the renewal of the very act of reading suggested in Ibsen and Strindberg, the establishment of reading as a wholly self-grounded communication which, by insisting on the otherness of others, would prevent both the pretended belief in reality and the dangerous delusion of uniform response.

9.

The parallel between *Mario* and *Rhinocéros* is thus very close. And although the focus is completely different, since the role of the uncompromising individual is now taken by Mario, who is not offered as a target for identification, there is perhaps still a kind of dialectic of rescue in the novella. For our criticism of the narrator includes finally the understanding that Cipolla's death is *not* "predestined and residing in the nature of things" (p. 658). It is, rather, the purest accident, which does nothing but raise unanswered questions if we try to regard it as fated. Why is the murder committed by Mario and not by some other humiliated victim? Why is it "predestined" to occur just when it does, not at some earlier performance? How is *any* judgment possible here without "personal" knowledge of Mario (p. 705)? Above all, why does Mario happen to be carrying a gun? These difficulties about the ending are concentrated in the German word "fatal" ("ein höchst fatales Ende" [p. 711]), which suggests the idea of "fate" but actually signifies "annoying" or "disruptive," referring to something that does *not* fit smoothly into a causal or destined flow of events. Cipolla's death, then, is our escape from the story, a "befreiendes Ende" for us as much as for the narrator (p. 711), not only in that we now stop reading, but also in that the act of interpreting, which had entrapped us, now becomes a mere transparent gesture, since no serious attempt is made to understand

Mario. Or perhaps even this gesture is dangerous, this seductive sense of being able to manage the literary as a mere game. Perhaps Cipolla's death, if we acknowledge it as a turning of the uninterpretable against itself, then makes sense after all, so that our restored individual reflectiveness cannot but interpret it, thus become entrapped yet again, and so on.

But if *Rhinocéros* and *Mario* thus exhibit practically the same self-critical literary strategy, what has happened to the specific function of *drama* as a now militant antifascist church of literature? To deal with this question, we must remind ourselves, first, that our aim is not to distinguish drama from the rest of literature, not to define drama, but rather to understand what drama accomplishes *for* literature. For the present argument, thus understood, is *supported* by the existence, in other genres, of such works as *Mario und der Zauberer*, works in which the relation between fascist politics and an aesthetic conception of literature is grasped firmly and imposed on us in the form of a dialectic that leaves us alone with the task of mastering our now thoroughly problematic situation. The narrative pieces with which Ionesco anticipates his plays around the time of *Rhinocéros*, it seems to me, represent an insistence upon just this crucial continuity between drama and literature as a whole, upon the status of drama not as a kind of separate space, characterized by its own unique laws (which would be one way of understanding the statement "theater can never be anything but theater"), but rather as a site, within literature, of maximal literary self-reflection, where the historical problems and tensions of literature are brought most keenly into focus.

Of course the manner of drama's operating, both in general and in the case now under consideration, is different from the operating of other literary genres. What in *Mario* is an extremely subtle dialectic, involving our sense of individual critical freedom and our sense of being trapped in the process of reading—as the self-consciously critical narrator is trapped in Cipolla's theater—is developed, in *Rhinocéros*, as a relatively large and powerful dialectic, between the conditions of spectator and audience, which we recognize as belonging to the very form of theatrical drama. Perhaps we can generalize from this situation, and suggest as a hypothesis that the very form of drama is an enactment of crucial and subtle and otherwise hidden problems in the fabric of literature, a place where those problems actually *happen* in form. In the matter of fascism as a literary phenomenon, a case could be made for this assertion. The idea that the literary work is constituted by our response to it, hence the idea of uniformity of response, is insidiously close, though in spirit directly opposed, to the idea of literature's meaning what we mean by it, requiring our active participation (as the seat of memory) in the building of a human history. And is this relation, this perverse proximity of the aesthetic and (let us call it) the poietic, not mirrored in the very structure of drama by the closeness, yet noncoincidence, of the dangerous dialectic of spectator and audience and the fruitful tension between virtual reader and actual spectator? Another way of looking at this situation is suggested by Ubersfeld's perception that the space of the theater, as mere space, represents, or as it were enacts, the problem of multiple readings of a text.

These ideas, however, would remain speculative even if they were supported by a complete systematic theory of drama of the sort that I am not confident is possible in the first place. For the business of drama is resolutely empirical, in the sense not of responding to experience, but of condensing *into* experience certain obscure or contradictory qualities of our existence which are otherwise accessible only theoretically, only by way of the complex interplay of literature and its interpretation as historical processes. The salient point, for our purposes—as is also suggested by the persistence of Nestroy's or Schnitzler's "theater" beyond the exit-doors—is that drama tends not to close itself into an object of systematic study, but always to *open itself* to its own "outside" or "other," whether in the form of the real world (where it is situated as theater) or in the form of something like fictional narrative (to which it is neighbored as a literary type). I think there is a misconception involved in what I take to be, for example, Handke's sealing off of the theater as a strictly special type of space. Drama is not a church in the sense of a sanctuary or secret inquisitorial dungeon, but is always thrown open to its outside, always in danger (and in need) of becoming indistinguishable as itself. Only thus does its existence retain the quality of an ever still uncompleted *act* on our part; only thus can the boundary effects that mark it as a literary type (and so, paradoxically, keep open its theater as a problem) be constantly developed anew.

Drama is what it is only by refusing to be sealed off from what it is not. Drama does not detach itself from experience, or seek to engender a new form of experience; its aim, rather, is to enact and develop the problematics of self-reflection that is present in all our experience anyway. If drama is not continuous with our experience as a whole, especially with our literary experience, it accomplishes nothing. The reader of the future envisaged by the theater of readers in Ibsen and Strindberg, who practices his or her reading as a communal endeavor, is not a *new* kind of reader but simply a reader whose theoretical grasp of the nature of reading is at last fully integrated into actual practice. The inherently defective or uncompleted form of drama not only pleads for such a reader, as if from a distance of objectivity, but also itself marks the literary defect represented by that reader's absence. Or yet again, whereas *Mario und der Zauberer* leaves us with the task of shaping our experience so as to *exclude* the equivalent of that story's own structure, such exclusion is itself excluded by the very form of drama. In *Rhinocéros*, the literary defect that opens the way to fascism is enacted in such a way as to leave us, still, in its inexcludable presence, supported for a moment by the possibility of identification with Bérenger, who is himself defective as a model, then supported by nothing but our own "self," whatever that is. The theoretical arguments I have attempted still seem to me valid, to the extent of showing that drama as a form, within the whole structure of the literary, is the site of a unique self-revelation. But in each particular case the operation of drama tends to become utterly pragmatic, involving the sacrifice of its own formal closure for the sake of a specific historical task.

Like Bérenger in the final tableau of *Rhinocéros*, drama is uniquely what it is only by being defective, by having (in each particular case) its walls penetrated to admit its own "outside." The paradox of the "frame," that which belongs to the work of art precisely by marking the point where such belonging ceases, is not only applicable to drama, but is in a sense its very center, in the form of a pattern of *reversible* frame relations, text and performance, literature and theater, address to the spectator and address to the audience, real world and fictional world. Drama, as it were, is *nothing but* its own frame, its own "outside," whence it seems to me that the whole of my argument on the dramatic and the absurd eventually follows, and whence it follows, in addition, that public statements of an author like Ionesco are here more easily readmitted into the fabric of the endeavor—the whole, ultimately world-shaping endeavor—than in the case of other artistic types. Drama remains for us as eminently public an affair as it was for the Greeks. The dramatic theater, when its tenseness, its keeping open of questions, is developed to the full, becomes in a strong sense the center of our existence, but only by unceasingly carrying out the sacrifice of its *own* center, a gesture of sacrifice that creates not only the locus but also the image of an adequately experienced humanity—and so is comparable to Bérenger yet again, who is an individual in the very act of having no reason or justification for being such.

10.

I realize that the argument finishes by making large claims, not the least of which is the claim that both it and its object (both the argument on drama and drama itself) operate in a region of thought or discourse where any conceptual system that might mediate between them would itself automatically assume a dramatic or gestural character, as the enactment of a defect, and so undermine its own validity as a system.[10] The complexity of this situation, moreover, and the power of the notion of the defective, can be measured by the consideration that it is possible for a dramatic work to be *too* exactly and completely interpretable in the theoretical terms I have sketched.

Much more is involved in the structure of Jean Genet's *Le Balcon*, for example, than just the irony of play-within-play. The first words of the text, for the spectator, are not words at all, but a visual image, that of the chandelier that remains the same in every scene.[11] As a sign, the chandelier evidently conveys the notion of inside, "intérieur"; and its presence in the fifth scene, Irma's room, which is exterior with respect to the brothel's "salons," and then even in the sixth and eighth scenes, where the whole building, "Le Grand Balcon," is seen from without, suggests that the furtive, dreaming insideness of the first four scenes is entirely inescapable, that the movement from inside to outside merely replicates the conscious self-manipulation that characterizes the inside to begin with—that even we, the audience, as Irma herself informs us in her last speech (4:135), will take the insideness of this theater with us when we leave. The last words of the text, however, are not Irma's, but another stage direction, the sound of a machine gun, which, throughout the play, evidently signifies "outside." And with respect to this sign, too, the provisional or reversible quality of the distinction inside/outside is insisted on. In the sixth scene, where the machine guns are actually seen (4:92)—but not heard—we observe, under the chandelier, between Roger and Chantal, what is still evidently a

[10]See my "Nietzsche's Idea of Myth: The Birth of Tragedy from the Spirit of Eighteenth-Century Aesthetics," *PMLA* 94 (1979), 420–33, where the treatment of the systematic aspect of *Die Geburt der Tragödie* describes in detail what a systematic version of the present argument would have to look like, and where Nietzsche's use of conceptual relations as at once a dramatic and a historical gesture is discussed.

[11]Jean Genet, *Oeuvres complètes*, 5 vols. (Paris, 1951–53), 4:39. Further references to vol. number and page in parentheses.

brothel-fantasy. And the final machine-gun burst, after Irma's direct address to us, suggests the outside of the theater as much as that of the brothel.

The theater, namely, is the domain of reversibility into which the distinction between inside and outside—as represented primarily by the ideas of mind and world—is plunged. Especially the reversibility of the relation of stage and auditorium is insisted on. The play's very title refers both to a stage setting and to a common architectural feature of theater auditoriums. And Irma's room, in the central scene, manifests the same ambiguity. Equipped with an apparatus for spying into the various salons, it corresponds to the auditorium from which *we* see into the salons, and so represents an objective outside with respect to all those secret passionate self-enactments. But that room, by virtue of its equipment, is also the hub, the center, the inside, from which the salons radiate, and is accordingly characterized by its own secret passion, to which the Envoy later alludes: "Our spies keep us informed as accurately as the peepholes in your salons do you. And I must admit that we consult them with the same delicious thrill" (4:105). Indeed, Irma and Carmen metaphorically reduce the whole "house of illusions" to a miniscule interior within the interior of each client's mind (4:71); and the range of this metaphor clearly includes by implication the house of illusions in which *we* are now sitting as well, but which is also located *in us*.

"Le Grand Balcon" is thus at once (1) a kind of huge head—which it even resembles visually when its shutters open like eyelids in the eighth scene (4:108)—an infinitely self-mirroring mind composed of interiority within endless interiority; (2) a theater, an endless ceremony of metaphor and imposture, of the separation of image from person (4:120), where the situations of player and spectator are repeatedly confounded; and (3) the world, insofar as the movement toward the outside, by which "world" is arrived at, always turns out to be nothing but the move of self-exteriorization which characterizes the mind's own relation to itself, and which is enacted in the reversible relation between stage and auditorium or in the failure of the theater to distinguish itself from the mind. The status of the brothel as "world" is the most tenuous of these metaphorical relations, but also the one that is most insisted upon thematically—by Irma's and the three clients' adequacy in representing the real versions of their roles, by the Chief of Police's conception of a satisfying destiny in "la nomenclature des bordels" (4:122), by Roger's capitulation in the last scene. Thus Genet aims to actualize in his theater what we recognize as the whole triple structure of Hamlet's metaphor of the "seat" of memory or consciousness.

The level of the theater mediates between the levels of mind and world and becomes the site of a reversible relation between them, the reversible frame relation par excellence. But the reversible relation between mind and world is essentially the content of what we have called drama's "hermeneutic ceremony." And here as there, *enactment* is the only possible way of coming to grips with the truth in question, since any form of systematic doctrine or statement inevitably reduces that truth to a quality *either* of the world (a particular state of affairs) *or* of the mind (a dynamics in our experience of world). It is clear, moreover, how this type of philosophical enactment unfolds about the complex nucleus represented by *two* mirror-theaters ("Le Grand Balcon" and our actual theater) which bear, to each other, a reversible relation of exteriority (we recall Irma's equipment) that draws in and confounds the categories of mind and world. Either the brothel is the detached or exteriorized image of our real theater, which must therefore be recognized as prior (as the original of the image), as having the quality of historical establishment or "world" with respect to our present situation in it; or else our theater becomes by suggestion an exteriorized image of the brothel, therefore an extension of our own mental interiority, constituted by our interpretive response to its content.

It must be recognized that Genet is not content to set forth these ideas on the level of meaning or metaphor. The theater here aims *actually* to burst its last limits and incorporate the whole of its "outside." And in fact, with regard to the outside in the sense of "history," it claims already to have accomplished that move. For history as event, as *res gestae*, not only dictates or determines, but also submits to determination *by* the writing and reading of history as account, as *historia rerum gestarum*. When Irma, in considering whether to accept the role of Queen, hints at the possibility of a genuine justification in her ancestry, the Envoy replies, "Fiddlesticks, Madame Irma. Genealogists work day and night in our cellars. History is what they make it" (4:105). And later: "Ce qui compte, c'est la lecture ou l'Image" (4:114), "What counts is the reading or the Image." History itself is subject to the way we agree on seeing or reading it. "World," in its realization as history, does not need to be captured magically by the theatrical process; the predilection for such captivity, the recognition that its reality is only "la réalité que le jeu nous propose" (4:87), "the reality that the game offers us," belongs to its very nature.

And the element that completes this structure, and embeds it in our *immediate* experience of the theater, is supplied when the Envoy continues: "Ce qui compte, c'est la lecture ou l'Image. L'Histoire fut vécue afin qu'une page glorieuse soit écrite puis lue," "What counts is the reading or the Image. History was lived only in order that a glorious page be written, then read." The full absurdity of this statement is drawn forth when Roger then repeats it with reference to himself: "Mon histoire fut vécue afin qu'une page glorieuse soit écrite, puis lue. Ce qui compte, c'est la lecture" (4:130). If the only purpose of life is to be realized in writing, then why live in the first place? What is the *content* of historical writing? The specific qualities of experience as experience, of "le vécu"—if such qualities can even be said to exist—need have no effect whatever on what such writers as the Envoy's "genealogists" put down on their "page glorieuse." Experience, "le vécu," the immediate substance of history, operates not by *what* it is, but by the mere fact *that* it is, by its mere being there to be written on, by its sheer spatial and temporal extension—by the only specifically nonliterary qualities, in other words, that can be attributed to *the theater in which we are sitting*. The theater is here utterly merged with its "double," which is life, "le vécu," the always immediate outsideness of world.[12] The whole basic substance of the world, of history, is compressed into nothing but our taking up of time in a theater that takes up space.

Thus we arrive at an interpretation of *Le Balcon* that mobilizes practically all of the theoretical material developed so far: the quality of the theater, precisely in its physical immediacy, as a vessel of literary self-reflection; the operation of drama as hermeneutic ceremony; the reversible frame relation as a decentering of the form. And above all, the admission into the form of its own strict "outside," as represented in earlier arguments by the openness of *Rhinocéros* vis-à-vis both narrative form and the effects of its author's public statements, by the historical quest for formal self-supersedure in Ibsen and Strindberg, by the groping into open spaces between scenes and beyond exit-doors that characterizes Nestroy and Schnitzler, by the presence on stage of things and people whose

---

[12]See Antonin Artaud, *Oeuvres complètes*, 7 vols. (Paris, 1956–69), 5:272–73. Artaud's formulation, in his letter to Jean Paulhan, includes ideas that would not ordinarily belong to the concept of "le vécu." My point, however, is that Genet's conception of what his theater reincorporates into itself is broad enough to include *everything* Artaud speaks of—but indiscriminately, hence not in the manner Artaud actually envisages. And Artaud's definition of "le Double du Théâtre" as "the real which is *unutilized* by people of the present" is directly translatable into the idea of an "outside."

actual engagement with the world will continue undiminished (we know) even when the semiotically determined identity they now bear evaporates into nothing.

But as I have said, I question whether Genet's play is perhaps *too* perfectly interpretable in these terms, whether it does not *devour* the outside, rather than simply admit it.[13] The machine-gun fire that threads its way through the action, and attempts to destabilize the structure by insisting on an "outside," is perhaps really only a sign of dramatic bad conscience, the forlorn wish that there *were* still an outside that might be admitted, a kind of deadly sewing machine, stitching the closed structure ever more tightly together in spite of itself. The simple devices by which a play such as *Rhinocéros* contrives to admit its outside without engulfing it or laying claim to it— for example, the device of offering identification with Bérenger as a possibility of closure, a barrier *against* the outside, but a barrier that crumbles when we try to take advantage of it—are missing in *Le Balcon*. Genet's play does not simply open onto our problematic situation in a real political and literary world, but rather it *haunts* us in that world, represents for us the corrosive "intérieur" from which our outward existence can never tear itself free. Nor is it a question of our carrying *the theater* away with us, as an ironic lever for use in real life, which is what we do when we are pursued through the exit-doors by Grasset's "Sie werden uns nicht entgehen." The theater, for Genet, is not portable in this sense, but philosophically located and closed, a contentless extension in which absolute Out-

---

[13]The sense in which I use the concept of closure is different, for example, from what Frank Kermode means in *The Sense of an Ending* (Oxford, 1968), where *Le Balcon* would probably represent something close to a maximally effective avoidance of closure. Kermode says, "Even when there is a profession of complete narrative anarchy . . . it seems that time will always reveal some congruence with a paradigm—provided always that there is in the work that necessary element of the customary which enables it to communicate at all" (p. 129); that is, closure at some level is entirely inescapable, for it is already implied by *the possibility of interpretation*. In this view, the inevitability of closure and the necessity of nonclosure, of breaking out of convention into reality (into an "outside"), make up an irresolvable literary tension that becomes manifest only historically, only over the time necessary to establish a sufficiently clear hindsight. My point, by contrast, is that this tension, the whole problem of admitting the "outside" into the form, becomes the immediate business of literature *in the genre of drama*, which, as a type at once both literary and concretely theatrical, itself represents that tension; and that *Le Balcon*, by attempting (or achieving) a kind of closure with respect to precisely this quality of the genre, may perhaps confuse the issues to which drama—as an activity, a communal human endeavor in history—responds. *Le Balcon*, like *Faust*, "makes . . . the gesture of attempting to swallow us up," to engulf its own outside; but *Faust*, in making this gesture, also renounces the possibility of being strictly a drama. See my *Goethe's Theory of Poetry* (Ithaca, 1986), pp. 292, 215–22, 310–24.

side and absolute Inside become indistinguishable, a secret place which we, by being in any particular condition at all, are in the condition of having left behind us, yet never having escaped, more or less as we never escape our childhood.

It is possible, as with Frisch at the end of Chapter 2, that I am being unjust to Genet. Perhaps there is a form of openness in *Le Balcon* that I have not considered. And even if the preceding discussion is entirely valid, it does not follow that *Le Balcon* is a trivial work. Perhaps a play of its type is needed in the economy of the genre, as a kind of antiplay, an articulation by radical negativity of what we mean by drama. But none of these qualifications invalidates the point for the sake of which I make the argument. I exhibit at least my version of *Le Balcon* as a sign of precisely the defect that its own structural completeness denies, the sign of a defect, of a resistance to closure—hence also a resistance to adequate systematic treatment on the level of theory—which I contend it is the very business of drama to keep open in the literary universe.

Perhaps, at this point, I should repeat my general apology for my procedure. What I have to offer is a collection of related arguments; and I think that the reader will find it more useful if I simply present that collection, with its rough edges and imperfect joints, than if I were to qualify each argument to death in the futile attempt to make the collection into a system. System, again, is a quality that I claim is already excluded by my subject matter. But I do not claim that qualifications are unnecessary or irrelevant. Is the "communicative ethics" in late Ibsen, for example, especially in its use of traditional mimetic style and its tendency to uphold communal order, not at least in effect a *conservative* ethics—or from the feminist perspective a patriarchal ethics, despite all that has been said about Ibsen's female figures? It might be replied that the nineteenth-century historicist view of reading, against which Ibsen's initiative is directed, is far more insidiously conservative and patriarchal; but the historical comparison becomes too complex to settle the matter conclusively. Then in Chapter 2, in the midst of a hermeneutic argument that takes cognizance of the impossibility of noninterpretive reading, I contended that we "experience" reading or film viewing as a direct "reception" of the work. Even supposing that the context, a comparison with how we experience drama, gives the contention some validity, we must still worry about the extent to which "experience" is or is not informed by the knowledge that the argument itself presupposes. I think that this particular problem is in fact symptomatic of the discussion of drama, that artistic form where the

realm of the textual or the intellectual and a realm of insistent physical immediacy not only meet but interpenetrate, each operating in
the constitution of the other. And in the case of Genet, finally, the
problem is one of valuation. I use *Le Balcon*, in this chapter and in
the next, as a negative example, to bring out by contrast certain
significant simplicities in Ionesco and Pirandello that might otherwise pass unnoticed. But is the usefulness of this text then *restricted*
to the present argument? Does the argument itself, precisely to the
extent that it is valid, not assign *Le Balcon* a special usefulness in the
historicity of the genre? And does it not do this in the very process
of showing a *discrepancy* between its own conception of the genre
and Genet's?

CHAPTER FIVE

The Trees Are Sentences:
Semiotic Ceremony and Pirandello's Myth of the Theater

Up to a point, I think it is possible to assert that the reversible frame relation—or the disclosure of reversibility in the frame relation as such—*characterizes* dramatic form. The reversible relation of understanding and interpretation fits the pattern, as does also, for instance, even Strindberg's cubism, which can be understood as the achievement of reversibility in the relation of past and future, as frame, to the otherwise privileged dramatic present. This chapter treats yet another form of ceremonial reversibility that characterizes drama, in the realm of semiotics. But the idea of a "characteristic" is subject to radical qualification, because the notion of a dramatic essence or center or character remains excluded, now by the very quality of reversibility (which is the center? which the frame?) that suggests it. Drama represents literature, as its church, by always establishing for literature a *further* level of valid theoretical self-reflection—"literature" being itself a maximally self-reflexive version of language—which keeps problems open and resists conceptual closure.

1.

Genet's *Le Balcon* seems to me an exemplary instance of the problematics of drama. And if *Rhinocéros* represents one possible way of dealing with that problematics, a different possibility is seen in Pirandello's *Quando si è qualcuno*. This play is deceptively simple, and in its simplicity is useful not only from a theoretical point of view,

179

but also as a gateway to the apparent simplicity—by contrast with such earlier works as *Sei personaggi* and *Cosí è (se vi pare)*—of all of Pirandello's latest plays. The main character, known only as *** in the text, and never referred to on the stage by any name except "Dèlago," the pseudonym under which he had published lyrics purporting to be those of an unknown young Italian-American, is an established author who feels his experience of life impaired by the public image he cannot help dragging around with him; his very thoughts, he complains, have been interpreted into a fixed pattern, a "precise conception, determined in every smallest part,"[1] which he himself is no longer able to change. Like Genet's Chief of Police, *** is in effect dead (5:985), and in the course of the play becomes literally a statue of himself, except that he resists this process whereas the Chief of Police welcomes it.

A more important difference from Genet, however, has to do with the way in which we, the audience, are involved in the separation of image from person that is shown to us on the stage. In *Le Balcon*, a developed version of the dialectic of spectator and audience insists upon our presence in both our actual theater and the theater of "Le Grand Balcon," which are in turn, interchangeably, outside or inside with respect to each other. And this situation of being spectators to ourselves—hence not freed but *trapped* in our spectating, in the state of spectator as object, the state of "audience," which now becomes the object of a new reflexive spectating, and so on—is potentiated yet further by being itself wholly represented in the action shown us. We are drawn into a vortex, a self-tightening spiral focused upon the secret center of the dramatic as such, the perfect identity of spectator and audience, of subject and object. In *Rhinocéros*, the political allegory keeps that untouchable center at a certain radial distance, which makes available circumferential distances or areas in which the dialectic of spectator and audience can be deployed fully, and perhaps dealt with politically. But the same dialectic is cramped, loses its articulation, in *Le Balcon*. "My history was lived only in order that a glorious page be written, then read," says Roger; and this speech is *itself* at once both a living and a reading of the "history" it speaks of, a struggling of the spiral toward the quality of a pure point. *Le Balcon* thus exposes a crucial difficulty in the practice of drama. If the dynamics of the reversible frame relation is adequately thematized *in* drama, then the goal of precisely that dynam-

---

[1]*Opere di Luigi Pirandello*, 6 vols., 4th ed. (Verona, 1967–69), 5 (= Maschere Nude II):984. Further references to Pirandello by vol. number and page in parentheses.

ics has vanished—namely, the constant self-decentering of drama (and thence of literature as a whole) which, in a different context, we might speak of as literary "irony." Where does this leave the idea of drama as a focus of maximal self-reflexive intensity in literature?

It seems to me that this difficulty is dealt with effectively in *Quando si è qualcuno*. The play shows us, simply and directly, the private life of a public person, and so casts *us* as the public by which *** is victimized. For it is only by our distinguishing a particular individual's public from his private existence, and only by our focusing upon the latter, only by our attempting to ferret out the individual's personal secrets, that this individual's *public* image (an image precisely of his supposedly private life, of the effects of aging in ***'s case, for example) is created. By attempting to live his *own* private as opposed to public life, therefore—with Veroccia, who is onomastically a cross between truth ("verace") and ferocity ("feroce")—*** only plays into the hands of his fictional public, of the play's public (us), and of the half unwitting, hair-cutting Veroccia-Delilah herself. Moreover, once we understand that the conventional privileging of our audience perspective is thus retracted here, the assumption that we (from the safety of the auditorium) do see *** as he "really" is— once we recognize that even the convention of the monologue is subverted, at the end of act 2, by ***'s addressing his words to Veroccia, which reflects an inevitable "public" conditioning of what he says—it follows that the very idea of a private existence has been discredited, and we find ourselves poised to undertake a semiotic analysis of human identity in general, of identity as nothing but "outside," nothing but a product of interacting semiotic differentials. Hence ***'s name, which is not a name, distinguishes him but does not locate or describe him, and so presents his identity as nothing but distinction, nothing but identity, which means in effect the absence or failure of identity.

In other words, *** is the strategy of identity as such, a strategy that is prior to the identity of any particular person *whose* strategy it might be. He is the projection of a truth about ourselves that is concealed from us precisely by our inveterate enactment of it, by that clinging to an identity which represents existence itself for us, by our unceasing subjection to the illusion of "being someone." What is interesting for our purposes, however, is that projection considered as a dramatic or theatrical strategy. In Genet, the spiral or vortex, driven by an inexorable dialectic, calls our identity into question by tending to obliterate the difference between the condition of being in the auditorium and the condition of being on stage, under the omnipresent chandelier of "Le Grand Balcon." In *Quando si è qualcuno,* on the other hand, the difference between stage and auditorium is insisted upon. The spectator's personal identity is not obliterated, but simply *redefined,* precisely by the difference between stage and auditorium; being-myself is now understood not primarily by the difference from being someone else, but by the difference from a purely public identity, from nothing-but-identity, as represented by ***. Our personal identity, as we sit in the theater, is thus permitted to persist. Our identity *must* persist. Without it, we would not be in a position to assess by analogy ***'s need for a valid private identity; and we would not be able to recognize that in making such an assessment, we carry out the function of ***'s "public," which in turn ensures that his identity will *be* strictly public, that it will be that nothing-but-identity from which our own personal identity is distinguished. Yet at the same time, this redefinition is also a radical questioning of our personal identity, since the difference, or the process of differing, from the nonidentity of nothing-but-identity, *is* still precisely the happening of nothing-but-identity; it is not yet the establishment of my particular identity in the sense that I am different from someone else. And this questioning, this failure of our personal identity after all, is then itself projected, and reflected back at us, in ***'s failure to be other than (we might say) "la lecture ou l'Image."

In the theater of *Quando si è qualcuno,* therefore, our personal identity is both insisted upon *and* called fundamentally into question. Our condition is that of being on the brink of our own identity—except that, strictly speaking, it cannot yet quite be "we" who occupy this condition. The content of this theater—including both stage and auditorium—is thus an enactment of the very *happening of identity,* exactly the happening that the play's title refers to with the wonderfully appropriate impersonal construction that Italian makes available. The attempt is made neither to obliterate our identity nor to collapse the differential structure of the theater, as in Genet. On the contrary, the difference between stage and auditorium, and the differences that distinguish both what I am and the way I am, are *exploited,* played off against one another so as to shadow forth their quality as representing nothing-but-difference, the enactment of an aboriginal semiotic event.

2.

Even supposing all these points hold, how do they make *Quando si è qualcuno* any less a self-contained philosophical ritual than *Le*

Balcon? The internal articulations of theatrical experience are given more room to deploy in Pirandello, but the theater as a whole is apparently as self-contained as Genet's; the theatricality of even the spectator's existence, and even of our existence outside the ritual public present (given the reversible frame relation of public and private existence in which we now participate), is no less a thematic focus for being less obviously realized as an image. I contend, however, that the semiotic elaboration of this self-reflecting structure does also manage to open the structure as a whole to its outside, and that this opening is evident especially in the use of the idea of the *author*.

Is *** "really" a mask for Pirandello himself? Does the "real" subject matter of the play touch the personal life of Luigi Pirandello? The answer to such questions is both yes and no. If we assume that the play offers us a glimpse into Pirandello's private life (and this assumption is contained in the question itself, which I cannot see how we can avoid asking), then it follows from the preceding argument that Pirandello's private life is precisely what we do *not* see, since our seeing has already transformed it into the public image named ***. "QUALCUNO, VIVO, NESSUNO LO VEDE" (5:1027), "Someone who is Somebody, as he actually lives, is seen by no one." Precisely ***'s namelessness, plus his being, in the fiction, a well-known author (which raises, inescapably, the question of his relation to the play's well-known author), thus names him "Pirandello" after all—in a degree that we cannot measure, but that does not need to be measured exactly to constitute an intrusion into the play of the play's own public "outside." This intrusion, moreover, is *real* in a manner in which the stylized machine-gun fire of *Le Balcon* is not. And it is a more direct way of dealing with the difficulty we started from than even the actual naming and discussion of Pirandello at the opening of *Sei personaggi* (4:50–53)—more direct and effective also, for example, than the naming of Ionesco in *Rhinocéros*. For in *Quando si è qualcuno* the naming of Pirandello is effected by devices that can still be understood as belonging wholly to the play's internal economy of signification, to the complex relation of public and private existence. The author is not dragged in, in a manner that obviously violates the work's closure; but rather he turns out simply to *be there*, in that artistically closed "inside" where he has no business being.

Le Balcon is interpretable as a self-contained exercise in the interchangeability of inside and outside—which is a contradiction, since self-containment is precisely what is denied. The final intrusion of the outside, in Irma's closing address to the audience, is a logical development of the mechanism of the play as a whole. One can think of other ways in which the play might have ended; but once we are shown that last scene, we understand clearly how it is related to the thematic treatment of "inside" and "outside" in earlier scenes, how it grows out of that theme. A relation of priority is thus established; the external dimension follows *from* the internal development. And the case of *Quando si è qualcuno* is quite different. The strictly external, the naming of "Pirandello," is inextricably involved in the play's internal mechanics; but since its externalness is constituted by the person of an individual who (as the referent of a proper name that does *not* actually occur in the text) participates directly in none of the relations that make up the content or structure of the fiction, it cannot be understood as a *development* of that internal mechanics. "Pirandello" is a concept that we have to *bring with us* into the theater; otherwise it is not there.

"Pirandello," then, is an element of the play's strict "outside" which is still undeniably present in the play's internal economy, but without being logically or artistically *implied*. In *Le Balcon*, the relation between inside and outside, like that between spectator and audience in *Rhinocéros*, is dialectical, an instance of mutual implication that evokes perversely the same organic model of art that it turns away from. In *Quando si è qualcuno*, by contrast, the relation suggested between outside and inside is that of a *semiotic differential*, a relation in which A is present in B, and B in A, not because each implies the other (as if A and B each had a substantial being capable of generating implications), but rather because their very existence is the product of a dynamics of differences (including the specific difference between them) which is strictly prior to any positive quality they can be thought of as having. Their presence in each other is a residue (or Derridian "trace") of their differential genesis. A and B, or in this case "inside" and "outside" with respect to the work of art, are *signs* in a semiotic universe whose structure has no level prior to that of difference as such. Outside and inside are present in one another in the same way that, say, green and red are, but without implying each other any more than green and red do.

I say that this play of Pirandello *suggests* a semiotic speculation of the sort indicated. To say that this or that relation *is* "semiotic," as distinct from another type of relation that is not, would be nonsense; the semiotic perspective, once adopted, must inform our understanding of any relation whatever. My point is that the suggestion alone—by way of the phantom naming of "Pirandello" and the semiotic criticism of identity implied in the structure of the fiction—opens the way to a satisfactory account *in general* of the pattern of reversible frame relations in drama. For the frame relation, as a type, is eminently amenable to semiotic analysis, being a relation of difference that is immediately understood as prior to the existence and respective identity of its arguments; and it is semiotic analysis that displays the inherent reversibility of such relations. If we agree, then, that such relations as text/performance, spectator/audience, work's world/author's world, and especially understanding/ interpretation, are basically frame relations—if we agree, for example, that interpretation encloses and closes off the domain of understanding, yet still insists that there be a definite room for understanding—and if we recognize that drama brings prominently into play the reversibility of these relations, then it follows that we have already adopted a semiotic perspective vis-à-vis the form, a perspective that no particular play can claim to create for us, but which *Quando si è qualcuno* does exploit and reveal with special intensity.

Here, as always, it must be understood that the question of drama makes sense only as the question of what we mean by drama, the question of our stake in it. And in response to this question, the reversible frame relation, the exchangeability of outside and inside, presents drama as a site of maximum semiotic awareness, a ritual or ceremonial focus at which the eternally unconcluded logic of semiosis become available—one is tempted to say, miraculously—*in* our experience, as a content of self-reflection. Semiotic thought constantly finds its way back to a logic that seems occupied primarily with the undermining of its own foundations, with a paradox that is perhaps also the general form of the paradox of history as both act and fact. In particular, the universe of signs, in which difference as such is the primitive generating and organizing principle, can never be stabilized into a system that might serve as a permanent ground of communication. For every difference, and every conceivable system of differences, must itself be the product of a difference or differing, and so on ad infinitum; as soon as we can identify a particular difference well enough to use it in communicating, that difference, by definition, has already revealed itself as a product of meaning, not a source. Communication, or intelligible signification (assuming that this is something that really happens), therefore requires, repeatedly, a decisive inaugural *act* of signification that creates its manner of signifying anew; without such an act or choice there is no ground sufficiently stable to support what we experience as communication. But the act in question, being itself a signifying, cannot happen without being grounded in just such a system of differences as has yet to be established.[2]

This logic, unless we insist upon some form of "transcendental signified"—which would take us out of the domain of semiotics in the sense I mean—must be recognized as characterizing our existence, but does not ordinarily characterize our experience, for roughly the same reasons that exclude the strictly absurd from experience. In fact, the logical unfolding of the paradox appears to depend specifically on the assumed presence, in our experience, of a relatively naïve sense of successful communication. But the argument on Pirandello, so far, suggests the possibility of regarding drama as an opening of experience to that whole impossible logic nevertheless. And this argument can be carried further.

3.

Let us turn back to *Quando si è qualcuno* and note that the handling of the concept "Pirandello" is echoed and reinforced by the play's simultaneous exclusion and inclusion of the *authorial function*. Exclusion of this function is normally part of what we mean by drama. In narrative (or in any form that is locatable in the space defined by narrative, lyric, and prose exposition as coordinates) the authorial function, while it can be suppressed or distanced to whatever extent one pleases, cannot be strictly excluded. In the most opaque irony or the most transparent persona, there is still always at least room for an ultimate authorial voice. That room, that "dedans," that active or vital possibility, is what minimally distinguishes "parole" from "langue" in the first place. And drama is characterized precisely by our insistence on *retracting* this condition. We may recognize that a dramatic character "speaks for" the author, or expresses opinions that we know to be the author's; but it is still the character's voice that we hear, not the author's, for the authorial *function* is excluded. (And as far as the nonverbal aspect of the play is concerned, we recall the importance of the quality of stage properties as real things that could just as well exist in relations having nothing to do with the present artistic structure. The carrot in *Waiting for Godot*, again, is

---

[2]For a concise discussion of this paradox, see Jonathan Culler, *The Pursuit of Signs* (Ithaca, 1981), pp. 38–41. For a thoroughly elaborated and detailed treatment of the state of affairs at whose center this paradox resides, see Gilles Deleuze, *Différence et répétition* (Paris, 1972).

not *the* carrot meant by Beckett, is not wholly determined by what *any* particular authorial voice "means"—but is simply *a* carrot.) Even if a character named "Ionesco" appears in a play by Ionesco—and even if Ionesco himself played that role, which it happens he did not in *L'Impromptu de l'Alma*—the situation is no different. What amuses and interests us here, as in the explicit or implicit naming of "Pirandello," is the presence of the author *without* an authorial function.

But the exclusion of the authorial function in drama is not absolute, not a result of something like natural laws governing the form. It is, rather, a convention, part of what we mean by drama, and as a mere convention it is subject to being violated. In fact, to the extent that we recognize it as an established convention, the possibility of violating it becomes available as a powerful signifying device. In late Ibsen, for example, the authorial function is reincluded in drama, and receives signifying force not from any specific qualities or statements of the implied author, but from its mere presence as a function, from the presence of that person-as-such (the author) who serves as the spectator's partner in a communal endeavor by which mimetic style is established as a ground of communication, in defiance of the logical and historical-stylistic tendencies that oppose it. Or we think of the authorial function in what Szondi calls "Ich-Dramatik," especially in Strindberg's expressionism, where its mere presence—a presence that would be conventionally normal in narrative, hence without special signifying force—represents an attack on the self-contradictory pretense of objectivity that is implied in impressionist style. Even in Nestroy, we have observed, the authorial function occasionally leaps out of the wings and makes faces at us, compels us to reflect on whether we are not perhaps merely dupes in the theatrical economy. And in such plays as Frank Wedekind's *Frühlings Erwachen*, or in any number of Brecht's plays, the authorial function is entirely obvious, obvious perhaps in a manner that cancels out its own operation and reestablishes the historically given conventions of drama as it were on a higher level.

What strikes us in *Quando si è qualcuno*, however, is precisely the uncompletedness of a strong movement toward inclusion of the authorial function. The *idea* of such a reinclusion is suggested repeatedly: first, by the phantom naming of "Pirandello"; second, by the namelessness of the play's central figure, his reduction to nothing but the function of author, his failure to maintain even the name "Dèlago" as a mask behind which to exist as something other than a function; third, by our recognition that *** himself, precisely in seeking to have an exclusively personal existence, creates the distinction between public and private being to which he then falls victim, that he himself is thus in truth the "author," the initiator, of what is apparently inflicted upon him—a suggestion that also emerges from the large segments of dramatic time in which he is silent while other figures speak for him; fourth, by the otherwise gratuitous use of movable walls and facades and statues in the stage-sets, which suggests, in this context, a world whose reality is somehow infected and compromised by an arbitrary authorial imagination; and fifth, of course, by the actual appearance in written form of the final words spoken by ***. But by being focused insistently on the figure of ***, who is still inescapably a character *in* the fiction, this idea, the idea of a reinclusion of the authorial function in drama, interferes with its own realization in the play we are actually watching. The authorial function is displayed to us as a thematic figure; it is not an integral element of our relation to the play, as it is in Ibsen and Strindberg.

In *Quando si è qualcuno*, then, the *possibility* of an included authorial function is suggested strongly enough to raise for us the question of why that function is *not* included, why, in the case of drama, the authorial function is understood to govern the work strictly from without, why there is no room for a direct authorial voice in the language or images of the play. Is the exclusion of the authorial function a necessary result of the complete distribution of speech and action among fictional characters? Why should it be more necessary in drama than in narrative? A play, after all, *has* an author as much as a novel does—and in the play we are watching, the author is in fact the object of a cryptic naming. If *** can in a sense *be* "Pirandello," what keeps his function in the play from being a strictly authorial function? To the extent that we worry about this question, to the extent that we ask why *** can speak with *an* author's voice, but not with *the* author's, it becomes ever clearer that the exclusion of the authorial function has no objective basis at all, but is an arbitrary act originating with *us,* part of what *we* mean by drama. Nor is this thinking at all farfetched in this particular context. What the play is about, after all, is the manner in which the quality of an author's very existence is conditioned by arbitrary judgments on the part of his public. The relation between Dèlago and *** is for the fictional public what the relation between *** and the "real" authorial function is for us, the "real" public. In both cases, the public simply refuses to accept this relation as one of identity.

Once we have come this far, however, the one step further that involves us in a perverse semiotic logic is practically unavoidable. For it is now clear that the authorial function is not something that exists prior to the question of the work's genre, and that the "author" is not someone ("qualcuno") who exists prior to his assuming an authorial function. Rather, the authorial function is now revealed as a semiotic *product*, a result of the differences enacted by our own working out of what we mean by various genres, especially what we mean by drama. And it is at this point that the paradoxical logic of semiosis threatens to enter and disarrange our experience in the theater. For the authorial function—along with its location, either inside or outside, with respect to any particular fixing of the text or the work—now offers itself to us as the token of a free act on our part, an inaugural signifying act now actually in progress, while at the same time the content of that act, the very idea of an *authorial* function, involves an acknowledgment of our situation as mere recipients in a process of semiotically regulated communication—a process whose quality as action belongs to the past, belongs perhaps to someone named "Pirandello." We are caught in a typical semiotic paradox; our communicative situation is revealed both as our own inaugural act and as the necessary prior condition of our acting. To look at it differently, the name "Pirandello," here in the theater, has the quality of an impending action, by being known but not (or not yet) spoken, while at the same time it also reflects the influence of an outside, a larger and prior system of codes without which we would not be in a position even to ask the questions that open the possibility of our acting. Our experience thus undergoes a profound rupture. It seems to me that when Artaud speaks of a "metaphysical" disruption or shaking or tearing apart of our experience in the theater, his demands are answered as directly by Pirandello's theater, in the sense of this argument, as by the Oriental theaters he takes as models.[3]

Obviously a great deal remains to be said about *Quando si è qualcuno*, especially as regards the semiotic criticism of identity. The very title exhibits a kind of fracture, in the ambiguity of "qualcuno" ("somebody special," "anyone at all," hence the paradox of a person's own identity as the projection of identity elsewhere) and in its impersonal reflexive verb—"si è," analogous to "si capisce, si deve, si sa, si può"—which is scarcely even approachable in translation. Shall we try to sell tickets to a play entitled, "When being-somebody happens in an articulating relation to itself"? Or we might consider the play's whole development as a self-engendering progression of differences that establishes identity in the very act of exploding it.

[3]See, e.g., Antonin Artaud, *Oeuvres complètes*, 7 vols. (Paris, 1956–69), 4:56, 61, 92.

The tension between self-as-subject and self-as-object (compare Strindberg), in ***'s need for a mirror at the beginning, is replaced, in a process that itself mocks growth or aging, by the tension between youth and age, which is imagined not only as yet another form of mirror relation (5:1027) but also as something like the relation of actor and character; and then all these versions of tension or difference are collected and distilled in the final vision of a man now actually turned statue while speaking no longer of youth ("giovinezza" [5:1027]) but of that mystery of a childhood ("PUERIZIA" [5:1044]) which has an effective existence only in its uncompromised condition of absence. But there is no need to carry out these arguments in detail, provided we agree that not only the interpretive appropriateness of semiotic speculation, but also the existence of something like a semiotic level of *experience* for the play's audience, has been shown.

4.

It is true that the main focus of Käte Hamburger's *The Logic of Literature*, and the field in which her insights are best known and most respected, is fictional narrative; and it is true that the philosophical suppositions on which her argument is founded have by now lost even the limited currency they still enjoyed at the time of the book's final version in 1968. But Hamburger does make a number of valuable theoretical points about drama. She sees drama as belonging entirely within "the fictional or mimetic genre," but also as representing an anomaly, in that its language does not show any of the characteristic features (for example, "epic preterite") by which this genre normally proclaims itself. Dramatic dialogue is clearly fictional, in being composed not of "reality statements" that articulate a subject/object relation, but of sentences that "constitute" the person who speaks them.[4] Yet at the same time, dramatic dialogue is also structurally indistinguishable from the language of "reality statements," and therefore never establishes or inhabits a *linguistic boundary* of fictional language. Drama, as Hamburger puts it, "has its locus in the system of literature within that enclave in the general system of language which is formed by epic literature"; but that locus is situated "far from the frontier which the fictional narrative

---

[4]Käte Hamburger, *The Logic of Literature* (Bloomington, Ind., 1973), p. 203. Further references by page number in parentheses.

function draws against this general system" (p. 199). The terminology of this argument is suspect, but the basic perception is valid nonetheless. The language of drama, we might say provisionally, *uses up* its creative power in constituting the figures who speak it, and does not challenge or threaten our general sense of language in the same way that narrative does. The language of fictional narrative is *about* language in a manner in which that of drama is not.

By thus rephrasing Hamburger, I mean not so much to dismantle her thought as to turn it (so to speak) inside out, preserving its structure. I have already argued against the whole idea of *defining* either literature itself or any particular literary genre, hence against the idea of a "system" in which particular areas or indeed "enclaves" might be marked out. I have insisted instead on the idea of "what we mean" by literature, what our "stake" is. But it must be conceded, I think, that this insistence has at least as strong a hortatory as it has a logical or a critical component. As soon as we say anything definite about *what* it is that we "mean," say, by drama, or by literature—and we cannot simply avoid being definite on such points, since we would then "mean" nothing at all—it becomes correspondingly difficult for us to maintain our sense of "meaning" as strictly a type of act; that act's supposed freedom is now loaded down with a particular content. It must be conceded, in other words, that besides "meaning" literature to be what it is, we also *recognize* literature for what it is, especially in relation to language as a whole.

Of course we can still avoid the idea of a definition of literature or of particular literary genres. Geoffrey Hartman and Paul de Man, for example, do not require the concept or practice of definition in order to talk about how literature is recognizable as literature. We can convince ourselves in general, and justifiably, that our recognition of the literary is not formally reducible to a definition, that it is the recognition of a particular sort of operation or influence exercised upon the *life* of our language. We might say that when we sense the energizing or destabilizing or disordering or radically questioning effect of a particular text upon our language as a whole, we tend then to speak of "literature." But even here, the ghost of Hamburger's thought, or of the shape of her thought, of definitions and lines of demarcation, has still not been put to rest. For the effects by which we recognize literature are still necessarily always *boundary* effects; they are not recognized as occurring except at the point where "literature," as if from outside, *touches* our language as a whole. And this thought is disturbing in the theory of drama; for as

Hamburger points out, at least one crucial literary boundary, which she names "fiction," is not touched or occupied by drama, does not offer drama the opportunity to make itself recognized, by boundary effects, as literature.

Hamburger's main point with respect to narrative is that a small number of simple grammatical and structural features locate its language in an area clearly distinct from that of "reality statements," whose structure and operation are governed by the subject/object dichotomy, by an understanding that the utterance originates in a particular real subject and either refers to, or in some way acts upon, an entity possessing some form of objective reality relative to that subject (even at the minimum represented by the primitive object named "I"). If we wish to turn this point inside out, in order to avoid assuming the validity of the subject/object distinction, we might say that the language of fictional narrative—by being clearly distinct, yet still bordering on that ordinary language which seems to require subjects and objects—always *calls into question* the subject/object relation, hence the whole scheme of grammar, rhetoric, and logic, as a means of understanding or organizing our life in language. But if drama, so to speak, operates entirely within the shelter of this questioning, never mounting its own direct challenge to the language of "reality statement," then by what boundary effects will it manifest its own literary or poetic quality? Is drama merely a kind of public advertisement for what is really the linguistic achievement of the narrative genres?

It seems to me that the existence of this problem goes a long way toward explaining the phenomenon of theater-on-theater, the strong tendency of drama to talk about itself, to thematize its own qualities and problems as a genre. In the case of narrative, the operation of the literary upon or within language in general, the characteristic gesture by which the work makes itself recognized as literary, is carried out entirely in what Hamburger calls the "narrative function," and does not depend on the work's content. But in drama the "narrative function . . . has become nil" (p. 200), which means, apparently, that the linguistic boundary effects by which drama asserts its literary nature must be produced with the aid of content after all. Hence theater-on-theater, theater as its own content; drama apparently must *talk about itself* to assert its quality as literature. And this point brings us into the vicinity of Pirandello, for the content of the "theater" plays, *Sei personaggi in cerca d'autore*, *Questa sera si recita a soggetto*, and *Ciascuno a suo modo*, is built entirely out of the conditions of their performance, so that the relative "reality" or self-identity of the spectators, vis-à-vis the dramatic characters, is called into question dialectically, and the subject/object relation, the constitution of the subject prior to its operation in language, is threatened in what we recognize as a "literary" manner.[5] Nor is it only in the theater plays that this type of questioning is undertaken. In *Enrico IV* and *Cosí è* (*se vi pare*), for example, the subject/object relation is made to collapse under its own weight. The essential fragmentariness of the subject's perspective in reality—which for Hamburger, incidentally, is an important component of the dramatic spectator's situation (p. 202)—is mirrored repeatedly in these plays, and remirrored, in the structure and presentation of the fiction as well as in its content. We are offered a self-compoundingly fragmentary view of the fragmentariness of even our presumably accurate sense of how fragmentary our experience of reality is, and both subject and object are threatened by a kind of mathematical infinitesimalness.

But these literary boundary effects are philosophically mediated. They are not the same simple operation of language upon itself as those of narrative, which they imitate in their focus on the subject/object relation. They presuppose at least a rudimentary philosophical awareness on our part, hence also the given verbal medium of that awareness. In effect they presuppose a valid epistemological and hermeneutic terminology. And it seems to me that toward the end of his career Pirandello becomes ever less satisfied with these avenues for asserting what he often calls the "poesia" of drama. *Trovarsi*, for instance, and of course *Quando si è qualcuno*, no longer fit the pattern of the theater plays, no longer focus on a questioning of the subject/object relation. A new sort of questioning now seems called for; and the character of this new questioning, as we have seen, will be semiotic.

Boundary effects, in a sense broadly comparable to that of the argument in Chapter 2, are again an issue, but the situation has become more difficult. In discussing those boundary effects by which the generic identity of drama is asserted in the modern period, we found it convenient simply to assume that drama is understood to be, among other things, a literary type. A basis was thus established for developing such ideas as the tension between text and performance; the quality of performance as both an interpretation of the work and an operative element in its constitution; the significance of the multiplicity of performances, of the presence of

---

[5]See the detailed argument on *Sei personaggi* in my *Modern Drama and German Classicism* (Ithaca, 1979), pp. 273–79.

actual things on the stage, of the notion of an ontological integrity in texts, and so on. Moreover, the historical relativity of the boundary effects we discussed, vis-à-vis cinema and opera, the recognition that comparable but *different* boundary effects must be expected in different periods, plays into the hands, as it were, of the idea that generic boundary effects mark "what we mean" in a dynamic sense, as an *action* on our part. The evident historical mutability of the boundary effects we observed keeps open at least the possibility of referring them to a continuing activity, whose activeness is manifest precisely in historical change.

Now, however, we find ourselves on the horns of a typical semiotic dilemma. For we must inquire into the differential ground of that presumed activity; and in the process—to the extent that our inquiry is *successful*—we risk compromising precisely that quality of activity without which the very concept of literary genres becomes pointless. We must ask *how* we recognize drama as a literary type in the first place. The argument of Chapter 2, I think, remains valid within its limits; we do recognize drama as a literary type, even if it is not clear how. But the question of how, as it is brought into focus by Hamburger, or by her argument turned inside out, is a thoroughly uncomfortable one, especially since the corresponding question with respect to narrative admits such a clear answer, in the form of strictly linguistic boundary effects that produce a structural difference between "real" time or space, as governed by a subject/object relation, and the time suggested by narrative tenses or the space of narrative perspective. If the question of how narrative is recognized as a literary type could not be answered, then perhaps the question with respect to drama (or any other form) could be dismissed as an untouchable mystery in our historical and verbal existence. As things stand, the question must be asked: where does drama set itself off, in language, as a literary type?

5.

I maintain that there is, after all, a type of strictly linguistic boundary effect, an operation of language directly upon itself, that is proper to drama and available to no other literary form because it cannot be produced without the aid of the theater—or more precisely, because its strictly intralinguistic quality depends, paradoxically, on the operation of an extralinguistic factor (the theater) in defining a poetic type.[6] I maintain, further, that this boundary effect occurs automatically in drama, that it belongs to drama in the same manner as the narrative function to narrative, that it is not an achievement of any dramatic work, but simply the focus of drama's recognizability as a literary type. Thus the dilemma we have discussed, concerning the quality of the literary genre as an act or activity on our part, is brought strongly into play, and brings with it the other problems we have learned to expect. For if the operative existence of the theater is really required, then the identification of our manner of recognizing drama as a literary type depends (circularly, paradoxically) on our *having* recognized drama as a distinguishable literary type; otherwise the question could not have been asked to begin with.

If the operation of narrative is in a broad sense hermeneutic, having to do with the relation of subject and object in language, then I contend that the operation of drama is semiotic, involving a *reversal* in the direction of certain semiotic processes by which the very nature of language is adumbrated. This is the deepest sense, or the sense turned inside out, of Hamburger's argument that in drama, *"the word becomes figure and the figure word"* (p. 201). In particular, drama foregrounds the process of verbal *reference;* for in the theater, actual objects, to which the play's words and speeches may be taken as referring, are made available to the audience in a manner in which comparable objects are made available to no other type of literary audience. Richard II says, "Give me the crown" (4:i.181), and the actor is then handed an object that we do recognize as a crown. Word and referent are both present on the stage, confronting one another.[7]

This is a special feature of drama. For literary language is ordinarily understood to "mean" primarily by *signifying,* not by referring. It is possible that in reading *Madame Bovary* I recognize a typical human situation, and that I recognize the same situation in the household of my neighbors. But this does not imply that the novel, in any sense whatever, refers to Mr. and Mrs. Smith. In making the connection, I understand that I am arbitrarily delimiting a segment of the novel's signification and applying it in a way that has less to

---

[6]Julia Kristeva, *Révolution* (Paris, 1974), pp. 17–19, approaches the matter the other way around, and is entirely right in asserting that it is the problem of the extralinguistic that first makes necessary the articulation of a semiotic approach to language and literature. My contention is that drama is the home, or the beachhead, of the extralinguistic *in* literature.

[7]See Anne Ubersfeld, *Lire le théâtre,* 4th ed. (Paris, 1982), pp. 34–36; Michael Issacharoff, "Space and Reference in Drama," *Poetics Today* 2 (Spring, 1981), 217.

do with literary meaning than with my own social situation and perceptions. Similarly, I may know a great deal about the actual people Dante names in the *Commedia*, but it does not occur to me to suggest that the poem means such knowledge; the poem does not refer *to* those people so much as it signifies *through* them. Hence the special quality of drama, since reference does figure prominently in the dramatic establishment of meaning. This is not to say that reference ever comes close to exhausting the meaning of a word or phrase in dramatic dialogue, or that reference plays no part whatever in generating literary meanings outside of drama. But the difference, even if it is only a difference in degree, is significant. Reference unquestionably *happens in the theater*, with a directness not found elsewhere in literature; and it is unquestionably much easier to make sense of Dante without knowing that Guido Cavalcanti was a real person than to make sense of a performance of *Richard II* without knowing that the word "crown" refers to the object the actor is holding.

Drama, as I say, foregrounds the process of reference. But on the other hand, reference as it occurs on the dramatic stage is also known from the outset to be a sham; it is not so much that the word refers to the object as that the object is there for the purpose of appearing to be referred to by the word. What is dramatized in drama, therefore—since we recognize that without the put-up job of performance, the play's words would "mean" only in the sense of literary signification—is not merely verbal reference, but also the *disjunction* between reference and signification.[8] This disjunction, so

---

[8]The method of distinguishing between signification and reference in philosophy or linguistic-semiotic theory does not ordinarily effect a disjunction, but tends rather to establish a *hierarchical* relation. P. F. Strawson, "On Referring," *Mind* 59 (1950), 327, says, "Meaning (in at least one important sense) [i.e., signification] is a function of the sentence or expression; mentioning and referring and truth or falsity [the last two in the sense of accuracy and its opposite], are functions of the use of the sentence or expression." In other words, something very like a drama—a more or less perspicuous order of circumstances—is needed for the happening of reference. But when translated from the domain of practice into that of theory (e.g., Strawson's), the distinction becomes problematic. For that very "use" which makes reference possible also *presupposes* reference—reference as a particular established relation between the utterance (or its linguistic context) and real circumstances—which embarks us on a journey of thought that can end nowhere but in the idea of a comprehensive system of codes in which reference is but one type of coded relation. Nor does it help that Strawson continues, "For to talk about the meaning of an expression or sentence is not to talk about its use on a particular occasion, but about the rules, habits, conventions governing its *correct* use, on all occasions, to *refer or assert* [my emphasis]." Now the hierarchy is simply reversed; meaning, or signification, is simply subordinated to reference, which latter includes all the presumably valid relations between language

to speak, is the linguistic action in which the foregrounded quality of reference plays a part, an action in which language itself takes the opportunity to resist any unified view of its own mode of operation. Reference and signification both happen on the dramatic stage, and evidently have to do with each other. But in the theater it becomes clear that they have to do with each other only at a distance, in a sense that inevitably involves "mere" convention, not in the sense, for example, that reference is either the true destiny (utilitarian view) or the true origin (sensationalist view) of linguistic signification.

Drama thus enacts a disjunction that belongs to what we might call in general the *semiurgic indeterminacy* of our situation with respect to language. (That is, indeterminacy in our manner of making signs and working with them.) Signification and reference are evidently related processes. Indeed, in the realm of theory, it is difficult to maintain even the distinction between them, since theory must always ask either (1) how can reference operate without a prior encoding of its elements in some system of signification? or (2) how can signification get started, and how can it impinge on our immediate sensory or material existence, without some prior referential contact between meaning and reality?[9] But on the other hand, if we do make the distinction (as the form of drama insists that we do, in its playing off of literary signification against the immediate refer-

---

and real circumstances that are named "rules, habits, conventions." To explain reference, that is, is always to destroy it, by either nullification or universalization. And yet, reference still *happens*, in a manner distinguishable from signification, which is a curious (all but miraculous) fact that is nowhere offered more directly to the intellect than in the dramatic theater.

[9]C. S. Peirce, for example, does his best to maintain the distinction when he begins by saying, "All dynamical action, or action of brute force, physical or psychical, either takes place between two subjects . . . or at any rate is a resultant of such actions between pairs. But by 'semiosis' I mean, on the contrary, an action, or influence, which is, or involves, a coöperation of *three* subjects, such as a sign, its object, and its interpretant, this tri-relative influence not being in any way resolvable into actions between pairs" (5:484). And this necessary triadic structure, which is not reduced even by the infinite series of interpretants relative to the same object (2:92), permits the object to be understood as a referent without the concession that anything other than signification (the production of interpretants) ever actually *happens*. Peirce can thus emphatically avoid denying the immediacy of perception (5:53–55). But still, "perceptual judgments" (5:115–16, 180–86), which are easily confused in experience with perception itself, condition all thought and so prevent reference from ever becoming an independent communicative possibility. What counts ultimately is the production of triadic relations and their order (2:233–42). In fact, signification overwhelms reference to the point where even the human sign-user is identifiable only as a sign (5:283, 313–14). The citations in parentheses refer to vol. number and paragraph in the *Collected Papers of Charles Sanders Peirce*, ed. Charles Hartshorne and Paul Weiss, 8 vols. (Cambridge, Mass., 1931–58).

ence to objects on the stage), then neither process can reasonably be understood as subsuming the other; they operate, as it were, not only *with* each other but also *past* each other, and so constantly keep open an uncertainty or imbalance in our sense of exactly what language does. If reference were merely a type or aspect of signification, then it would follow that our "real world" is in truth constituted by our linguistic relation to it, which is a position that can be maintained in abstract philosophy but conflicts violently with the shape of our experience. (Do we never experience anything *new*, for which we then find or invent or are taught words?) And if signification were merely an aspect, a result or development, of reference, then it would follow that language is but one particular device by which we come to grips with a fully preexisting world, which is a position that seems to accord with a certain limited area of our experience but fails very quickly when it is reflected upon. To grasp its failure, we do not even have to worry about whether or how or in what degree "abstract concepts" are referential. We need only consider the linguistic possibility of lying, which does not arise from the process of reference alone, no matter how complicatedly that process is folded back on itself.

It is true, of course, that the revelation of semiurgic indeterminacy, in this sense, is not exclusively the domain or the task of drama. In fact it is clearly part of the business of literature in general. That literary language, especially in the aspect of the fictional, always rejects the subsumption of signification under reference, requires no argument. And the converse movement, the exclusion of pure signification, of a signification untrammeled by reference (or by what is otherwise called the "sensual"), belongs to what has been meant by the border between poetry and philosophy at least since Plato, belongs already, I think, to the foregrounding of metaphor in literary language. But if this particular operation of language upon itself, the keeping open of semiurgic indeterminacy, thus characterizes literature as a whole, still it represents a case where drama is situated a good deal closer to the "frontier" than in the case of fiction and the "narrative function." It seems to me that we might even reasonably speak of a unique revelatory reification of metaphor in drama, of theatrical reference as a ceremonial display of the ineradicable referential residue in all metaphorical language.

Theoretical points of this type, however, are not our main concern at the moment. We still need to ask how drama is recognized as a literary type, and the argument so far is clearly a circular one; even to ask the question, we have had to make use of the assumption that drama *is* a literary type. This circularity belongs inescapably to the whole idea of the literary type as a form of activity on our part; we cannot reasonably expect to find circumstances or criteria that *compel* us to recognize (passively) such a type. But by following the line of thought we have embarked on, I think that we can understand in increasing detail what drives that circular movement in the particular case of drama, how that circle, which *is* drama for us, maintains and reproduces itself.

6.

Our next step is to understand that the foregrounding of reference calls attention to the *reversibility* of reference in the dramatic theater. I mean that the things, and especially the people, on the dramatic stage, in the very process of being referred or alluded to verbally as the play unfolds, also refer *to* the words that name them and require them as objects. (This is part of what I mean by saying that reference in the theater is a sham, that the referent is recognized as being there *in order* to be referred to.) Physical things, including real people (the actors), are the *signs* by which the theater refers to figures in the text. (A "figure" here means any semiotically distinguishable unit in the text, any result of applying an "s-code" to the text.)[10] Those physical things are signs, moreover, in a manner that is structurally indistinguishable from the manner in which words are signs referring to things. Just as the word can never become strictly a proper name, focused upon nothing but one real object,[11] so neither the actor nor the prop is ever focused perfectly upon the textual figure, but always brings with it its own horizon of associations. (The carrot used in performing *Waiting for Godot*, we recall, is not *the* carrot signified by the word "carrot" in the text, but rather *a* carrot that could as easily do other things besides be eaten in *Waiting*

---

[10]See Umberto Eco, *A Theory of Semiotics* (Bloomington, Ind., 1976), pp. 36–40.

[11]Consider the sentence "XYZ is a person," where the predicate is chosen as one that is easily verifiable in fact. Even if XYZ *is* a person, and indeed the only person ever to bear that name, the referential focus of the word "XYZ" is still not perfect. For the sentence, in order to mean anything at all, bears the traces of other possible sentences, including obviously inaccurate ones, sentences in which the word "XYZ" participates (as it were speculatively) and so develops a semiotic identity beyond any referential function. Conceivably—in response, say, to an olfactory stimulus—I could say the word "rose" or "pancakes" in such a way as to imply no sentence whatever; but in this case, the word has become not much more than its own sound, as an involuntary bodily reaction.

for Godot.) Given that we are talking only about the process of reference (since the signified, by definition, *is* focused upon perfectly by
the signifier), it thus appears that things, on the stage, *act like words*
with respect to the enacted text, and so always enact their own
semiotic or verbal translucence *as* things. Just as the word, when it is
understood to refer, becomes translucent with respect to a particular
thing that we recognize is *different in nature* from the word's "meaning," so the thing or person or performance-figure (i.e., the result of
applying an "s-code" to the performance), on the stage, becomes
translucent with respect to the words or text-figures behind it—
even if we do not happen to know, at the moment, exactly what
those words are. I say "translucent," not "transparent," for both the
word and the thing, when seen each through the other in this reversible process of reference, lose their sharp outline, their directly
knowable or tangible identity as themselves.

And I contend that this quality of translucence, in things on the
stage, then becomes the token of an insubstantiality, a translucence
with respect to language, of things in general. In the same way that
the relation of subject and object in language is threatened by narrative, drama, by way of the theater, challenges or threatens directly
the assumption that language and its range of reference are strictly
distinguishable realms, the idea that language can possibly happen
in a world of semiotically inert objects. Pirandello's *Lazzaro* is an
allegory in this sense. Diego Spina's religious faith includes the belief in a vile material world that is available as the strict object of
scientific reference; precisely his belief in the divine or immortal
therefore compels him to insist on the strict referential applicability
of the concept "morto," "dead."[12] (Even the particular concept is
significant here; for a language that claims to be strictly referential
contends in effect that its object is *always* dead, inert.) And it is the
untenability of this position that becomes manifest when Diego
Spina is then forced to acknowledge his own present existence as a
resurrection from death, as an instance of the concept "miracolo,"
"miracle." But once *this* concept is admitted to have referential validity, the floodgates open and "miracles" are everywhere. Lucio re-
vokes his irrevocable decision; Arcadipane's and Sara's impermissi-
ble union turns out to be permissible after all; and Lia, whose

---

[12]Eco, p. 66, even in the process of showing that referents can only operate as
"cultural units," acknowledges that real things in someone's "experience" can be
referred to—with one exception, since "death, once it has occurred, and only then,
constitutes the one and only referent, or event which cannot be semioticized (in that a
dead semiotician no longer communicates semiotic theories)."

paralysis is now seen to be merely the enforced inflexibility of an object-world tyrannized by linguistic reference, rises from her wheelchair and walks. For a miracle is a sign that does refer to an eminently real object, but only reflexively, only to its own real miraculousness or miraculous reality—which is precisely its quality as a sign in the first place, since it is a sign only by *really* happening. The miracle, as a referential sign, thus suggests in general that the ultimate referent of signs is never anything but the act of referring itself, which makes nonsense of the idea of reference as a one-way process. A similar challenge to our sense of referential language is of course also mounted by semiotic and literary theory, in the idea of a world constituted by signification, a universe of signs, a "general text." But the challenge in this form is philosophically mediated, whereas in the dramatic theater it is an operation of language directly upon itself, by way of actual things whose supposedly extra-verbal nature (whose *apparent* interruption of the self-referred operation of language—especially literary language) has become a "naked mask."

Among the various possible objections to this argument, I think the most significant is that the concept of linguistic reference appears to be overstrained. Even the idea that the relation of thing to word in drama is structurally indistinguishable from the relation of word to real referent on the stage, the idea that the thing or person or performance-figure must first signify in its own right, and then, in view of its signification, be recognized as pointing at a text-figure that had existed (really) prior to its signifying, appears to push matters too far. One might reasonably ask exactly *how* the text-figure exists prior to its representation, or indeed *whether* it exists. Justification is present in the text of *King Lear*, for example, to permit using the most perfectly beautiful actors available as Goneril and Edmund, actors markedly more beautiful than those who play the constrictedly virtuous Cordelia and Edgar; but there is also a case to be made for letting Goneril's and Edmund's evil show in their persons. Depending on how this choice is managed, therefore, the same two characters on the stage will represent *different* text-figures; they will bring this or that text-figure into manifest being, not merely refer to it. Why, then, not simply regard those actors as signifiers, as signs that operate like Peirce's "interpretants" with respect to the text?

Or yet further, supposing the structural parallels I have indicated are actually part of the audience's experience, do they not suggest philosophically something more like Heidegger's argument in *On the Way to Language?* Shall we insist on the idea that the thing *refers* to the word? Is it not enough to suggest, with Heidegger, that the thing—in its quality as being, or for the sake of its entrance into or envelopment in Being—*is referred* to the word (or the Word, language in general)?[13] Heidegger's argument attempts to preserve an asymmetric or one-way relation between language and its objects, while at the same time avoiding the simplistic idea of valid external reference, the idea of a strict separability and absolute relatability between language and the range of objects it points to. Language is still separable, still different—in that the word "is not" in the same manifest sense in which things "are"—yet is also never absent or inoperative in the things from which it is different. A crucial component of this argument, however, is the reduction to indistinguishability (in a procedure not fundamentally different, for instance, from Peirce's) of the processes of signification and reference. And drama—which has a text that signifies literarily, yet also insists that the words of that text be used in a clearly referential manner on the stage—*does* distinguish between signification and reference, along the same line that separates virtual reader and actual spectator. The performance-figure does act like an interpretant, in its bringing the text-figure into manifest being; but at the same time, on the stage, it is clearly referred to by spoken words and is clearly something *other* than what the text-figure "means." It is, again, *a* carrot, not *the* carrot.

Objections of this type, therefore, do not seriously affect the argument I have proposed, not because that argument is impregnable, but because it avoids theoretical attack by appealing to a situation that it claims is strictly *real*, the "happening" of reference in the theater. If this sort of argument is to be questioned, and not simply either accepted or rejected, it must be questioned on different grounds. We must ask *what is to be gained* by distinguishing reference from signification, by insisting (as dramatic form does) on what I have called the semiurgic indeterminacy of our relation to language. Or to take the questioning a step further back, what exactly do we mean by linguistic "reference" to begin with? The process of reference cannot be distinguished adequately from that of signification if it does not include a strictly nonlinguistic or nonsemiotic component; the referent must be something *different in nature* from any sort of sign that might be taken as the signified of the referring word— this being the difference between *the* carrot and *a* carrot in Beckett. But then where does the *code* come from, the system of relations,

[13]See Martin Heidegger, *On the Way to Language*, trans. Peter D. Hertz (New York, 1971; orig. 1959), e.g., pp. 86–90.

that permits reference to happen? ("Indexical" signs will not do the job; the referent still has to be identified, semioticized, encoded, before it can be referred to even by an indexical sign.) In the process of reference, if it is really fully distinguishable from signification, something entirely different in nature from the word's "meaning" is nevertheless "meant" by the word. This event, assuming it happens, is thus a kind of mystery, indeed a "miracle." (It is fairly clear that our earlier discussion of the word "miracolo" in *Lazzaro* can be refined in exactly this direction.) Heidegger refers this mystery back to language itself, as the mysterious or miraculous or challenging quality of "being" with which language endows the objects of a process in which reference operates as reference (on objects different in nature from itself) without being clearly distinguished from signification. I will call this quality of the referent, its quality of being different in nature from the referring sign, not "being" but "opacity," by contrast with what seems the relative "translucence" of the word or sign that is associated with it.

But the question remains: what is to be gained by distinguishing strictly between signification and reference? The quality of mystery or challenge in our relation to language, as Heidegger shows, can be quite adequately articulated without the aid of that distinction—hence without the insistence upon or enactment of that distinction in the form of drama. Let us therefore approach the question the other way round. What are the consequences, what is lost or sacrificed, if we do *not* distinguish clearly between signification and reference? And with this question we find ourselves again in the vicinity of *Lazzaro*. For it will now be seen that the linguistic condition represented by Diego Spina's insistence on a wholly self-ordered material world, by that tyrannical insistence on the limitedness of the real with which he punishes both himself and others, is the tyranny not of reference as such, but of a reference utterly inseparable from signification. The paralysis of Diego's world—and of his daughter—is the condition of a world in which things are permitted to *be* nothing but what is signified by the words that refer to them. Or in the terms of the previous chapter, any acceptance of the ultimate indistinguishability of signification and reference, whether on metaphysical or on strictly semiotic grounds, leads in the direction of what I have called a fascist insistence upon uniformity of literary response.[14]

---

[14]Thus I enlist Pirandello in what I contend is drama's inherently antifascist campaign in the field of literature, even though he himself was a member of the Italian Fascist Party, which he made a public gesture of joining shortly after the murder of

It may seem to us in practice that there is room in the real world for any number of different responses to a literary text; and it may follow theoretically from the idea of infinite semiosis, the unending chain or field of interpretants, that this room is not restricted even when we regard reference as a complex form of signification. But if reference is always subject to a valid semiotic analysis in terms of higher or more comprehensive codes, then it follows in principle that the literary text, or any text as a signifying entity, is *systematically definable* in terms of an expanding array of codes that eventually includes all possible responses to it, hence that the text, in principle, can be *defined* in terms of reception or response, that the existence of any clear signifying unit guarantees on some level a uniformity of response, or at least the asymptotic approach to uniformity. That this reasoning holds "in principle" is sufficient. The question is not whether we can find, in any particular case, the system that organizes as aspects of itself, thus reduces to uniformity, our various responses to a text. The question is whether we *think* of the text or the work as definable by our response, whether we think "aesthetically," whether uniformity of response operates as an unacknowledged literary *value*. And I contend that the subsumption of reference under signification—however good the arguments by which it is supported—always includes a tendency to think in this manner.

If *Lazzaro* is a complex allegory of this state of affairs, and this train of thought, then Pirandello's *La nuova colonia* is a relatively simple one. Padron Nocio opens the proceedings by dismissing Nuccio's tavern as "questa tua tana . . . di ladri e vagabondi" (5:1066), "your den of thieves and vagabonds," whereupon he becomes entangled with Tobba in a discussion of whether the latter is "meant" by those words. The point here, and throughout the Prologue—as in *Lazzaro*—is that at least a certain group of people are not permitted to *be* anything but what is signified by the words that refer to them. Once a jailbird, always a jailbird—even if, as the Fisherman's protest apparently proves, it is not "true" that you have committed a crime (5:1082). Signification and reference thus merge and become an instrument of oppression, from which the "uomini cattivi" of the Prologue (5:1066) can escape only by founding an entirely new society

---

Giacomo Matteotti. See Gaspare Giudice, *Pirandello: A Biography*, trans. Alastair Hamilton (London, 1975), chap. 7, esp. pp. 149–51. That widely differing ideas of "fascism" are involved here, does not get rid of the problem. Pirandello was a Fascist, albeit an increasingly disillusioned one; his work, especially in its semiotic aspect, is antifascist.

and, in effect, a new language that no longer names them "bad men." Therefore, accompanied by the "miracle" of La Spera's milk (5:1087), they flee to the island. The trouble is that to operate as the foundation of a new society, their new language must shape itself as a system of signification, and must insist on its *own* referential validity. We must all become "different from what we used to be," says La Spera (5:1097); but as Currao points out, even this new freedom from what we "were," from what language had made us, must itself take the form of *law* (5:1101–2). And when this new combination of signification and reference is then destroyed by a new intrusion of the real, of what is different in nature from what language (now the new language) signifies—I mean, when the island is invaded—it follows that the result is not only a defeat, but also a kind of philosophical victory, a new wrenching apart of signification and reference, which is then reflected in the newly miraculous La Spera, perched with her child upon the waves.

Again, the question of whether signification and reference *are* distinguishable, or whether one may be subsumed under the other, is undecidable. The question that counts is how we *think* of this matter. Again, my point is that literature, considered not as an isolable area within language but as the act of maximal linguistic self-reflection, has a clear *interest* in distinguishing reference from signification. And that interest is served most directly by drama as a form, by the at once defective and effective church of literature.

7.

We must be clear, however, about *why* it is in the interest of literature to resist the theoretical collapse of the distinction between reference and signification. The idea of fascism as a literary category and an aesthetic phenomenon goes a certain way toward answering this question, as does the idea of a keeping open of metaphor, a celebrating of its stubborn referential residue, its quality as comparison. But nearer the center of our concern is the reversibility of the process of reference on the dramatic stage, which arises as a consequence of the separation between reference and signification, between actual spectator and virtual reader. For in that reversible process, the word (or the text-figure in general, the signifying linguistic unit) becomes *opaque* with respect to the sort of brute physical object to which it normally only refers translucently. Of course the word still refers to the object, and in this sense is still translucent;

the reference of word to object on the stage is precisely the model by which we are enabled to recognize the reverse process. But the word, or the text-figure, is now also a referent, an opaque object of the act of referring, which means that language, at least for a moment, has lost its primacy in the domain of reference. Language, so to speak, is *dethroned* in the theater—and I am not sure that this meaning is not secretly present in Richard II's handing over his crown.

It is easy to assume that the interest of literature is best served not by the dethroning, but by the dominion of language, that literature, as Heidegger suggests, is the site where language most powerfully asserts its quality as the "house of Being."[15] And it is true that the operation of literature tends normally to favor a literarization of our existence as a whole—a phenomenon we discussed earlier in connection with Schnitzler. But I contend that this imperial tendency in literature is a danger—and a danger *for* literature—which, in order to be counteracted, in order to be mastered fruitfully, requires the influence (as in Schnitzler's theater) of a relation of outsideness. It requires, so to speak, exit-doors by which we can really leave. Precisely literature, I contend, requires the operation of the strictly nonverbal in a form that is *not* subsumable under its own play of signification. Otherwise literature runs out of substance and becomes mere speculation, or is reduced, at best—as Artaud says of Western drama—to exploring the complications of empirical and moral psychology. If literature is the place where language knows itself most intensely, then the question must always be: knows itself in relation to what? as the outcry against (or of) what "esprit d'anarchie profonde"?[16] And I contend that semiotic reversibility in the theater is literature's most efficacious device for dethroning language without *en*throning some "transcendental signified" that would obscure Artaud's threatening and challenging "anarchy."

Let us consider the matter of literary polysemy. Polysemy, first of all, is already implied by the idea of the literary utterance (or the literary work or genre) as an inaugural act; for if the meaning of a literary unit can be exhausted by a finite number of interpretations, then it becomes possible to regard that unit as nothing but a passive response to its own meaning. Therefore we are reluctant to speak of the literary or the poetic where we cannot detect at least the pos-

[15]Heidegger, pp. 5, 21–22, et passim, with reference to his earlier "Letter on Humanism."
[16]Artaud, 4:51. Further quotations by vol. number and page in parentheses.

sibility of a virtually infinite polysemy. But if the literary work harbors an infinity of as yet unarticulated meanings, then it has become thereby a model of language as such, in the sense of "langue," while at the same time still remaining, itself, an instance of "parole." And this combination, when we consider it successful, gives us the sense precisely of an inaugural act, a kind of primordial speaking, a breaking-into-speech of language as such.

This train of thought, however, has a tendency to slur over what we mean by an *act* in the first place. If the quality of an inaugural verbal act is something we *recognize* in literature, then that quality of act also disappears; the act is now merely a fact, not an act *for us*. Literary polysemy, in itself, suggests not action so much as the deferral of action, a kind of indecision between possible statements. Hence the literary importance of drama's dethroning of language, of the confronting of language with an outside in which, for us, the original miraculous articulating act can be grounded. Drama in this sense always enacts the act of meaning, the act of difference which founds meaning—whereby we perhaps also think of Ubersfeld's idea, mentioned in the Introduction, of that limitlessly polysemous "espace scénique" in which an entirely particular reading of the text is performed nonetheless. Or to put the matter less radically, the semiotic activity of drama can be seen as a keeping open of *questions:* Where does the literary act come from? Why does the polysemous literary work not have the character of merely a *field* of potential meaning? How does it become "parole"? For again, as soon as we lose sight of these questions, as soon as this questioning is replaced by a supposed knowledge or recognition, the quality of action, for us, disappears in favor of fact.

In any case, when I speak of the *opacity* of the word in drama, it will be clear that I am attempting to approach Artaud's notion of a substantializing or spatializing of language, but by way of concepts fundamentally different from, say, that of "incantation" (Artaud, 4:56). However, one apparently insurmountable obstacle remains. Semiotic reversibility, on which everything depends, has been defined and (I think) demonstrated only in the domain of linguistic *reference*. Is the domain of *signification*—the literary domain par excellence—immune to this infection? Can the people and things and events on the stage be said to *signify* the words or figures of the written text? Ordinarily we should tend to regard the performance-figure as a Peircean "interpretant" with respect to the text, a sign that signifies not the word itself as signifier, but rather the signified of the word. And perhaps, given our earlier argument on the exchangeability of understanding and interpretation, this relation *is* to an extent reversible; perhaps the word can become an interpretant of the performance-figure. But is this limited reversibility sufficient to render the word opaque, to dethrone language?

Can the word be toppled from its position as a privileged signifier, as the arch-signifier, the original model of all signifying relations? *Can* the word in this sense be substantialized, be made opaque? *Can* Heidegger's house of Being somehow live inside itself and "be" after all, in the same way that what it names "is"? Obviously words can become the objects of a signification that means some particular lexical or semantic or syntagmatic or paradigmatic or historical relations. But a strictly reversible verbal signification would require that the word as *nothing but* signifier, nothing but sheer signifying power, be signified. And the word in this sense, it appears, is always too transparent, does not present an opaque target, always leads signification one step further, in the direction of *its* signified.

8.

Let us return to Pirandello's late "myths," and approach them now with regard to the question of drama and theater as separate arts, but arts that require each other and so inevitably come into *conflict*. Pirandello himself repeatedly complains about the sullying of drama's "poetic" quality in theatrical performance; the theater, as it were, is a cradle in which the promising infant of drama is exchanged for a caricature of itself. And drama, in turn, reduces the theater to an interpretive device, robs it of its quality as the locus of sheer semiotic revelation. In *I Giganti della Montagna*, Cotrone says to Ilse:

Voi attori date corpo ai fantasmi perché vivano—e vivono! Noi facciamo al contrario: dei nostri corpi, fantasmi: e li facciamo ugualmente vivere. [5:1341]

You actors give a physical body to fantasms, that they might come alive—and they do live! We, on the contrary, make fantasms of our bodies; and we make them come alive equally.

The *actual* theater gives bodies to ghosts, to the fantasmal signifieds of the text; but there is perhaps also another kind of theater, a *true* theater, which makes bodies into ghosts, makes them semiotically translucent, or indeed transparent, and reveals their nature as signs.

How shall the true theater be made actual? Pirandello's earlier "theater" plays are an attempt to deal with this problem by reintegrating theater and drama, by making theater not only the vehicle, but also the content of drama. And yet, can drama and theater be reintegrated, given "nostre condizioni morali e sociali"? Our trouble is that "noi sentiamo troppo, *soffriamo* troppo: la nostra vita è per sé stessa drammatica, però non possiamo aver la serenità di concepire il dramma, da che noi stessi vi siamo impigliati" (6:870), "We feel too much, we suffer too much; our life is in itself dramatic, but we cannot attain the serenity necessary to conceive the drama in which we ourselves are entangled." Our cultural situation is such that we *require* the nonintegration of drama and theater. We need the theater as a *barrier*, as the establishment of a contemplative distance, between ourselves and that drama which is otherwise merely our enveloping unconscious life and so never attains the quality of drama to begin with.

It is thus *we* who bring about the conflict between drama and theater that leaves us dissatisfied. If *Lazzaro* is an allegory of semiotic retribution in this sense—showing our own responsibility for our world's paralysis—*La nuova colonia* is an allegory of cultural or historical retribution. A fully reintegrated theater, from our point of view, would be an island of paradise, a reattainment of our semiotic dominion over existence, a place, as La Spera says, "fuori!—dove non sono mai stata. . . . Dove le parole—tu non sai com'è—le dici—le ascolti—ti diventano nuove" (5:1071). A place where *words become new,* a miraculous rescue from our being the mere objects of signification used as reference, our rescue from a world, for example, where a "jailbird" is a "jailbird" no matter what he does. But in this reintegrated theater the presence of a Crocco is inevitable, and is *equivalent to our own presence as spectators.* For the theater is paradise only by being known as such, which presupposes our conscious point of view beyond its limits. The theater as boundary, as barrier, is necessary even here; the new colony, without such a barrier, throws itself open to precisely the corrupt society against which it carries out its definition of itself. And the "miracolo" of La Spera is thus left floating on the waves of perfected disintegration.

Or we might look at both *La nuova colonia* and *Lazzaro* differently, as enactments of the mutual interference of drama and theater. *La nuova colonia* does, after all, represent an escape from semiotic civilization, into a realm where "words become new," where words are newly made and thus subject to our control, rather than in control of us. And in the play considered *strictly as theater*, the limited space of the stage obviously represents just such a realm, just such a precariously existing island. Or at least the stage *would* have this character, *if we did not know what the play means*, if the play had no poetic or literary component whatever. It is our knowledge of the play's semiotic purport, our knowledge (like the characters') of that inherently unknowable paradise, which robs the island-stage of its pure theatrical significance (precisely its quality as paradise), thus as it were "colonizes" it; for that knowledge, as such, presupposes inescapably a prior fixing of semiosis, hence the impossibility of a truly new semiotic beginning after all. And if the literary here interferes with the theatrical, the reverse is the case in *Lazzaro*. For if this play were nothing but literary, if it were presented, say, as prose narrative, then the miracles on which it is focused—understood as the miraculous dissociation of signification from reference—would in a sense be *valid* for us, for the reader, since the literary, after all, is precisely the domain of free signification, untrammeled by reference. But those miracles, for all their validity, would then also no longer be miracles at all; they would be merely regular features of the domain of literary signification. Therefore a domain of the referent is required, something like a theater, in relation to which Diego Spina's resurrection and Lia's healing can become fully what they are. And yet the theater, once we establish it, strips these miracles of their miraculous quality altogether, interferes with even their semiotic miraculousness, by way of our knowledge of its *interpretive* character, hence its ability to provide only artificial representations of the miraculous.[17]

The necessary conditions for a reintegrated dramatic theater are therefore also impossible conditions. *La nuova colonia* could mean what it means only by our not knowing what it means; and *Lazzaro* can do neither with nor without its performance. The theater is simply not reintegrable *for us*. We can develop this point, and gain some perspective on the geography of Pirandello's late plays, by considering again the idea of the author. For when we read narrative, the "narrative function" tends to supplant the authorial function; the author's existence can be pared down to the point where language simply operates on itself in the manner we discussed earlier in connection with Käte Hamburger. But the location of the

[17]See my *Modern Drama and German Classicism*, pp. 16–17, on "realism" in drama, and on the distinction between the imaginary and the artificial.

dramatic function in a theater clearly distinguishable from the drama, and in tension with it, disrupts this linguistic self-operation by *preserving* the author as a task for interpretation—in defiance of our actually only conventional insistence (we recall *Quando si è qualcuno*) on his absence. The ideal operation of language on itself is interrupted by the author's continuing presence, like the presence of the dead poet in *I Giganti della Montagna*, "il cancro che ci ha mangiati fino all'osso" (5:1324), "the cancer that has eaten us away down to the bone." And the presence of the author, by way of his work, is answered or complemented by the presence of the *audience*. "Gente a noi!" (5:1312), "People are coming!" are the first words of *Giganti*, and refer not only to the Countess's troupe, but also to *us*, as we sit there. Without us, and without the work brought by the Countess, La Scalogna is a pure, dreaming, ideal theater, a theater in which "truths" are "invented" (5:1342), in which bodies become semiotically translucent ghosts. But that ideal theater, now that it must produce an authored work, and especially now that *we* are here watching it, belongs irretrievably to the past. The two main aspects of our effect as an audience are mirrored exactly by the unseen giants themselves and their rowdy servants. Like the giants, we support the theater with our goodwill; but like the servants, we also thereby destroy the theater, at least in its ideal character. And of course the association between authorial function and the role of the audience or public recalls our argument on *Quando si è qualcuno*, where the intrusive authorial function, to an extent, *is* eliminated, but only at the cost of our recognition that its absence depends on an arbitrary, hence inherently temporary decision made by *us*.

Again, the dramatic theater, for us, is simply not reintegrable as an operation of language on itself. And all the various factors that interrupt or interfere with its potential realization as a revelatory linguistic process self-reflection—the authorial function or the presence of the authored work as an object of interpretation, our presence and our interpretive activity as an audience, the "social and moral conditions" of our culture—are represented, given concrete form, by the sheer physical reality of the stage and its contents. That sheer physical reality, interposed between work and audience, is semiotically necessary; the body cannot become a sign (a "fantasm") without first *being* a body. But that same bodily quality, which we must begin by assuming, also inevitably interrupts the literary effect. There appears to be no way out of this dilemma. The true dramatic theater cannot be realized except via the destruction of precisely that intractable physicality, that association of a literary genre with a brute historical accident, which makes it needful or desirable in the first place.

And yet, I contend that in *I Giganti della Montagna*, or as much as we have of it, there is a kind of answer to the problem of the true theater. For the content of *Giganti* is not theater as a present reality but the *myth* of the theater, the theater of Misfortune, La Scalogna, which is always irretrievably lost in the mythical past when the words "Gente a noi!" ring out from behind the cypress. The physicality of stage, actors, and props thus functions as a kind of *dramatic preterite*; that physicality as such (merely that the objects are there for us) is the token of an absence, of a *pastness* of the theater it represents. The people and things before us, not by being *particular* physical objects, but simply by being physical objects to begin with, become signs that betoken an *absent* theater in which, perhaps, signification is (or was) truly reversible. Those people and things, in enacting this particular fiction (the collapse of Cotrone's theater), therefore enact precisely the ground of their own signifying, the ever recurring death of the true theater. The crucial point is that the physical theatrical signs signify simply by *being there*, and do signify a well-defined textual figure—the impossibility of realizing Cotrone's true theater—but without *referring* to it, which would require a correspondence with their particular quiddity. Signification itself has thus become reversible. The true theater dies in enacting its own death, and in this act of dying demonstrates its existence after all.

These paradoxes can be developed as far as one pleases. It is the nature of the sign to invoke the presence of its object in the very process of enforcing the object's absence, putting it into the distance of pastness, which is exactly what the intractable physicality of Pirandello's mythical stage does. And in this sense, the plot of *Giganti* becomes yet another form of allegory: the sign (the Countess's real theater) intrudes itself before its signified object (Cotrone's true theater), but only in order to disclose the signified, which means in a sense to effect its own destruction. Thus *Giganti* becomes the drama of signification as such. The things and people on the stage all signify the word "La Scalogna" (misfortune), which in turn signifies *both* the inevitable exile of the true theater from our experience *and* that true theater itself. Or indeed, the suggestion of semiotic transparence in the very physicality of the stage before us is *itself* a sign for the perfected semiotic transparence of objects in the true theater, a transparence that is perfected precisely *by* the true theater's not being quite there for us, since its achieved presence or self-identity would make an opaque object of it.

We should perhaps not speak of *Giganti* as an achievement, since it is not finished. But there are plenty of indications, starting with "la lingua verde" (5:1312) on the roof, that the project is conceived in terms of linguistic and semiotic theory. Or we might ask, why, on his deathbed, does Pirandello tell his son that he has "solved" the whole problem of the last act ("ho risolto tutto" [5:1371]) with the idea of a Saracen olive tree in the middle of the stage? Why not any other kind of tree? "Un olivo saraceno." It seems clear, at least to me, that the word "saraceno" suggests the *sentence* "sarà cenno," "it shall be a sign, a token, a gesture, a hint, a summary," which produces a semiotic circle. The object signifies the sentence that signifies nothing but the object's quality as signifier; thus a perfect miniature emblem of semiotic reversibility is created. Or yet further, the other suggested sentence, "the olive shall be a sign," alludes to the mythical founding of Athens in the sense in which that city becomes the source of our whole dramatic history. Stefano Pirandello tells us that his father was "very pleased" with his last scenic idea. But perhaps he was amused as well. Perhaps it even occurred to him that the tree at the beginning of the play, the cypress, also signifies a sentence, and a very curious one: "ci presso," whose verb means specifically to press *olives*. Does this physical object thus signify a sentence in the first person singular, which would suggest a signifying relation between the physical interruption in true drama and the authorial interruption? And is the object in that sentence "us," the restored community of a miraculously restored theater?

9.

These remarks would perhaps be mere inconsequential play, on my part or on Pirandello's, if they did not correspond to certain thoroughly pervasive qualities in the texts and in the general theoretical situation. For despite all the complexity we have had to work through, there is still a clear sense in which it can be maintained that semiotic reversibility, even in the domain of signification, is characteristic of *all* drama, and of drama in the actual, not ideal theater.

Let us begin with the question of the relation between drama and the illustrated book. Are the illustrations in a book not interpretants of the text, in roughly the same way that performance-figures are interpretants of a dramatic text? This analogy does not affect most of the arguments I have advanced, since the addition of illustrations to a text, in history, does not mark anything like as clear a generic boundary as that between drama and either narrative or exposition. But if we restrict our view to semiotic issues, the question does arise: do performance-figures signify in a manner that is fundamentally different from the operation of drawings or photographs added to a book?

Umberto Eco, in *A Theory of Semiotics*, paraphrases the sentence "this is a cat," spoken by someone actually pointing at a cat, as follows: "The semantic properties commonly correlated by the linguistic code to the lexeme /cat/ coincide with the semantic properties that a zoological code correlates to that *perceptum* taken as an expressive device." His point is that this explanation, in terms of a relation between the contexts of "sign-vehicles" (the actual perceived cat being taken as such a vehicle), would not in the least disturb us if we were talking about the *picture* of a cat. And he goes on to argue that in truth, the two cases are not really that different. For in the formation of the sentence "this is a cat," or indeed already in the act of perception, "the [real] referent-cat is no longer a mere physical object. It has already been transformed into a semiotic entity."[18]

This argument is familiar, and is valid within its limits. But we have also seen that drama, in the sense of what we mean by drama, insists on the semiurgic indeterminacy of experience nonetheless, reminds us constantly that there *is* a difference, in experience, between signification and reference, hence a difference between the cat and its picture after all. This is the difference between *a* carrot and *the* carrot in *Waiting for Godot*—*the* carrot being what would appear in a film or a text illustration. Or, with the valuation in a sense reversed, it is the difference between *an* enactment of Lia's walking, in *Lazzaro*, and *the* unique miracle signified by the text.

The important point now, however, is that in drama, because of the simultaneous existence of virtual reader and actual spectator, *both* of the carrots are there in the one thing, both *a* carrot (for the spectator) and *the* carrot (for the virtual reader). The illustration depicting a cat, as an interpretant, signifies only *the* cat, the signified of the word "cat" in the text. But somehow, in Beckett, both *a* carrot and *the* carrot manage to be there at the same time. How can this possibly happen? To the extent that this question is actually part of our experience in the theater, the signified of the theatrical sign (of Vladimir's actual carrot) now necessarily includes the *relation* be-

[18]Eco, p. 164.

tween the carrot's two modes of existence—which relation, in turn, *is nothing but the sheer signifying power of the word "carrot" in a literary text,* the power that can somehow invest *a* thing with the quality of *the* thing. The word, that is, strictly in its quality as signifier—not in any context of referring—has become the signified of the physical theatrical sign, and the semiotic is now revealed as fully reversible.

I have qualified the argument by saying: To the extent that this question—the question of how *a* thing and *the* thing can both occupy the same pocket of existence—is actually part of our experience in the theater. Perhaps it is *not* part of our experience, as Pirandello appears to concede, and as Artaud insists. The matter is not strictly decidable. But if that question, along with its consequence of semiotic reversibility, is not part of our experience in the theater, then, since the abstract argument still holds, the fault must lie *with us,* in the way we respond to the theater, perhaps in our "social and moral conditions," and is not a structural failure in drama itself. In other words, the true dramatic theater, in Pirandello's sense, is always there, waiting for us, as soon as we are able to live up to it.

Indeed, that true theater is perhaps really nearer at hand than it appears we have any right to suppose. For the absence of the true theater (if it is really absent), hence the very nature of the actual theater as a communicative form, is entirely a function of *our* attitude—as is, for example, ***'s authorial situation—hence at least potentially *under our control.* We find ourselves in a situation like that of the perfected "new colony" (if it could be perfected), a situation where words, if we only try hard enough, *can* "become new," a fresh beginning where we are offered dominion—indeed, are already exercising dominion, perversely, by omission—over the very structure of the semiosis that establishes our existence. And this dominion evidently includes the human dominion over history which we have discussed several times, both in its large philosophical aspect (memory's "seat" in the "globe") and in its practical aspect as a response to the literary danger of fascism.

Can we take the one short step that is still needed? Can we *change* our basic attitude toward the theater? Where shall we find the fulcrum, the leverage necessary to effect such a change? These questions, if we ask them, have to be answered with "No, there is no such fulcrum, a miss is as good as a mile." Yet these questions also contain the assumption that our actual theater is not somehow, secretly, *already* the true theater; and this assumption is by no means unshakably established. For just as there is no fulcrum for changing ourselves, so also there is no perspective for knowing ourselves (knowing exactly what our "attitude" and its limitations are) in this sense. The condition of having a true theater, in other words, and the condition of knowing such a theater to be impossible, do not necessarily exclude one another. Or as Artaud puts it:

> Il ne peut y avoir théâtre qu'à partir du moment où commence réellement l'impossible. . . . Une vraie pièce de théâtre bouscule le repos des sens, libère l'inconscient comprimé, pousse à une sorte de révolte virtuelle et qui d'ailleurs ne peut avoir tout son prix que si elle demeure virtuelle, impose aux collectivités rassemblées une attitude héroïque et difficile. [4:34]

> There can be no theater except from the moment at which the impossible begins in reality. . . . A true theatrical work disrupts the tranquility of our senses, liberates the repressed unconscious, pushes toward a kind of virtual revolt—which, moreover, achieves its full value only by remaining virtual—imposes on assembled collectives a heroic and difficult point of view.

Precisely in being real, the true theater also remains "virtual"; and it is this "difficulty," perhaps even a certain "heroism," that is opened for us by Pirandello's last plays, especially *I Giganti della Montagna*, which does not manage, as a work, even to thrust its own whole bulk into existence.

Pirandello calls those last plays "myths," and what they in fact establish is *the myth of the theater*. For what else is a myth, if not a recounting of past events whose pastness is attributed not to the mechanical working of time so much as to our own inability to live up to them? And if the disappearance of the mythical material, its impossibility, is something *we* are responsible for, then the possibility of our also *having* it—if in an infinitely problematic sense—is not excluded after all.

10.

Is it legitimate, finally, to invoke Artaud in an argument on drama as a *literary* type? It is true that I have spoken of a dramatic dethroning of language for the sake of literature, and that parallels to this idea can be extracted from Artaud, parallels even to an idea of the "poetic" efficacy of the dramatic theater (e.g., Artaud, 4:280–81). It is true that when Artaud speaks of the solid or materialized word in the theater (e.g., 4:87, 149), we are perhaps justified in thinking of the word's semiotic opacity, and that the idea of "elevating ordinary objects, including the human body, to the dignity of signs" (4:112) seems to point toward a theory of semiotic reversibility. And there are suggestions in Artaud of a theory of anticharacter—or a non-theory—that appears to resonate with Cotrone's idea of the actors' making their bodies into "fantasms" (e.g., 4:48, 139).

But what is the significance of these parallels? Does the present text, my text, do anything even remotely associable with the attempt, in Artaud's text, actually to perform chaos or anarchy? If this book were to be considered primarily as an attempt to come to grips with Artaud, it would obviously lay itself open to exactly the type of criticism that Derrida, in *Writing and Difference*, directs at Maurice Blanchot. The very form of the statements I have made tends inescapably to circumvent "that which irreducibly amounts to Artaud," to accuse Artaud of a kind of "error."[19] Why does Artaud not himself make my arguments? Why does he not recognize at least the possibility of something like Pirandello's achievement?

Artaud's actual effect, when I import him here, is mainly to expose the limitations of the present endeavor. In particular, I have tried to focus on drama in the sense of what we mean by drama, and the trouble with this focus, from the point of view of an Artaud, is the word "we." Of course it could be maintained that the same "we" exists under the surface in Artaud, or perhaps that the first person plural is there divided in two: into the civilized "we" who are responsible for the persistence of a decadent European drama of psychological dialogue, and a repressed, unconscious "we" who can on occasion be moved to admit that we do, after all, know what is meant by such theatrical terms as "chaos," "anarchy," "magic." But still, Artaud's bifurcated "we" does manage to remain in a region of conflict, collision, confusion, whereas the word as I have used it— despite my attempts to depersonalize it, to anchor it in history and in logic—inevitably suggests the appeal to a *consensus* that I do not really mean, and in fact even perhaps flirts dangerously with precisely the fascist notion of uniformity of response that I have placed in a radical opposition to the dramatic.

And yet, I am an Artaudian. I claim that my invocation of Artaud is legitimate. To argue this point, I will turn not to Artaud himself, but to those texts of Derrida that call my claim into question. I will take Derrida's argument, so to speak, as a fixing of Artaud, the

---

[19]Jacques Derrida, *Writing and Difference*, trans. Alan Bass (Chicago, 1978), p. 171. Further references designated by W&D plus page in parentheses.

establishment of a position between Artaud's and mine, where the question of legitimacy becomes discussible. For there are numerous points in Derrida's unfolding of Artaud that border very closely on my argument. "Artaud promises the existence," says Derrida, "of a theater that is a text because it is no longer enslaved to a writing more ancient than itself, an ur-text or an ur-speech" (W&D, pp. 174–75). Does semiotic reversibility in drama not accomplish exactly this, by demolishing the *priority* of the written "original"? And is the story of the individual stolen from himself, confused with his double, which Derrida develops from Artaud's texts (W&D, pp. 179–81), not a paraphrase of Pirandello's "La Favola del figlio cambiato," the unfinished intratext of *Giganti?* And is the problem of colonization, especially the idea of "the theater which is no longer a colony" (W&D, pp. 188–90), substantially different in Derrida, in "La Conquête du Mexique" (Artaud, 5:21–29), and in *La nuova colonia?*

Perhaps more crucial, however, is Derrida's analysis of Artaud in terms of a struggle with "the autonomy of the signifier" (W&D, p. 178), which reflects a concern that goes beyond just the Artaud essays in *Writing and Difference*. We recall the problem developed in Derrida's discussion of Claude Lévi-Strauss in "Structure, Sign and Play in the Discourse of the Human Sciences":

> To take one example from many: the metaphysics of presence is shaken with the help of the concept of sign. But . . . as soon as one seeks to demonstrate in this way that there is no transcendental or privileged signified and that the domain or play of signification henceforth has no limit, one must reject even the concept and word "sign" itself—which is precisely what cannot be done. For the signification "sign" has always been understood and determined, in its meaning, as sign-of, a signifier referring to a signified, a signifier different from its signified. If one erases the radical difference between signifier and signified, it is the word "signifier" itself which must be abandoned as a metaphysical concept. [W&D, p. 281]

Evidently the perfected *reversibility* of semiosis would provide at least a response to this problem, and it follows that not only Artaud's struggle with the signifier, but also Pirandello's semiotic project, perhaps looks toward the dramatic theater as the church of "literature" in an even broader sense than we have yet suggested.

In any case, it is interesting that Derrida begins the first Artaud essay in *Writing and Difference*, "La parole soufflée," by developing from Michel Foucault the idea of the infinite closeness, even in their opposition or rupture, of "the work and madness," and then extends this idea to include the closeness of critical to clinical commentary (W&D, pp. 169–74). What, after all, is the difference between Artaud and Pirandello, if not the difference between madness and the work, which in turn corresponds to a highly problematic difference we have observed in the structure of the true theater itself, the difference or distance, which turns out to be a tantalizing proximity, between its utter impossibility and its potent actuality. "Artaud kept himself as close as possible to the limit: the possibility and impossibility of pure theater" (W&D, p. 249). When Derrida thus summarizes his discussion of Artaud, I think we can be excused for detecting a closeness to our discussion of Pirandello. But discussion is obviously not the end for Derrida. The two Artaud essays enclose an essay on Freud; thus the complicated relation of critical and clinical discourse is structuralized, bearing with it, inescapably, the closeness of madness and the work; and Derrida, in the end, thus flirts with the paradoxical closeness of his own text to Artaud's.

CHAPTER SIX

Approximately Five Questions
on Dürrenmatt's *Die Physiker*

Is drama as difficult a matter as it appears in the last chapter? Is it necessarily a question of balancing on the edge of madness, or concentrating centuries of philosophical thought into an instant of deathbed inspiration? Let us turn to what appears, on the surface, a comparatively relaxed dramatic style, and ask the following questions about Dürrenmatt's *Die Physiker:*

1. Why does Möbius enter the insane asylum in the first place? Is his own explanation of his decision adequate? Does that explanation also justify the abandonment of his family, and then finally the killing of nurse Monika?

2. Can we say anything about the status of Möbius's world system *as* a scientific discovery or achievement? Is the history of science, or of thought in general, one of the play's concerns?

3. Suppose the play's outlandish premises were true in reality. Suppose a crazy psychiatrist were actually to gain control of the world in the manner shown by the play. What would be the consequences outside the asylum walls? To what extent would *our* world be different?

4. Who is insane, if anyone? What, precisely, does the concept of insanity refer to? Why, in his final speech, does Möbius say not merely that he sees Solomon but that he *is* Solomon?

5. Why is the opening "stage direction" permitted to balloon into a long, mildly satirical essay on modern Europe and the traditional poetics of drama? And why are "21 Points" appended to the printed

text? Are these pieces merely an author's commentary, or do they affect our sense of the work's genre?

1.

Möbius opens his own defense of his actions as follows:

> Here we are, three physicists. The decision that we have to make is one that we must make as physicists; we must go about it therefore in a scientific manner. We must not let ourselves be influenced by personal feelings but by logical processes. We must endeavor to find a rational solution. We cannot afford to make mistakes in our thinking, because a false conclusion would lead to catastrophe. The basic facts are clear. All three of us have the same end in view, but our tactics differ. Our aim is the advancement of physics. [P. 78/61][1]

But is Möbius's real aim "the advancement of physics"? He himself denies this only a few speeches later.

> There are certain risks that one may not take: the destruction of humanity is one. We know what the world has done with the weapons it already possesses; we can imagine what it would do with those that my researches make possible. . . . Fame beckoned from the university; industry tempted me with money. Both courses were too dangerous. I should have had to publish the result of my researches, and the consequences would have been the overthrow of all scientific knowledge and the breakdown of the economic structure of our society. A sense of responsibility compelled me to choose another course. I threw up my academic career, said no to industry, and abandoned my family to its fate. I took on the fool's cap and bells. I let it be known that King Solomon kept appearing to me, and before long, I was clapped into a madhouse. [P. 80/62]

His aim, it turns out, is not the advancement of physics but the preservation of humanity. Or is it? We *do* know "what the world has done" with atomic and hydrogen weapons; since Nagasaki the

[1]Translations are from Friedrich Dürrenmatt, *The Physicists*, trans. James Kirkup (New York, 1964). Further references indicate the page number from Kirkup's translation, followed by the page in Dürrenmatt, *Die Physiker* (Zürich, 1962). When an asterisk follows the first page number, it means that I have altered Kirkup's translation.

world has done practically nothing with them, precisely *because* they are as powerful as they are. Why should the invention of more powerful bombs make a difference, especially if the publication of the necessary theory is controlled by a scientist who will not reserve it for just one side of the cold war?

This last is a minor point and serves mainly to alert us. The crucial question is this: if Möbius is really operating on the principle that "we have to take back our knowledge" (p. 81/63), that "today it's the duty of a genius to remain unrecognized" (p. 82/63), then is his course of action a logical one? Why ruin his family financially? Why call attention to himself by appearing to go mad? Why *not* take a job in industry and simply do well-paid routine work? Or if this is still too risky, why try to "disappear" in a madhouse? Why not change his name and take an obscure job somewhere, say as an electrician? By having himself officially committed as insane, he only makes himself easier to trace. One can quibble about this matter. One could suggest that Möbius's becoming a madman will keep other physicists from taking his published dissertation seriously—to which it could be answered that the same end would be served by his deliberately publishing a series of routine papers, thus establishing for himself the reputation of an unoriginal mind *without* ruining his family. The point is that there is no specific or compelling reason for his madman's pose, if his motives are as he states them.

But does there have to be a compelling reason? Are we perhaps taking too seriously a question of motivation that is not really a principal question in the play? Given that the play insists upon its clear relation to not one but three narrative genres in which obscure or concealed motivation plays a central role—the murder mystery, the spy story, and science fiction (in the last case, consider Isaac Asimov, whose work almost always turns on a character's concealed interest or motive)—I think we can dismiss these doubts. The question of Möbius's true motive is definitely obscure, and is definitely indicated as a significant interpretive question.

2.

Once this question is asked, moreover, the answer, up to a point, is obvious. In speaking of the "advancement of physics," Möbius has in fact let the cat out of the bag. He pretends to go mad because the asylum offers him the leisure and privacy he needs in order to work out his theory without the worry of being compelled or tempted to publish it. For all his fear of the consequences, a fear he had felt *before* going "mad," he still wants to see what his theory looks like in full. He himself admits that he has calculated the practical effects of his discovery "out of *curiosity*" (p. 75/59, my emphasis). He quickly covers himself on this point by continuing, "Why play the innocent? We have to face the consequences of our scientific thinking. It was my duty to work out the effects that would be produced by my Unitary Theory of Elementary Particles and by my discoveries in the field of gravitation" (p. 75/59). But surely he had already calculated those "effects" in considerable detail *before* going "mad"; otherwise there would have been no obligation to suppress the theory, and his own reasoning collapses. Therefore it is not "duty" that had moved him. On the contrary, the asylum represents for him an endless sabbatical, where he can work untroubled by governments or colleagues—or by his family.

Once we have come this far, the rest of our initial diagnosis of Möbius's condition follows easily. He questions Kilton about freedom and Eisler about power, for he is confident that freedom and power are precisely what he has preserved in *his* relation to science and to the world. In the asylum he can think about whatever scientific problems he wishes; and as long as his theory remains private, he holds absolute power over the world, a power he can realize at any time (as Dr. von Zahnd does later), although he seems to have no intention of doing so. Even his withholding of his theories is an exercise of power, a shaping of the world as he wants it—albeit presumably for the world's own good. Hence his need to work out the theory and its consequences in full detail. He is enjoying, relishing, savoring a freedom and a power such as, in his opinion, no person has ever known. And hence, of course, his association of himself with Solomon, the absolute ruler through wisdom. Möbius, at the end, *is* a defeated Solomon, and we are thus on our way to answering question number 4 as well.

But we must still ask why, of all places, an insane asylum? Dr. von Zahnd, without drawing any attention to herself, has used Möbius's theories to amass the fortune necessary to capitalize her huge corporate undertaking. If Möbius is in any degree tempted or corrupted by the power his theory gives him, why does he not simply make himself financially independent and hide in his *own* villa, somewhere, to work? Why the asylum? As far as I can see, there is only one possible answer to this question. Möbius is corrupted by the dream and the reality of enormous power; but he is also conscious of his corruption, and in this consciousness he has declared himself insane, he has diagnosed his own mental condition as a form of insanity. With the inconsistency of despair, he later insists to Dr. von Zahnd, "Do be reasonable. Don't you see you're mad?" (p. 90/69). But he himself has lived this inconsistency; he has been, or imagines he has been, reasonable enough to recognize his own insanity. "We're caged in, like wild beasts!" says Eisler, and Möbius replies, "We are wild beasts. We ought not to be let loose on humanity" (p. 83/64). This is his clearest statement of why he had gone "mad"; he had *recognized* himself as a madman, a mind unbalanced by power, a would-be Solomon, a wild beast, a danger to humankind.

We must be more precise, however, about the nature of the madness Möbius recognizes in himself; otherwise we shall find ourselves arguing that his entering the asylum (to enjoy his power) is the reason for his condemning himself to the asylum. The point is that Möbius considers himself a madman *as a physicist*; in the end, by an extension of the logic he applies to himself, he succeeds in having all three physicists judged mad. His own conception of this madness appears clearly in his relation to his three sons. The first wants to become a minister, the second to study philosophy, and the third to become a physicist, which last provokes a violent reaction from Möbius. "But you became a physicist yourself, Papi—" says Jörg-Lukas, to which Möbius responds, "I should never have been one, Jörg-Lukas. Never. I wouldn't be in the madhouse now" (p. 40/32).

The progression minister-philosopher-physicist makes evident why Möbius associates the study of physics with madness. The sense of this progression is a decrease in the firmness of human values. The minister simply believes, simply accepts certain values as absolute; the philosopher, in criticizing values and beliefs, still takes them seriously, still attempts, like Nietzsche, to establish some kind of basis for the institution of values. But the physicist, presumably, has struck out into a realm where belief and value utterly evaporate; he has blasted off on an intellectual spaceship that leaves the "breathing earth" (p. 44/36) of human considerations and sensibilities behind. Advances in physics do not build a world we can live in, a world accessible to our experience and activity, but rather they refute any such world, they make nonsense of it. Möbius says:

> In our science we have reached the limits of the knowable. . . . We have reached the end of our journey. But humanity has not yet got as far as that. We have battled onwards, but now no one is following in our footsteps; we have encountered a void. Our knowledge has become a frightening thing. Our researches are dangerous, our discov-

eries are lethal. For us physicists there is nothing left but to surrender to reality. It has not kept up with us. It disintegrates on touching us. We have to take back our knowledge. [Pp. 80–81*/62–63]

Physics destroys reality, in the sense that reality is for us an order of beliefs, traditions, established attitudes, illusions. Humans, as Nietzsche says in "Vom Nutzen und Nachteil der Historie," cannot exist without their illusions, without a horizon, a "breathing earth," to frame their thought and activity; and physics, in Möbius's view, is the systematic destruction of illusions. Therefore, if sanity is the willing and effective participation in a human life accessible to such participation, it follows that the physicist, by profession, is insane.

These are the grounds on which Möbius judges himself mad. And his use of the ideal environment of the asylum to continue the study of physics only confirms him retroactively in his judgment. He *is* King Solomon, but "no longer the great golden king who sang of the Shulamite, and of the two young roes that are twins, which feed among the roses" (p. 43/34). Solomon, in the person of Möbius, "crouches naked and stinking [in the sanatorium bedroom], the pauper king of truth, and his psalms are horrible" (pp. 43/34–35). His research has carried him beyond the sphere of human values ("my wisdom destroyed the fear of God" [p. 93/71]), and without value there can of course be no "wealth," no achievement or satisfaction. Möbius—in his own view, heroically—has taken up the burden of being Solomon in spite of himself, being the enjoyer of a power generated by wisdom, but a power so great as to render itself meaningless, unenjoyable, terrifying.

3.

Even if the foregoing is accepted, however, one essential question of motivation remains. Why does Möbius go to the extreme of killing his nurse Monika? We can understand why he goes "insane" in the first place, but why is it so desperately important to him to *remain* insane, and to be considered insane by others? The other possibilities mentioned, to take a routine job as either a physicist or something else, remain open to him, even after he trades in his old wife. He no longer even needs the asylum as a place to work; his system is now finished and (he thinks) safely destroyed. It would be convenient, and would flatter his judgment of himself, to remain in the asylum. But are these considerations a sufficient motive for murder, and the murder of a woman he claims to love?

We shall return to this question after we have said something about Möbius's discoveries *as* science. Möbius claims, "In our science we have reached the limits of the knowable. . . . We have reached the end of our journey." Are we to infer that he has found the final answers, the most comprehensive and accurate answers possible, to all questions of physics? Of course such an inference would require a naïve view of science on our part. But is this the view we are meant to adopt for the sake of this play?

I contend that we are obviously not meant to adopt a naïve view of science. The inherent limitations of scientific knowledge are already insisted upon in the conversation between the inspector Richard Voss and Newton.

NEWTON: Do you understand anything about electricity, Richard?
INSPECTOR: I am no physicist.
NEWTON: I don't understand much about it either. All I do is elaborate a theory about it on the basis of natural observation. I write down this theory in the mathematical idiom and obtain several formulae. Then the engineers come along. They don't care about anything except the formulae. They treat electricity as a pimp treats a whore. They simply exploit it. They build machines—and a machine can only be used when it becomes independent of the knowledge that led to its invention. [Pp. 22/20–21]

The physicist does not claim to "understand" electricity any better than the police inspector. He develops a mathematical theory by which "electricity" is defined and described in the abstract, and he postulates a relation between this abstract idea and certain experimentally isolable phenomena. That this postulated relation happens to make possible the building of machines that work more or less as predicted, prompts the layperson to conclude that the relation between theory and reality has been proved, that the physicist "understands" the phenomena in question. But the physicist knows better; he has a much clearer idea of how tenuous and provisional the relation between theory and reality must always be. And the audience, if they pay any attention at all to what is being said, must know better as well.

Therefore it does not surprise us to hear Möbius making a similar concession about his own theory. We have reached "the limits of the knowable," he says. But then he continues immediately: "We know a few precisely calculable laws, a few basic connections between incomprehensible phenomena and that is all. The enormous remainder is a secret closed to the rational mind. We have reached the end of our journey" (p. 81*/62). He does not claim to have explained everything; he claims only to have ordered theoretically everything that can be ordered theoretically. And even this claim is placed in a relativizing context by the presence on the stage of two people dressed as Newton and Einstein. (Hence, incidentally, the principal reason Dürrenmatt does not use Galileo, even though Galileo's recanting suggests a strong analogy with Möbius.) For Newtonian mechanics and Einsteinian relativity are the two main examples, in the history of science, of *universal* systems, theories purporting to make possible the theoretical ordering of everything that can be ordered theoretically. If either Newtonian mechanics or Einsteinian relativity fails at a single point, then the whole system collapses—as in fact Newtonian mechanics has collapsed (as a theory, even though our machines still work!) before the relativistic world-view, and as we must assume that relativity has been superseded by Möbius's theory. Möbius's claim, therefore, that the untheorized "remainder" of physical reality is "closed to the rational mind," can be valid only insofar as we understand it to mean closed to any rational mind that operates within *his* system, which is the most comprehensive physical system yet devised. The actual presence of Newton and Einstein on the stage, as well as Newton's little lecture to Voss, reminds us that the supersedure of universal systems is to be expected in physics; and Möbius's system, for which absolute completeness is not claimed, can be no exception.

But then why does Möbius talk *as if* his system were an ultimate? Why does he insist, "We have reached the end of our journey"? We can begin to answer this question by noting an inconsistency in Newton's remarks to the inspector. Newton opens by conceding that he does not "understand" the phenomena he theorizes about; but then he heaps scorn on the engineers who use his formulas without mastering the "knowledge" behind them. He thus claims for himself precisely the type of knowledge or intellectual mastery whose existence he has just finished denying. He says to the inspector, "But, if you don't understand anything about electricity, why don't you refuse to turn on the light? It's you who are the criminal, Richard" (pp. 22–23/21). We might reply, however, by asking, Does the physicist actually "understand," in a substantially better way than the policeman, what happens when he turns a light switch? Newton himself has already answered this question in the negative.

The physicist is thus as much a "criminal" as the engineer or the ignorant switch-turner, for he too, with his formulas, is creating powerful and ultimately ungovernable effects in reality without any real knowledge of how the effects are produced; indeed, the physicist is more a criminal, since he knows more about his ignorance. Newton's indictment of the inspector, whether he realizes it or not, is an indictment of himself, and the importance of this state of affairs is that it is in turn a model of Möbius's self-indictment. Möbius exiles himself from humanity not for having discovered the truth but rather for having turned a switch, for having made possible incalculable effects in the real world without actually understanding why those effects should be there.

This still leaves us, however, with the question of why both Newton and Möbius, in the very process of admitting their ignorance, also claim knowledge in something close to an absolute sense. Actually—paradoxical as it may seem—the claim to knowledge follows logically *from* the admission of ignorance. For if it is true that scientific theory, hence human thought in general, can never achieve direct contact with a strictly external reality, then it follows that at any given time, the prevalent scientific world-view in effect *is* our reality, and the scientific theorist can, after all, in a sense be said to know about reality, or at least to know more than the layperson. Conversely, if scientists insist absolutely upon the insufficiency of theory vis-à-vis reality, then their thought contains a contradiction. For in order thus to plead ignorance, they must claim to *know* of at least the existence of a reality beyond theory, which knowledge is denied precisely by the plea of ignorance. By insisting on the quality of theory as "knowledge," therefore, the scientist avoids a certain hypocrisy and accepts responsibility for the effects of his or her thought in the human world, responsibility for *determining* the human world via theory. Or at least this appears to be true in Möbius's case; Newton develops the paradox one step further, in talking with Voss, and uses the idea of his superior knowledge in order to *deny* responsibility.

That this argument is not merely a paradoxical quibble, but belongs to the play's basic structure of motivation, becomes plain when we work it out in detail. The responsible physicist must recognize that his work is *in effect* a "knowledge" of reality, of the reality in which humans actually live. This recognition, however, is based logically on an acknowledgment of the limits of theorizing, on an awareness of being ignorant. The responsible physicist is therefore always under an obligation to convince himself of his ignorance, of the insufficiency of current physical theory; and the only conceivable way in which he can carry out this obligation (without falling into the trap of a hypocritical assertion of ignorance) is by striving to *supersede* current theory, by seeking a more comprehensive theory, thus more "knowledge" and, inevitably, more machines. Precisely *by* being responsible, therefore, precisely *by* recognizing a responsibility to humankind, the physicist is involved in the process of providing human beings with ever greater destructive forces, thus placing humankind in ever greater danger. It follows that physics itself, *as* physics, may be regarded as a kind of violent, suicidal madness. Therefore Möbius judges himself mad and consigns himself to the asylum. The self-propelled mechanism of scientific madness, he decides, shall stop here, so that humankind might have a chance to survive.

4.

As we might expect, however, there are at least two weak points in Möbius's reasoning. In the first place, he proclaims himself willing to accept the responsibility for his theory as a knowledge with tangible effects for other human beings. But in accepting that responsibility, he finds it necessary to think of the knowledge in question as *his* knowledge, which opens for him the possibility of interrupting the insane progress of physics by placing *himself* in a mad-house. Thus he actually only avoids responsibility, in the very gesture of accepting it. It is Dr. von Zahnd who makes this point clear—especially if, at Möbius's own suggestion, we read "Möbius" where she says "Solomon."

> Möbius . . . tried to keep secret what cannot be kept secret. For what was revealed to him was no secret. Because it could be thought. Everything that can be thought is thought at some time or other. Now or in the future. What Solomon had found could be found by anyone, but he wanted it to belong to himself alone, his means toward the establishment of his holy dominion over all the world. [P. 89/68]

A physical theory, by its nature, cannot be hidden, since it can be thought, if not by one mind then by another. Möbius's only truly responsible course would have been to publish all his results, which would have prevented their being discovered and exploited in one of the think tanks described by Kilton and Eisler. The parallel between Newton's rhetorical strategy in lecturing Voss, and Möbius's strategy in entering the asylum, is now complete. Both physicists assert the quality of their theory as "knowledge," an assertion that in itself is an acceptance of responsibility, but that is used by both Newton and Möbius as a means of avoiding responsibility. Newton's little banter with the inspector is thus a complete model of the larger action that culminates in the play's two hours or so.

This point is fairly obvious, but the other difficulty in Möbius's thought is a bit less so. Möbius insists that the insane progress of physics must stop here, with his theory, because reality in the sense of human reality "has not kept up with us . . . disintegrates on touching us." It is his opinion, apparently, that in the pre-Newtonian and Newtonian ages, and even in the age of relativity, humanity as a whole had somehow managed to come to terms with the universal systems presented it by physics, but that now it has become impossible to reconcile physical theory with a genuinely human reality; the "breathing earth" has now been left behind by the spaceship of physical theory. This opinion, however, presupposes a knowledge of *the limits of the human*, limits beyond which humankind, or individuals, cannot pass without forfeiting their humanity. It is not clear, on the face of it, that such limits exist, let alone that they are knowable. But Möbius's self-imposed exile from humankind expresses the belief that he, as an individual, with his theory, has crossed the boundary into the inhuman. Therefore it is of the utmost importance to him *that other people consider him insane.* The whole plan behind his action is based on the idea that there exists a relatively comfortable human reality from which he is excluded; if other people accept him, treat him as a human being, include him in their world, even love him, then the whole Solomon-and-spaceship mythology he has built up for himself collapses, and his supposed self-sacrifice becomes senseless. Here, and only here, therefore, we have an adequate motive for the killing of nurse Monika. Möbius must not only become insane; he must also remain insane and be considered insane by others. Otherwise his idea of the human, on which his whole life is now based, is revealed as an illusion.

Of course it is evident—to us and to Möbius—that the other characters in the play do not regard him as seriously insane, as a "wild beast," as a fundamentally nonhuman creature. But for his purposes it is sufficient if they at least believe that he has hallucinations, and believe (as Monika does not believe) that those hallucinations are symptoms of a disabling illness. To know the true basis of his insanity, the true sense in which he is a "wild beast," people would have to know about his physical theory, which his whole aim is to keep from them. That Monika can accept him, even with his hallucinations, is thus a serious problem, but a problem that can at least be solved by murder—although the weakness of the reasoning involved does become apparent in the idea that the preservation of traditional human values requires an extreme violation of just those values. If, however, it were to prove possible for other human beings, or human society, to accept Möbius *even with his theory*, then his whole strategy would be in ruins, since it would be demonstrated that normal humanity does *not*, after all, exclude the thinker of such thoughts. Therefore Möbius is desperate to convince Newton and Einstein that, by their knowing acceptance of him, they too have become in truth "insane."

And as I have suggested, there is a serious "mistake in thought," a "Denkfehler," in this position. Möbius is convinced that by thinking and working out his theory he has passed the limits of the human, trapped himself on an intellectual spaceship far from the "breathing earth." On the basis of this conviction he devises a strategy for sacrificing himself to permit human values to survive. *His* action is therefore eminently human—self-sacrifice for the sake of the welfare of the whole—and is carried out in the full knowledge of a theory that supposedly bursts the bounds of the human. It follows that his theory *can* after all be integrated into a human or humane scheme of values and responses; his own action is an instance of such integration. What he has done, then, in essence, is to arrogate the human to himself, to insist on carrying out himself a task he would have done better to entrust to the humanity of humankind at large. "What concerns everyone can only be resolved by everyone" (p. 96/77). His strategy therefore itself turns out to be less human, less easily reconcilable with humane considerations that transcend individual wishes and needs, than the supposedly inhuman state of affairs to which it responds. "Each attempt of an individual to resolve for himself what is the concern of everyone is doomed to fail" (p. 96/77).

5.

Let us look at this matter from another point of view. By being spectators in the theater, we are carrying out an emphatically human act; we are engaging in a regulated activity with other people, consenting to give our attention and intellectual effort to human problems without any prior guarantee that those problems will make a difference in our lives; we are participating in a ritual by which human problems are not treated in the abstract, but rather allowed to emerge from the acts and words of relatively plausible human beings by whom our emotions might be engaged. When the truth about Möbius's theory is revealed in the second act, therefore, that theory already *is* firmly embedded, for us, in a human context. Even our situation in the theater thus contradicts Möbius's implied claim to know the limits of the human, to have located a point at which human activity violates some necessary minimum of simplicity or ignorance without which humanity can no longer be said to exist.

That we are not given an opportunity actually to understand Möbius's theory, that most of us perhaps do not yet understand relativity, makes no difference. Physical theories, as Möbius suggests, communicate with us by way of their "effect" (cf. pp. 96/76–77), the machines they make possible. We do live in a world with atomic and thermonuclear weapons; we can extrapolate from whatever conception we have of these weapons' power; and yet we are still sitting in a theater. The question of the limits of the human is thus translatable into the question of the limits of dramatic form, and the question of whether drama is still a reasonable human activity in the present age. Are we, by sitting in the theater, perhaps deluding ourselves disastrously about our real condition? This question, at some point, needs to be answered. But for the time being, our situation in the theater is still a practical refutation of Möbius's tyrannically absolute ideas concerning what humanity may be permitted to think about.

It is true, as Möbius insists, that our humanity includes a responsibility to shape and preserve, to define the human, to *decide* what is humanly permissible and what is not—at least as long as "memory holds a seat / In this distracted globe." Transgression, the overstepping of all possible boundaries, must therefore belong to our world—or to our world-picture, which comes to the same thing. Otherwise the possibility of decision, of choice, vanishes. We have not only the ability but the duty to conceive of the preterhuman, to employ it in our judgment of the human. Even if Möbius's theory is preterhuman in the sense of being unsanctionable in the actual modern world, still that theory is also undeniably human in the sense of being humanly conceivable ("Everything that can be thought is thought"), and cannot simply be excised from the world.

It belongs to the world, to the whole of what human beings must come to grips with. "What concerns everyone can only be resolved by everyone," and in the theater it is we who, for the time being, represent "everyone"; it is *our* task, not the task of a particular individual, to reintegrate the human, to make sense of the play and its suggestions. Again, therefore, the strategy chosen by Möbius is both inhuman and futile.

It may be objected that in the theater we receive Möbius's theory and its consequences as a fiction, with which we can play, on which we can speculate without danger or the need for decision. This objection, however, brings us to question number 3, and to the recognition that the plot of *Die Physiker* is constructed so that even when the story takes "its worst possible turn" (p. 95/75), the events represented on stage *could happen in reality without making any appreciable difference in our daily lives.* Dr. von Zahnd is merely going to take control of the world's economy by means of a huge trust not essentially different from the corporate conglomerates that already control the world's economy. All we will notice, if we notice it at all, is another mysterious name in the newspapers, another unimaginably rich individual about whom we actually know nothing whatever. Every day, of course, there will be news of startling new technological advances; but we are accustomed to this sort of news anyway. For all intents and purposes, as we sit in the theater, we might as well be seeing reality itself played before us. Möbius's theory, and the whole plot of the play, may be fiction, but cannot be dismissed as fantasy; Möbius is not being carried light-years away from us on an intellectual spaceship. On the contrary, his thought and his situation are thoroughly integrated into the world as we have become accustomed to it, and we are thus confirmed in our sense of his theory as a manifestation of the *normal* self-superseding, transgressing quality of human consciousness. As soon as we think about the human, as soon as we take the human as an object of critical consideration—and Möbius himself insists that we are obliged to do so—we have already transgressed, overstepped the bounds, located our consciousness in the preterhuman, on a kind of spaceship. Our situation, as reflective humans, has always been such and will never be any different; this situation *is* our "breathing earth."

There is yet a further consequence of the recognition that what happens in *Die Physiker* could actually happen tomorrow, or could have happened yesterday, without making any special difference in our sense of ourselves and the world. For we can now formulate the central problem of the play, as a problem that does concern us directly, without resorting to the idea of the survival of the human race—which is not a "problem" to begin with. Namely, we live in a world where the scientific knowledge that shapes what we call "reality" is in principle accessible to us, but is deliberately kept secret from us by human agencies. Even if Möbius succeeded in his masquerade, the same would hold true; the theory that potentially gives a new ultimate shape to our reality would still be kept secret by a human agency, in this case by Möbius himself. From the very outset, in the very conception of his strategy, therefore, Möbius plays into the hands of the "secret services" represented by Newton and Einstein, and ultimately into the hands of Dr. von Zahnd.

The play, however, as its author insists, is "paradoxical" (p. 96/76); and at this point in the reasoning, accordingly, we find that we have also arrived at a *defense* of Möbius's position on the essential insanity of physics. A physical system, first of all, no matter how powerful its technological consequences, is still only a theory, an imposition of intellectual order upon our ultimately "incomprehensible" experience, thus not fundamentally different—we recall Möbius's two older sons—from a theological or philosophical system. But there are significant practical differences between physics and other methods of systematizing our existence. To be effective in the human world at large, a theological or philosophical system must be communicated, must actually penetrate, in some form, the consciousness of large numbers of people, who are thus in a position to reject or modify or criticize it. A physical system, by contrast, via the machines it makes possible, can profoundly reorder our existence while still being kept secret from us. Again, for all we know the world *has* fallen into the hands of a crazy psychiatrist; the extent to which we might be conscious of this fact would make no difference at all in the fact itself. In earlier ages, where (we assume) the shape and boundaries of the human world were understood mainly in theological or philosophical terms, every human being was at least theoretically in a position to influence that understanding; in the age of physics, despite all the popularizing literature, the notion of human self-determination (whether in the fifteenth-century version of a Pico, or in the eighteenth-century version of a Kant) has become for the vast majority of individuals an exploded illusion. Physics may therefore be regarded as a historical sickness of the human community, the degeneration of its very quality as a community; and Möbius's gesture, futile as it may be, is at least directed against a real evil.

Or one might maintain that in the age of physics the human

condition undergoes a special kind of dissociation, in that all contact is lost between the general historical shape of our *world* and the particular character of our *experience*. The plot of the play could be reality without making any difference whatever in our daily lives; our world could be transformed by an intellectual upheaval as complete as the Copernican revolution, and our experience of the world would not change in the least. We are in the habit of assuming that such a dissociation has not, until now, characterized human history. We may be theoretically skeptical about cultural or historical relativism, but such relativism nevertheless informs, for example, the way we teach practically all our courses in literature and history. Changes or differences in the large shape of the humanly conceived world, differences referable to language or scientific world views or to religious or philosophical attitudes, are presumed to reverberate eventually in the very fabric of experience. There is a certain comfort in this assumption; it implies that in our daily lives we are not, after all, entirely out of touch with the large movement of history, not utterly at the mercy of forces we cannot comprehend.

This assumption and this implication, however, if they were ever justified, are in the age of physics justified no longer. Now the large movement of history is thoroughly insulated from the intimate movements of experience. Even the physicist, and indeed even that physicist who has personally worked out the latest theory, the theory that now claims to represent "reality" most comprehensively for humankind, is no longer able to mediate between experience and history. The gap is too great, the insulation too perfect. Like Möbius, even that physicist has no choice but to retreat into an idea of the human, a mode of experience, which his own thought has rendered inconsequential. He as it were hermetically seals himself—and us with him—into a spaceship hurtling through an utterly alien environment toward a destination no one has the slightest conception of. And here too, the question of drama as a form comes to the surface. For if a principal function of drama in culture, as I have suggested, is to represent literature (to be its church, its instrument, its validation) in the project of making available to humanity an active and creative relation to history, not merely a passive acceptance of historical change, then it appears to follow that the insulation of experience from history in the age of physics, by making that function unfulfillable, invalidates the form. Does Dürrenmatt's play thus make nonsense of its own endeavor, by way of a logic characterized by the same combination of inevitability and inconsistency as Möbius's?

In any event, question number 3, the question of what difference the play's action would make to us if it were real, thus leads us in two exactly opposed directions. On the one hand, modern physics is an entirely normal manifestation of human reflective consciousness. On the other hand, modern physics occasions an unprecedented self-dissociation of human existence viewed as a whole.

6.

Let us retain, for the time being, a naïve view of the "influence" of intellectual events on culture, and ask whether the insulation of our larger historical world from our experience is really a phenomenon unique to the age of physics. The answer to this question depends on whether we view the human situation diachronically or synchronically. If the character of our immediate experience of life is influenced by, and changes with, the general constitution of the world or mythology or value system, then it does so only a certain amount of time *after* the books or acts or discoveries or inventions that mark the particular world-reconstitution we are talking about; it takes time for the effects of an intellectual or visionary revolution to percolate through the culture involved and become an integral part of the way we experience things. But if we look at the situation at any single point in time, then we shall expect to find experience every bit as insulated from history as it is for us in the age of physics. Even those contemporaries who actually knew of the work of Copernicus, or Kant, still *lived* in the pre-Copernican or pre-Kantian age. In fact, as far as the immediate quality of experience is concerned, Copernicus and Kant themselves doubtless lived in the past with respect to their own achievements, in the same way that Möbius, as a human being, lives in the pre-Möbian age. This anomaly, this schizophrenic insulation of the historical individual from the experiencing individual, which is the source of Möbius's personal difficulties, is a common and recognized characteristic of life. Plenty of people even nowadays live as if there had never been a Kant or a Romanticism or a nineteenth century; and to succeed in American politics—or for that matter in Russian politics—it is practically indispensable that one experience the world minus Marx.

But the synchronic insulation of experience from history is generally not an occasion for terror or despair; it is a comforting and life-promoting phenomenon. Winston Churchill, for example, as a painter, knew of Picasso and is reported to have declared himself ready, for the sake of art, to give the latter a swift kick where it would do the most good. We recognize that the history of art—perhaps even the history of the Western visual sense, the history of what happens when we open our eyes—was on Picasso's side and had left Churchill behind. But for Churchill, as for any number of old-fashioned painters and viewers, it was fortunate and comforting that he was spared this recognition; it was perhaps even fortunate for art in general, for the play of tensions and controversies that produces vitality in a cultural tradition.

Suppose, however, that Picasso had been in a position to drop bombs on Churchill, thus in a position to enforce recognition, but without being able to enforce comprehension. Then we should have had a situation comparable to ours in the age of physics. We as individuals, like Churchill (or like Möbius), are incapable of *changing* fast enough or far enough to keep pace with the history of our kind in times of revolution; therefore a certain amount of insulation or buffering is useful, both for us and for the revolution in question. But that salutary insulation of experience from history has become for us a kind of permanent hermetic seal, a spaceship, while at the same time it is also circumvented by the technological effects of revolutions in theoretical physics, by people's ability to drop bombs on us. On the one hand, experience is now absolutely and permanently insulated from history. Even if history, in the form of physical theory, were not kept secret from us, it is fairly clear that our direct experience of the world cannot adjust itself to relativity or to a big bang in the same way that it can to a Christ or a Freud; we can be cognizant of those physical theories, perhaps worry about them, but it is difficult to see how they can become a fully integrated part of experience. And yet, on the other hand, our insulated experience is forced into a *collision* with history by way of technology, the "effect" of physics, which is entirely palpable—not essentially different (Pogo Possum once remarked) from being hit with a shovel. It is as if Churchill, without being able to *change* for Picasso, had had to *yield* to him; the result is a Churchill turned against himself, torn apart, schizophrenic, a Churchill gone mad—or in Dürrenmatt, a Möbius gone mad, a King Solomon who is *both* a king and a filthy beggar.

The question of the nature and justification of Möbius's madness is thus vexed still further. But the question to which these considerations lead us more directly, it seems to me, is that of the situation of the audience in the theater, which for all intents and purposes *is* the collision between experience and history. Again, our daily lives would not be changed significantly even if the events on the stage were reality. We thus recognize the presence of a very strong dis-

junction or insulation between our own experience and those hypothetical events which, if they happened, would "make history" in
the most literal sense. This recognition, in turn, must affect our
judgment of Möbius, for we now see that his insistence upon an
idea of the "human" which, in its historical narrowness vis-à-vis the
play's scientific speculation, appears arbitrary to the point of being
tyrannical, is an attitude we ourselves could not conceivably avoid
in his place. His insistence on the "human" is no longer dismissible
as a Solomonic posture, a megalomaniac imposition on others of the
result of his own vague logic, but now appears as the inescapable
formulation of his (and our) sense of the utter gulf between immediate experience and the historical reality generated by advanced
physical theory. It is not necessary for us to put ourselves in Möbius's place; we *are* in his place, not only as human beings, but more
especially as spectators in the theater.

The insulation of experience from history is self-reflexively potentiated in the theater. We undergo this insulation, and also see it
being undergone, and also know we are undergoing it; even the
simple distance between auditorium and stage represents it for us.
But at the same time—as if a Churchill were compelled to recognize
the significance of a Picasso—we are also compelled, in Dürrenmatt's theater, to recognize history *as* history. We are brought into
collision with precisely the level of historical movement from which
our experience is insulated, since the events of the plot might as well
be history itself. In our day-to-day existence we collide with history
by way of technology, by way especially of our awareness that a few
individuals, continents away, are in a position to kill us whenever
they feel like it.[2] But in the theater this collision is more direct and
violent. We see history itself in operation, its generating center, its
secret "strong room" (p. 91/69), and there is nothing whatever we
can do about it; we, as ourselves, have no effective contact with it,
despite our knowledge.

"The world has fallen into the hands of an insane, female psychiatrist" (p. 92/70), says Einstein; and this statement is in its own terms
an obvious absurdity. "The world," by definition, is that general
context within which individual identity happens, and therefore
cannot actually fall "into the hands" of an individual; nor can any
criterion obtain by which the individual who determines the whole
order of human life might be judged "insane." But Einstein's inherently absurd statement, in the plot of the play, is strictly referential

2See Jean Baudrillard, *Les Stratégies fatales* (Paris, 1983), pp. 49–70, on "L'otage."

and accurate; and the plot of the play, in turn, might as well be history itself. Are we therefore, as Newton suggests, "all mad" (p. 89/68)? It is even suggested that we have reason to *want* Einstein's absurd statement to be factually accurate. Möbius at one point makes a move to attack Dr. von Zahnd, presumably to kill her, and is restrained by Einstein (p. 91/69). Why? Why not kill her? He has not stopped at killing Monika. "There is no point in attacking me" (p. 91/69), she says. But why should one not attack the insane dictator of the world? The reason, it seems to me, is that the forces consequent upon Möbius's theory have already been unleashed as history; if Dr. von Zahnd is killed, they will be in *nobody's* hands. Better a crazy psychiatrist than the blind, inhuman movement of history as such. Thus, in the very process of occasioning a more violent collision of experience with history than is possible outside the theater, the play also suggests, by negation, a collision more violent still that occurs on the fringes of our awareness. Just as Dr. von Zahnd's human (if insane) control of history to an extent softens the physicists' defeat, so, for us, our eminently human situation in the theater softens precisely the collision of experience with history that the theater effects. Or does it? Once we recognize this softening effect of the theater, must we not ask, softening by comparison with *what?*—whereupon the specter arises of an ultimate collision between experience and history, which we undergo, here and now, without beginning to comprehend it.

And yet, supposing this self-aggravating collision between experience and history does happen in the theater of *Die Physiker*, to what extent is it a *unique* happening? Can it be maintained that the collision of experience with history is a phenomenon that *originates* at some point in the history of human consciousness, not having been there earlier? Without such a collision, in some form, could "history" ever happen? If the insulation of experience from history were always worn away by time so gradually that we did not notice it, could it ever occur to us to speak of history, as distinct from experience, in the first place? We are faced with the typical problem of origins, a problem similar to the one which, in the eighteenth century, bedevils theories of the origin of language. For there to *be* a collision of experience with history, there must *have been* such collisions. Thus we are brought back to the question of the "human"; for just as it appeared earlier that physics is a normal manifestation of transgressing human consciousness, so it appears now that the collision of experience with history belongs to the normal human condition, and cannot be attributed to particular historical circumstances.

When Churchill offers to give Picasso a swift kick, is he not defending himself against the schizophrenia occasioned by accepting Picasso, thus admitting in effect that he *has*, schizophrenically, accepted Picasso? Does it not follow, in the terms of the play, that the human condition is itself essentially insane, that our history is the history of insanity? Is our situation in the age of physics, and also our situation in the theater, not merely an extreme manifestation of what we have always been, schizophrenically, in truth?

This brings us back to the question of Möbius's identification with Solomon. Möbius's project may still be seen, now on a different level, as an attempt to abolish the human condition (by avoiding the collision of experience with history), hence a tyrannical initiative. But on the other hand, does the idea that the human condition is a form of insanity not require a human point of view that opposes its insanity? What else is the history of culture but the repeated attempt, if not to abolish, then at least to restrain, resist, postpone the human condition? And is it not then, after all, the wise king Solomon, in Möbius, who adopts a self-sacrificing strategy in order to carry on this historical work? Monika must be killed in order for Möbius to be considered insane; Möbius must be considered insane in order for the rest of us to postpone our insanity a bit longer. Of course the sacrifice is futile. But then all such historical strategies, as self-aggravating symptoms of the very sickness they resist, are necessarily futile. History brings us inevitably to this insane theater, in which we can understand Möbius and make sense of the play only on condition that we thwart Möbius's project (precisely *by* understanding it), and thwart thereby the whole cultural project of which the play itself is a part. The king and the beggar become utterly one, and reality becomes idiocy.

7.

Does our critical reception of the play thus lead us *necessarily* into the same cul-de-sac that traps the physicists at the end? Let us note, first, that the argument so far depends on a form of relativism, on the idea that our individual experience possesses its own ultimately incommunicable character, which, though insulated from the movement of history, thus able to collide with it, is also the accumulated product of history, a particular historical niche from which we cannot escape. This assumption is difficult to avoid in practice. What do I refer to when I say "I," if not to this special character of experience, which difficulties in making myself understood lead me to conclude is different from the character of others' experience? What do we refer to when we say "we," if not to the larger communicative gulf between generations, cultures, ages?

But the relativistic assumption is still only an assumption. Suppose it does not hold. Suppose my identity, my separated, unique, ineffable individuality, is in truth only an illusion. Suppose Ernst Mach—who, incidentally, was also a physicist—was strictly correct in insisting that the word "I" refers to nothing whatever. Suppose our sense of being misunderstood, our dissatisfaction with language as a communicative vehicle, is in truth a purely linguistic phenomenon, an energizing tension within the organism of a language which thus in truth uses "us" in order to live, in the very process of our believing we use it in order to live.[3] Of course we cannot escape from the experience of individuality; without a belief in the uniqueness and cohesion and ultimate incommunicability of our individual experience, we become clearly insane, we have no self. But it is still possible for us to *know* that the experience of our individuality is an illusion, and in fact this knowledge is suggested very strongly in *The Physicists*.[4] "Everything that can be thought is thought at some time or other," says Dr. von Zahnd; and Möbius, in his last words before the final confessions of the three mad physicists, echoes her statement: "What was once thought can never be unthought" (p. 92/70). In the realm of physics, where ideas are tested against measurements, this seems an entirely reasonable proposition; the theory not worked out by one mind will eventually be worked out by another. But as seen in the play, physics is merely the human field where, nowadays, that world-articulating and world-creating work is carried out which had earlier been entrusted to other types of intellectual endeavor; the age of physics follows upon the ages of religion and philosophy.

Everything that can be thought is thought: perhaps this proposition applies *everywhere* in human intellectual endeavor. Perhaps human thought or discourse is, after all, a world, an organized finite structure in which our suffering individuality exists solely for the

---

[3]See my *Hugo von Hofmannsthal* (Cambridge, 1988), pp. 105–229, esp. 122–24, for a discussion and an example of how this idea, formulated in this relatively naïve manner, can be applied (within limits) to literary interpretation.

[4]This problematics, that literature and the study of literature have in a sense rendered obsolete a notion of the "self" that nonetheless continues to operate as an undeniable literary force, is treated with great clarity by Stanley Corngold, *The Fate of the Self: German Writers and French Theory* (New York, 1986), esp. the "Introduction," pp. 1–19.

purpose of realizing each element in turn. Perhaps even religious or philosophical or poetic thought is never, after all, the property or achievement of the thinker; perhaps the thinking individual, rather, is the dispensable vehicle of the thought. Perhaps even our failure to communicate is mere illusion; perhaps every individual's thought is all humankind's thought, if the individual could only remember it as clearly as Plato's philosopher strives to.

The national poet of the German-speaking Swiss (or at least a good candidate) is Gottfried Keller; and in *Das verlorne Lachen*, one of Keller's popular Seldwyla tales, the character Jukundus explains his thought on religion, in part, as follows:

> In everything that I do and think, even when unobserved and unsuspected by others, it seems to me that the whole world is present. . . . How this knowledge of everybody about everything is possible or is constituted, I do not know; but I believe that there is an enormous republic of the universe, which lives according to a single and eternal law and in which ultimately everything is known in common.[5]

Whether or not Dürrenmatt has this passage in mind, something of its spirit, something of the idea that self-enclosed individuality is recognizably an illusion, that our private experience has no specific character after all, is suggested by the idea of the supraindividual quality of thought in physics, plus the idea that physics is the same type of intellectual activity as religion or philosophy. And what is the effect of this suggestion on the argument concerning Dürrenmatt's theater as a historically inevitable theater of insanity, especially in view of the evident conflict between the quality of the theater *as* theater and the quality of insane theater?

8.

The first words heard by the audience in *The Physicists* are spoken by the Inspector: "All right if I smoke?" (p. 13/14). It seems to me that even if Brecht had not repeatedly made a point of permitting smoking at a dramatic performance, these words would still draw our attention to our situation in the theater. We are reminded of the

---

[5]Gottfried Keller, *Sämtliche Werke und ausgewählte Briefe*, ed. Clemens Heselhaus, 3 vols. (Munich, n.d.), 2:473–74.

regulation to which we submit, or which we impose on our behavior, in the theater, and this consciousness opens onto the idea of the arbitrary self-regulation of human existence in general.

The arbitrariness of such human self-regulation is insisted upon in the play by way of the idea of murder, which is shown not as a crime against nature, but as the object of a highly complex medical and institutional definition with respect to its criminality and punishment—not to mention that it is for us, the audience, an object of amused speculation: will the fairy-tale triplicity be achieved, and how? And if it is true *in general* that I am the shaper of my own world, then it follows that once the world has been given a particular shape, I can assert myself as its shaper and ultimate arbiter only by changing, elaborating, complicating what has been handed down to me. (The responsible physicist, we recall, precisely in order to maintain his sense of his work as mere theory, is compelled to strive for new theoretical advances.) The world never holds still for us. Precisely in order to recognize the world as *ours*, as our "breathing earth," we are compelled repeatedly to leave it behind, to blast off from it. Or if we agree that the idea of an established human world is equivalent to the idea of a specific character in our experience—since the character of our experience, for us, *is* the world—then it follows that the collision between experience and history, between a permanently charactered world and the inevitable mutability of all things human, is necessary precisely in order that we recognize and appreciate the security, the stability, the "human" quality of existence that is constantly lost to us.

Our situation in the theater, where smoking is prohibited but murder (at least for the sake of argument) has become acceptable, reminds us of these general truths of the human condition, *yet without being entirely subject to them*. For our experience in the theater, the ritual in which we participate, is composed of *nothing but* human self-regulation, without the quality of "world"—without that stability which, perversely, is always the object first of revolutionary dissatisfaction, then of nostalgia. In the world, human self-regulation, even in the sense of creative reregulation or transvaluation, is enforced; in the theater we undertake this task freely and, unlike Möbius, enjoy it, at least in the form of a scale model. The reality we create for ourselves temporarily in the theater does not supersede an established "human" reality, a "breathing earth" of which we might feel the loss. There is no nostalgia, no regret, in the theater, which is to say, the element of charactered experience, the experience of particular individuality, has in effect been removed from the human equation. For a short time, in the theater, it is as if we no longer had a specific individual manner of experiencing after all, but had only the experience of the race.[6] For a short time we become purely creative, purely historical beings, historical in the sense that our actions, our will, now *are* history, not mere experience. Our individuality is revealed as an illusion after all, a mere pose, a costume that commits us to nothing. The collision between experience and history, the insanity of the human condition, becomes a game, enjoyable precisely in its paradoxical complexity. "Life is serious, art is cheerful": this quotation from Schiller is hung up as a motto over the last scene of Dürrenmatt's *The Visit,* which travesties it.

But perhaps this transformation of the actual insanity of human existence into a philosophical game is merely a function of the work's fictionality, an instance of Aristotle's point about pleasure taken in the imitation of displeasing objects. As a reader, after all, or the enjoyer of an imitation in general, one is temporarily freed from the limitations and prejudices of one's everyday person, to the extent that one may be able, for example, to accept murder without repugnance. But in the theater the *self-regulatory* quality of this freedom is foregrounded as it is not for the reader. There is a substantial difference between individuality and collectivity here. Established rules and conventional moral responses are dispensed with in the theater; but the principle of *order,* in our attentive silence, in our not smoking, has definitely not been left behind. From the point of view of the individual, order must be externally imposed; but the collective in the theater is external with respect to *itself,* with respect to its reflection in each person, and so enacts the self-regulatory in a manner not available to the solitary individual.

The order inherent in the act of reading is far less palpable. As a reader, one can *accept* the suspension of one's prejudice against murder, but as a spectator one *affirms* that suspension by the self-regulatory gesture of denying oneself a cigar—or by the free act of paying money to place oneself in a situation where one knows a cigar (or whatever) will be denied one. The Inspector says to Möbius, when the latter demands to be arrested:

[6]Obviously we find ourselves talking Schiller here, which we might expect with Dürrenmatt anyway, given the obvious allusions in *Der Besuch der alten Dame* and *Romulus der Große* (which latter is *Wallenstein* written upside down). We think, in particular, of *Über die ästhetische Erziehung des Menschen,* of the idea of free creative play as the domain of the human, and of the idea of raising our experience to that of the human race. See Chapter 3, n. 18, and *Schillers Sämtliche Werke,* 16 vols. (Stuttgart, 1904), 12:6, 14, 59, 118.

Every year in this small town and the surrounding district, I arrest a few murderers. Not many. A bare half-dozen. Some of these it gives me great pleasure to apprehend; others I feel sorry for. All the same I have to arrest them. Justice is Justice. And then you come along and your two colleagues. At first I felt angry at not being able to proceed with the arrests. But now? All at once I'm enjoying myself. I could shout with joy. I have discovered three murderers whom I can, with an easy conscience, leave unmolested. For the first time Justice is on holiday—and it's a terrific feeling. Justice, my friend, is a terrible strain; you wear yourself out in its service, both physically and morally; I need a breathing space, that's all. [Pp. 64–65/52]

Again the Inspector reminds us of our situation in the theater. The values, the imperatives and prohibitions of our extratheatrical existence, are on vacation. We are of course not strictly free of those values; the Inspector's sense of self still depends on the idea of Justice. But in the theater, by way of the self-regulatory character of our situation, we experience those values as a free act. Our individuality is for a moment transcended, and we enact the self-creating experience of humankind as a whole; we live something close to pure history.

The trouble is that this Schillerian conception of our situation as an audience is reflected back at us, and travestied, by the three physicists, who renounce their individual identities and realize their being in the form of roles that they freely assume for the sake of the continued existence of humankind. Their fate traps them permanently in the insane asylum, but they affirm that fate on ideal grounds and so transform it Schillerianly into their own free action. They are "mad, but wise," in exploiting the "play-drive" for its true metaphysical end; they are "Prisoners but free," in affirming their fate; they are "Physicists but innocent" (p. 84/65), having overcome the state of individuated alienation that informs, for example, the myth of original sin. But they are also ineffectual and insane. Precisely in playing the game of madness, in order to conquer or master the real madness of human history—just as we, in the theater, conquer or master that historical madness by transforming it into a ritual of enjoyable self-regulation—the physicists fall into the trap set for them by an insane individual (that is, historically, a "normal" individual [p. 91/70]) whose actions will ensure that the human world remain as insane as ever.

The implications concerning the theater audience are obvious. We have seen that Möbius's supposedly human strategy can easily be seen as an act of self-indulgence or self-magnification. The same applies to our situation in the theater; the theater is a strategy by which we manage to tolerate, and even enjoy, an essentially intolerable human condition. Considered in the abstract, the theater may be a significant philosophical exercise, a device by which we are enabled to experience our human wholeness with a special refreshing intensity. But if we reflect on this quality of the theater, as Dürrenmatt's play requires, and if we fall into the trap, like the physicists, of preening ourselves on our humanity—of enjoying as individuals the supposedly preterindividual level of being suggested by the idea that all thought is thought in common by all humans—then we not only involve ourselves in contradiction, but we also blind ourselves to reality and, like the physicists, surrender the actual control of human destiny to those individuals or conglomerates or blind historical forces who simply deny their insanity, their futility, their absurdity, and justify themselves by sheer power. Precisely the availability of all thought to all humans places power in the hands of those who take it with no philosophical scruples. The plot of *The Physicists* not only could be reality, but *is* reality, and becomes all the more real, controls us all the more completely, to the extent that we are aesthetically gratified by this capture of reality in the theater.

Die Physiker thus traps us in the same disastrous dialectic of spectator and audience that we discussed in connection with Ionesco. But now neither the convention of absurd drama—the concept of a "convention" being itself, in this context, appropriately absurd— nor the figure of Bérenger, as a target for individual identification, is present to suggest at least the possibility of our maintaining ourselves in spite of the seductive theatrical dialectic. In Ionesco, as in Schnitzler and in some Strindberg, the exit-doors of the theater perform an integral function in constituting the work's meaning. But in Dürrenmatt, where the plot might as well be simply the way things are, the exit-doors lead right back into the theater again. The world in which Ionesco's theater operates is a world threatened by fascism in the form of universal uniformity of response; and we, precisely *as* individuals, by being different from each other, can meet this danger. But the world surrounding Dürrenmatt's theater, the age of physics, makes fascists of us no matter what we do; for the scale on which world-definition, and hence power, are now recognized (and indeed experienced) as operating, is sufficiently huge to reduce to uniformity any conceivable diversity or independence of response on our part.[7]

---

[7]On matters of this type—having to do, for example, with the status of the idea of

Is there, therefore, no hope at all, for either drama or the world? Is there not still a *difference* between the theater and the world, and does this difference not *make* a difference for both? Our human or humane posturing, our ineffectual Schillerian posturing as an audience, is after all *displayed* to us in Dürrenmatt's theater. Does this not put us in a position to modify our attitude, our posture, in a politically useful direction? Obviously we cannot simply discard our humane pretensions, even though we recognize that (for us, as for the physicists) they are a trap by which we immobilize ourselves and clear a path for precisely the least responsible or humane tendencies in our historical situation. If we could divest ourselves entirely of the illusion that our humane sensibilities somehow represent humanity in a sense extending beyond our individual concerns, we would become perfect realists, but also entirely unreflective and uncritical realists, lacking any perspective from which to decide to do anything about reality. And yet, does the theater, by showing this situation as clearly as it does, not offer us the possibility of a viable intermediate state? Does it not offer us the opportunity to become *critical* realists, without becoming either elegiac philosophers or the fanatics of some doctrine or program in the process?

The answer is no. For precisely as critical realists, we would have to understand that the transcendence of individuality, aesthetic or otherwise, is a chimera, that whatever we *do* in the world, we do as individuals. Human suffering and aesthetic enjoyment may in a sense sweep away temporarily the boundaries between individuals; and there is perhaps a historically imaginable point of view from which what I do or think appears as an action or thought of humankind at large. But from my own point of view, when I set about the business of original thought or creative action, I am operating, inescapably, as an individual; I am asserting myself, identifying myself vis-à-vis others. That Möbius regards his thought as *his* thought is thus not a mistake after all; it is, rather, the inescapable condition of his having an original or historically significant thought in the first place. The critical realist must recognize, at the very least, that what Möbius does is as much as any individual can do, which is in turn as much as precisely the critical realist in the audience can do. The statement that "what concerns everyone can only be resolved by everyone" now no longer offers us a program of action, but merely mocks us, and is *followed*, not preceded, by the statement that "each

---

historical uniqueness in the "nuclear age"—and on the specifically literary issues that attach themselves to such questioning, see Jacques Derrida, "No Apocalypse, Not Now (full speed ahead, seven missiles, seven missives)," *Diacritics* 14, no. 2 (Summer 1984), 20–31.

attempt of an individual to resolve for himself what is the concern of everyone is doomed to fail" (p. 96/77). By moving self-reflectingly from the transindividual exaltation of the ritual into the attitude of critical realism, we have taken a leap, like the physicists, from blindness into helplessness; and like the physicists, we have discovered that the two states are substantially identical.

The circle of paradoxes is complete. The play begins in a madhouse and, by making use of the situation in the theater as a component of its intellectual unfolding, develops an insane vision of the insanity of human history. Fortunately our situation in the theater also suggests a philosophical transcendence of this vision. But this suggestion is itself travestied. And then the attitude of critical realism that we arrive at by this route turns out to be the original, humanly unthinkable situation all over again. Thus we are "exposed to reality" (p. 96/77).

9.

There is perhaps still one way of responding to the work in a positive sense. The paradoxes, the absurdities, the futilities, the insanities, the movement of despair, do after all resolve themselves into a circle. The human condition, seen in the worst possible light, is thus in a sense mastered by the work, compelled to reveal itself in its entirety. Indeed, given that the structure of the vision involves not only our present situation in the theater, but also our reflection on that situation, it is perhaps not too much to say that *we*, by way of the work, have participated in an achievement of radical human self-mastery; we have experienced and faced and resolved into a kind of circular *object* the "worst possible turn" of the human "story" as a whole (p. 95/75). As long as the work continues to exist, as long as it is there, this human achievement stands in despite of chaos; like Nietzsche's Zarathustra, we, by way of this "comedy," have learned to laugh in the face of the worst conceivable truth.

We can perhaps even describe certain practical consequences of this achievement. In ordinary life, as in the particular case of Möbius, our pretensions to a direct experience of the historical life of the race are always psychologically reducible to postures conditioned by our situation as individuals. Individuality is inescapable. But perhaps an achievement like that represented by *The Physicists*, the resolution into form of the whole futile orbit of human possibilities, tells us something about ourselves (raises us to a level of existence) that is not less true for being entirely excluded from what we experience as "experience." Perhaps we are in a position now to take precisely our *individuality* as a posture, in its entirety. Perhaps I shall exchange being Bennett for playing the role of Bennett, and exist in a state something like what Eliot calls "detachment" in "Little Gidding." Again we think of the physicists, who begin by posturing as the shapers of history but then, after the catastrophe, assert the same postures in the form of helpless individuality. Of course the physicists *are* utterly helpless; but perhaps their helplessness is not a necessary condition of the assertion of individuality as a posture. Perhaps by insisting on my individuality as a posture, by renouncing utterly the chimera of historical being as experience, I can realize my historical being as something more essential than experience, perhaps even render effective in the world that quasi-divine level of human being which is presupposed, or indeed even demonstrated, as the adequate spectator of a resolution into circular form of the whole of the human condition. Perhaps individuality must thus be realized as sacrifice, so that Möbius's entering the madhouse (like our insisting upon living in the world as individuals) becomes a guiding symbol after all.

This whole train of thought, or of pathos, depends on the definitive existence of "the work"—which term thus threatens to reassume its medieval significance, as the repository of certain qualities and aspects of our being that are not adequately understood in relation to the concept of a person. We find ourselves talking a kind of theology. But does "the work," *Die Physiker*, the shaped object, really exist in the sense that is needed to support this thought? To what extent is the work "there"? This question brings us to the matter of the stage direction-*cum*-prologue and the "21 Points" in the printed version of the play. I think it is clear from the argument so far that when we read the play, we need to be aware of what we are missing by not actually seeing it performed in a theater. Imagining a performance is not enough; the positive activity of self-regulation in society, which we carry out as part of a theater audience, belongs integrally to the unfolding of the work's thought. But it is equally clear that we also *miss* certain important aspects of the work when we see it performed, certain features which, like the prologue and the "21 Points," are available only to the reader.[8]

And where, then, is "the work," the total shaped object? If it is

---

[8]See my *Goethe's Theory of Poetry* (Ithaca, 1986), chap. 8, on the collision of dramatic with narrative form in *Faust*.

wholly there for neither the reader nor the spectator, then for whom *is* it wholly there? Is it perhaps there only for some loftier version of ourselves, some pure spirit who can somehow *be* both reader and spectator at once? The combination of actual spectator and virtual reader is now entirely without efficacy. The prologue and the Points are there only for the *actual* reader. My argument does not mean to be mysterious. I do not mean that the mere inclusion of a preface or a commentary automatically decenters the dramatic work, or calls its very existence into question. I mean simply that the thought of *Die Physiker*, when we attempt a politically positive interpretation of it, compels us to *make demands* of the concept "work" that are so precarious, so inherently questionable, that the concept becomes vulnerable *even* to the apparently mild assault represented by that overblown stage direction. Again, therefore, the orbit of futility completes itself, again the text engages us only in order to abandon us, again the reader or spectator is enticed "into exposing himself to reality" (p. 96/77)—reality, however, not in the form of a comfortable order, a "breathing earth," but the reality of the interstellar void and the hermetically encapsulated self, the spaceship which, though it is perhaps in truth a significant human achievement, we inevitably experience as a trap or prison.

It emerges now, however, that the actual range of negativity in *Die Physiker* is not merely psychological or cultural or political, but specifically *literary.* For the self-demolition of this particular work, *Die Physiker*—which is not marked by any radical experimentality in either form or content—must surely also call into question the very notion of a "work," or at least call our attention to the ways in which this notion has always been questionable, to the problems of the boundary and the frame, of originality, of intention. Moreover, by pitting the spectator, so to speak, *against* the reader, *Die Physiker* attacks its own genre, the genre of drama, at a very sensitive point; for the combination of actual spectator and virtual reader, their simultaneity, is crucial in the development of both basic types of ceremony, the hermeneutic and the semiotic, by which drama exercises its energizing function in the literary at large. It is as if that fruitful tension, between actual spectator and virtual reader, were being cross-examined with respect to its status as a fact; and a tension that appears only in response to the question of "what we mean" by drama, or by literature, cannot sustain itself under such cross-examination. It is as if a musical string were stretched to breaking, and could now sound only in its breaking, like the mysterious string that sounds at the end of *The Cherry Orchard. The Physicists* is set in a cherry orchard of its own, "Les Cerisiers," and its theater, like Chekhov's, at once both represents (in the fiction) and contains (in actuality, for us as we sit there) the same "human" situation that it exposes to the full destructive force of "reality."

10.

Does this mean that *Die Physiker* is a counterexample, thus a kind of refutation, to the whole argument of this book? Not at all. On the contrary, it is a confirmation, and perhaps a clarification, of the argument. In the first place, an understanding of the full problematic depth of Dürrenmatt's play depends precisely on our willingness to examine the play in terms of the categories set forth in preceding chapters. If what we mean by drama were not more or less what I have suggested, then this play would not possess the consistency of negativity that we have observed in it.

In the second place, my overall argument is not such that it requires the conceptual closure of each—or indeed, of any—of the interpretations by which I have tried to substantiate it. "Theater As Problem" is my title, and I hope it will be granted at least that I have shown problems in *Die Physiker*, problems that unfold fully only by way of the work's theatrical aspect. If we agree that the business of drama is to resist and disrupt that constant movement toward theoretical self-closure which we recognize in literature as soon as we acknowledge that literary "study" is an integral *part* of literature, then *Die Physiker* is not in the least an anomaly. There are any number of genres of literary study (that is, of literary theory or criticism or scholarship) which attempt to preserve the integrity, not to say the sanctity, of the "literary" by dissociating *themselves* from it, by claiming to stand at a definite objective distance from "creative" or "imaginative" literature; indeed, this distance, perversely, is sometimes given the name "interdisciplinarity." But it is a distance that does not exist; and interdisciplinarity is never valid, never honest, except as the recognition or disclosure of proximity. What we say "about" literature is inescapably implicated in what literature "is," which sustains the possibility of closure and hence the needful function of drama in exactly the sense that *Die Physiker* is drama.

It is easy to say: "The validity of my interpretation of work X is established precisely by its own failure to arrive at a satisfactory positive conclusion." But this is not what I am saying. I am saying, rather, that *Die Physiker* takes as an object, and so endows with the quality of an object, the whole notion of drama that is modeled by the argument of the preceding chapters; in fact, from time to time, it subvocalizes the word "Schiller" as a name for that object. And that this object, *by* being made to operate as an object, is demolished, does validate my point that when we talk about drama, we are not talking about an object in the first place, but always only about what we mean by drama. Thus *Die Physiker* does after all assert and exploit its quality as drama in the sense I have developed, if perhaps in a manner as precarious as the manner in which we find ourselves saying the word "world" when referring to what we know is in truth an inherently breakable web of mere theory. And this, I contend, is a positive interpretation, even if it includes the recognition (as with Artaud) that in the very process of talking about its text, it is also itself talked about *by* that text.

CHAPTER SEVEN

Conclusion: Dramatic History
and the History of Drama

If we look back at what has been suggested so far about the history of drama, we find a number of apparent anomalies. The theoretical climax of the argument is the discussion in Chapter 5 of what I will call "Pirandello/Artaud," by which I allude not only to certain surprising resonances between dissimilar texts, especially the project of a semiotic dethroning of language in the theater, but also to the destabilizing proximity of madness and the work that Derrida talks about. And while the categories of madness and the work perhaps form a bridge to such later authors as Ionesco and Dürrenmatt, what has happened to the *specific* semiotic insights of Pirandello/Artaud? Has the very essence or structure of the genre, in a philosophical sense, been left behind? Derrida, for one, would apparently not mind doing without Ionesco, not to mention Brecht.[1] And how will an Artaudian react to the pervasive psychological and moral speculating of *Die Physiker?*

1.

Not only do I consider it politically dangerous to be willing to do without Ionesco or Dürrenmatt—not to mention Brecht—but I contend that neither Ionesco nor Dürrenmatt is in any sense marginalized by the history of drama, for the simple reason that the history of drama does not operate in a manner that might permit this. In the

[1]Jacques Derrida, *Writing and Difference* (Chicago, 1978), pp. 243–44.

first place, when we speak of the history of drama, we are referring to something much less continuous in time and place than in the case of other literary genres. Especially the development of relatively popular narrative types, such as the novel, can be traced satisfyingly as a process of challenge and response, of innovation and echo, of revolution and restoration, of aberration and parody—all of these qualities as defined *within* the domain of the genre, by chronologically reasonable relations among different works. But drama does not develop in this manner over long periods of time. It tends, rather, to flare up sporadically, and with a radical theoretical self-consciousness that disrupts what we might otherwise wish to consider a tradition. For drama, so to speak, does not have the same kind of historical *right to exist* as other literary forms. Once the novel has come into being—in the bosom of various types of epic, romance, and parody—it exists henceforward as a permanent literary *possibility* that presides, more or less unchanged, over the historical transmission and mutation of particular forms. But drama—dependent, as it is, upon the historical accident of the literary theater for its very definition—is never established as a permanent literary possibility in the same way. Precisely its mere possibility, its possible efficacy as a literary form, is what must be transmitted precariously from age to age, and so appears, in different periods, with a radical difference that precludes its governing the orderly unfolding of a "history."[2]

Another way of looking at this situation has to do with "boundary

2See my *Modern Drama and German Classicism* (Ithaca, 1979), esp. the preliminary argument in the Introduction and the summary on pp. 280–81. That book as a whole argues that precisely the *possibility* of drama, more than any particular forms, is transmitted to the modern period mainly from the efflorescence of German drama around 1800. This point, that the "history" of drama exhibits radical fragmentation in a manner matched by the history of no other genre, is no less important for being difficult to lay hold of. Walter Benjamin, *Ursprung des deutschen Trauerspiels*, ed. Rolf Tiedemann (Frankfurt/Main, 1978), for example, even in the process of opening for inspection the practically unbridgeable gulf between ancient tragedy and European "Trauerspiel," still finds it impossible to do without not only the idea of a "Trauerspieltypus" (p. 103)—which, by his own showing, is already in a sense superseded in *Hamlet* (pp. 117–18), and which permits very little interpretive refinement in the treatment of German Classicism—but also the idea of "[das] Reindramatische" (p. 99), the idea, from Wilamowitz, that "dramatic poetry" (p. 87) is sufficiently established in existence to admit of a division into types, the extremely seductive genetic idea, from Franz Rosenzweig, that "das Tragische hat sich gerade deshalb die Kunstform des Dramas geschaffen [!], um das Schweigen darstellen zu können" (pp. 88–89). I point here *even* to Benjamin, as an indication of the problems we face. As soon as we start talking about "drama" in the first place, we find ourselves attributing to it precisely the sort of coherent history whose absence still emerges implacably in the work of interpretation.

effects." If we agree that the boundary between drama and cinema—precisely because it is a questionable, permeable boundary—is crucial in our understanding of what drama is, then how do we deal with the absence of cinema, or anything like it, in earlier ages where we still speak of "drama"? The very idea of genre, at least as presented in Chapter 2, excludes the possibility of regarding the boundary with cinema as a mere symptom of what drama is "in essence." No such essence can be assumed for *any* genre; a literary genre can be said to exist (as that strict activeness which it must be) *only in its boundary effects*. It follows that the advent of cinema makes a difference not merely in how we see drama, but in what drama *is*, what we mean by drama. Even the longer-lasting boundary between drama and opera is affected, made substantially different, by the coming of cinema, by which it is interpreted now as an opposite boundary.

Of course new boundary effects also happen with respect to other genres. In fact the new boundary between cinema and narrative is crucial for the argument of Chapter 2, since it mediates a *literary* boundary effect for drama. Or we might consider, in the eighteenth and nineteenth centuries in Germany, the splitting off of the novella as an independent, frameless fictional form, which produces an interesting new boundary for the novel and may well have something to do with the characteristic German development of the *Bildungsroman* (as a movement away from the novella's focus on action and incident), by which, in turn, the boundary between the forms of novel and biography is affected. But in the case of the novel, there is always an array of *other* literary boundaries, in the sense of complex boundary effects (with, say, history, the philosophy of history, literary criticism, various forms of moral allegory and treatise), which would make it seem silly to say that the novel, because of its new boundary with the novella, *is* something different. And in the case of drama, those other persistent literary boundary effects are not present. The gulf between drama and other literary types, as I argued in Chapter 2, is in general *too* well marked to produce the sort of boundary effect that is required by our sense of a genre. For drama as a literary genre, therefore, new boundary effects are the only boundary effects there are.

2.

There is, then, no history of drama, if by "history" we mean a development through time which, at least upon hindsight, can rea-

sonably be regarded as self-shaping, as the result of certain principles of its own, as the working of a certain entelechy (however
well concealed or difficult to describe), by which it assimilates outside "influences," and by which certain particular cases, say Ionesco
or Dürrenmatt, can be dismissed as less important than others. And
yet, on the other hand, the very idea of a literary genre implies the
existence of such a history, at least if we understand "genre" in the
deeper sense, to mean a needful pattern of preunderstanding by
which we are enabled to read in the first place, by which we are
made confident of our ability to approach this or that text in an
appropriate manner. For this sort of preunderstanding (while never
fully articulable) must unfailingly stay in touch with itself over time.
A genre, in this sense, cannot possibly suffer a radical break without
ceasing to exist. We cannot simply start meaning something different by a type of literary unit, for our mere recognition of it as the
same type of unit is equivalent to our meaning by it something
reasonably related to what we *had* meant by it. If the conception of a
literary type functions as a genre for us, then it must at least *appear*
to have a continuous, coherent history; our mode of reading must be
based on what we imagine are earlier modes. And even this appearance, I think, is missing in the case of drama.

Does it follow from this contradiction that drama does not operate
as a "genre" after all? Is "drama" really only a word that we use
when an otherwise generically determined, intelligible literary
work—for whatever reasons—happens to be put onto the stage? I
think we have seen that this view is untenable. Drama is unquestionably a genre in the deep sense, in fact a genre par excellence. For
it operates not only upon our preunderstanding within its own particular domain, but also, directly and crucially, upon our preunderstanding, our attitude, our situation, our mode of existence, with
respect to the literary at large. Drama, especially, is the locus of: the
happening of the literary as a human *act;* the maintenance of the
"outside" and of semiurgic indeterminacy as literary conditions; a
constant resistance to the organic metaphor for literary form, and to
the idea of uniformity of response.

Drama does not have a history—indeed *cannot* have a history
without making nonsense, on a larger chronological scale, of the
opposition to the organic metaphor contained in its own textual
defectiveness. But on the other hand, drama (as a genre) *must* have a
history. And this contradiction is made less abstract by the recognition that it *appears* in history, in the form of drama's own curious but
typical tendency to theorize about itself, in the prominence, for

example, of the theater-within-theater strategy in Western drama. Drama cannot have a history, yet must have a history, and is therefore obliged to make—in the sense of to stage, to create in the theater—its *own* history.

This idea brings us back to Ibsen and Strindberg, whose works provide the scene for a stylistic history of their own form, a history that is then embedded—by way of the idea of a communication whose whole content is its own grounding—in something like a prophetic history of secular ethics. In the case of Nestroy and Schnitzler, the problem of the text opens the scene of *literary* history, where the needful movement toward a readerless literature is enacted. And it is interesting that the political dimension of this theater produces a configuration comparable to that of the true theater and the actual theater in Pirandello/Artaud. Just as *Giganti* can be either the destruction or the achievement of the true theater, so the undeniable power of the written text, in Nestroy, can be either an insuperable impediment to revolution or else the mere foil against which wit repeatedly reasserts itself in an achieved revolutionary society. And in Nestroy's theater, as in Pirandello's, we undergo the experience of finding it impossible to tell the difference between these alternatives, just as it is impossible to tell the difference between the aspect of doom and the aspect of promise in the words that follow us out of the theater of *Der grüne Kakadu*. In any case, the idea of a premodern theater of readers, in quest of clear literary boundary effects by which to gain leverage in the struggle against a de-volitionalized view of history, is evidently applicable to the two Viennese as well as to the two Scandinavians. But this theater is not merely a theater *for* readers. It recollects and enacts and foresees—and requires a definite ethical stand both upon and within—the *history* of reading.

When I say that drama needs to make or stage its own history, therefore, I do not mean the history of drama in a narrow sense. The dramatic stage attempts to be, not merely to reproduce, the scene of a *larger* historical order—the history of secular ethics, of reading, of social consciousness and criticism, of ideas of history—within which it itself (drama) will at last make sense historically. *Rhinocéros* is not "about" fascism, but rather the historical advent of fascism is made to happen in the theater as a whole, including the spectators, whereupon the play, in its specific quality as drama, makes sense as a model of the struggle to resist. And in *Die Physiker*, it is the diabolical complexity of what I have called "the age of physics" that happens in the auditorium—a situation comparable, in its hopelessness, to the social conditions in Nestroy, and a situation in which perhaps, therefore, as in Nestroy, the theater is erected as the self-demolishing quasi-material husk of a perfectly kinetic wit or "comedy" (Dürrenmatt's subtitle) by which the situation *becomes* different without our being able to say, in a visualizable manner, *how* it is different. In any case, if drama needs to make its own history, it cannot proceed otherwise; for it must evidently also provide the larger background against which its own history unfolds—there being no such thing as an unbackgrounded history.

3.

We find, however, that in rescuing Ionesco and Dürrenmatt, we have in a sense now marginalized Pirandello/Artaud. For the historical background to the semiotic revelation attempted in *I Giganti della Montagna*, for example, can be nothing other than the whole history of representation, the history of the sign, history in so utterly general a form that it can have the character of a mystery, but not that of a background, which would presuppose some reasonably adequate point of view for us. What is enacted here, it appears, is not the history of drama so much as the primordiality of drama, and this obscures the accidentalness that makes drama interesting and effective to begin with. What is revealed here, it appears, is the semiotic reversibility that always operates *inside* each drama, which confuses our sense of drama as the happening of a denial of any strict "inside" or "essence." If Genet goes too far in developing a self-disclosing and self-focused structure for drama, how shall a similar argument be avoided in the case of Pirandello? Surely an interpretation by way of the witty play of negatives, which works for *Die Physiker* (and perhaps even, in a different way, for Pirandello's own "theater" plays), would be trivial if attempted for Pirandello's "myths."

Let us return to the matter of boundary effects. In Chapter 4, the relation between dramatic and narrative versions of the same material in Ionesco was discussed in terms of the inveterate openness of dramatic form to its own "outside." But we might have gone a step further and argued that in *Rhinocéros*, the political manifestation of fascism is employed (against itself) to produce *a new literary boundary effect* for drama, a more direct and powerful boundary effect than the one marked by the relation between theater and cinema. As is made clear by the resonances between *Rhinocéros* and *Mario und der*

Zauberer, the unmasking of fascism as a literary-aesthetic phenomenon leaps the accustomed gulf between narrative and dramatic
form and creates a sudden uncomfortable *proximity* in which (by
way of the dialectic of spectator and audience) the public festivals of
the Nazis also threaten to participate. At this point, therefore, we
can begin to speak not of differences but of boundary effects between drama and narrative, effects that have to do especially with
the establishment of a target for individual identification, by which
the spectator's individuality is mobilized against a threatening theatrical or readerly dialectic. For it is clear that that target must be *a*
person (like *a* carrot), not *the* person or *the* target or *the* individual-as-
such, since the semioticized person, in this context, unbalances the
dialectic toward the disastrous condition of "audience." And it is
here that dramatic form makes the difference, the difference, for
example, between Bérenger—who, in the form of the actor, does
sketch a claim to the quality of *a* person—and Mario, who, in order
to be *a* person, must as far as possible (but never far enough) be
excluded from the story, since the development of a "character" in
narrative fiction always insists on *the* person signified in the text.

It might be maintained accordingly that a principal problem arising in connection with Pirandello, that of the recognition of drama
as a literary type, is altogether circumvented in Ionesco's procedure,
where the literary *operation* of drama, the unmasking of fascism as a
literary phenomenon and the unveiling of new boundary effects,
places us in the position of *having recognized* drama as a literary type.
And the case of *Die Physiker* is comparable. Here it is the age of
physics, in its entirety, that is unmasked as a literary phenomenon,
as the ultimate hegemony of writing, as the historical moment at
which the principle "Everything that *can* be thought *is* thought,"
which in effect includes all thought within writing, attains perfect
physical, political, and economic ascendancy in the world. Free or
private thought is no longer conceivable; thought simply *is*, in a
form equivalent to writing, like Möbius's undestroyed and in truth
indestructible manuscript. The deconstruction of a Western metaphysical privileging of speech or presence is no longer merely an
issue in philosophy, but has become demonstrable, indeed enforcea-
ble, by the bombs, or threat of bombs, that written theory engenders. And another new boundary effect emerges, now between
drama and writing as such, a boundary effect arising at the point of
threatening indistinguishability between our situation here in the
theater and our hopeless condition (as displayed by the physicists)
in the real, now thoroughly written "world." For this "world" is still

different from the theater, and different in a manner that is at once both surprising and predictable.

It is now the extratheatrical world that has become the domain of free semiosis, in which *esse est significari,* in which existence is equivalent to the condition of being a semiotic signified. There is no longer *a* thing in the world. Any thing that exists has already become *the* thing signified by whatever text now means the world for us. For this to be the case, it is not necessary that Möbius's document (or whatever "general text" is represented by it) actually mention, say, my fountain pen or my daughter; that text need not even contain these general concepts. It suffices that we understand why Möbius can acknowledge that his theory is merely theory, while at the same time insisting that it is final, that it establishes the limits of the knowable and organizes "all possible inventions." It suffices, in particular, that we understand (1) that our "world" is in truth never anything more than our *sense* of it, which is derived ultimately from (or is the signified of) the equivalent of writing, even if, ordinarily, the confusion of the actual texts involved in signifying "world" obscures the process of signification; and (2) that in the age of physics, however, certain brute practical criteria (especially the ability to bomb people) produce a rigid hierarchy of texts whereby that process of signification becomes all too plain. In effect, now, nothing exists (including the people, like Möbius, who write the texts) that is not the signified of something like Möbius's text. My fountain pen and my daughter are thus signified in the same manner in which any number of things can be "signified" by a text without being "meant" by it—a distinction we have no trouble applying on a smaller scale.

And the effect of its boundary with this utterly written world—or the effect that *is* its boundary—is to reserve for the theater the possibility of the existence of *a* thing. In Dürrenmatt's theater, semiotic tension between *the* thing (the signified, the interpretant) and *a* thing (the referent) operates in the reverse of its accustomed direction. What we see ordinarily in the theater is *a* thing, which is then invested poetically with the quality of *the* thing, while still not losing its original stubborn extraliterariness. Now, however, the same tension works to preserve the otherwise endangered quality of *a* thing. Of course this boundary is highly problematic—as is the boundary with narrative in Ionesco, which does not reduce the antifascist effectiveness of *Mario und der Zauberer,* but rather reveals it. How, after all, can we assert categorically that in the reality of the age of physics, the referent is overwhelmed by the signified, when we have also insisted, in the same argument, that everything depends on a "sense of world" that may be different for different people? Would it not be fairer to say that the age of physics is marked by an assault of signification upon reference, which must then produce the same tension between the two that drama does? Where is the boundary?

The point is that the boundaries established by drama, like any generic boundaries, are never located at anything comparable to a place, but rather exist only as boundary *effects*. Such a boundary does not mark off territory, as much as it articulates and exposes and brings into play certain special qualities of the larger situation in which it happens; and it follows that trespass or transgression—as in the case of the boundary of the "human" in the thought of *Die Physiker*, or as in the case of the general exclusion of the authorial function in drama—is not only possible but necessary. *That* the boundary is, matters; *where* does not. Since there can be no external guide for setting it, the boundary is set wherever one happens to be, like the city limits of Mahagonny in Brecht, which also expose and bring into play certain special qualities of their world. If the whole world now exhibits a semiotic tension otherwise characteristic of drama—or if (apropos Ionesco) literature as a whole now exhibits a resistance to its own aesthetic component—then this state of affairs depends on the assertion of precisely that boundary (of drama) which now appears to be violated by it.

The formulation can never be entirely satisfactory, but we do gain some clarity if we understand drama's repeated making of its own historical background as the bringing into play, by boundary effects, of certain latent operative configurations in history. The lack of available literary boundaries for the "theater of readers," in both its Scandinavian and its Viennese versions, now gives us a bit less trouble than before. For we can now understand the operation of this theater as itself a kind of double movement of boundary formation—comparable to the double movement by which otherness is achieved in Strindberg's cubism—as the attempt to create an actively self-effacing boundary within the history of reading, a boundary that exists only in order to be erased by the development, in response to it, of the new reader, the activated reader, whose reading will already itself be a making of history and will no longer require drama as a type.

And in this view of matters, again, it appears that the theatrical project of Pirandello/Artaud is merely a form of essentialism, the perverse attempt, despite its own focus on the tension between signification and reference, to assert not *a* boundary, but *the* boundary of drama. Or is it the other way around? Does the perversity not lie, rather, in using *against* Pirandello/Artaud, as a mark of essentialism, the fact that the semiotic categories with which their work operates are so widely applicable in understanding modern drama? In any case, the boundary of drama in Pirandello/Artaud, which involves the idea of a "true" theater whose literary quality is apparent in an operation of language upon (or against) itself, is not the same sort of boundary as in the theater of readers or the theater of resistance to totalitarianism. Even if we attenuate the notion of a true theater by calling it "l'impossible" or "mito," we thereby merely enter a domain of pure paradox and leave behind altogether the dramatically fruitful realm of concrete accidental events.

4.

The true theater of Pirandello/Artaud does not assert its own boundary so much as it claims to inhabit a heretofore only vaguely surmised boundary *of literature* (Pirandello and Artaud both say "poetry") within the larger geography of language. And yet this boundary, by being accessible only to the theatrically contaminated form of drama, is also a boundary *with* literature (between drama and literature), a boundary that is constantly violated to the extent that drama is recognized as a literary type, and in fact *must* be violated thus, since that recognition is its very reason for being.

This paradoxical logic can be regarded as yet another aspect of the essentialist move in Pirandello/Artaud. For it is clear that drama's making of its own history, its "bringing into play of latent operative configurations," always involves the unmasking of *the literary* in history. The history of secular social ethics is interpreted as the history of reading; fascism and the reach of modern physics are recognized as literary phenomena; social revolution and verbal wit become identical. The name of the background that drama sets up in order to stage its own history as a genre, its own boundary effects, is always, in the final analysis, *literary history.* Thus we have in practice a clear manifestation of the theoretical paradox in Pirandello/Artaud. The boundaries drama produces for itself are always boundaries *with* the literary; but that process of boundary making also presupposes drama's *participation* in the literary.

Nor is this favoring of the literary in history surprising, provided we agree that a certain amount of meaning has been accumulated by the idea of drama as the church of literature. Drama—to formulate the point as radically as possible—is the place where literature as a whole seeks to realize its inherent ambition to *become history,* to supplant all other historical forms or orders. This ambition exists, in the sense that it belongs to what we mean by literature. For within its own narrowly defined domain, literary history is history in the most perfect conceivable form. It is a self-writing history, a history whose whole content is the writing of itself, the account it gives of itself to itself. Or at least we can recognize that it approaches this perfect state, in which empirical error is no longer possible, if we agree, first, that "scholarly" literary history does not escape *being* literary, that it belongs to literature as much as lyric poetry does, and thus carries out an internal feedback by which more of its own content is generated; and second, that even the most imaginative or creative writing, say lyric poetry, is always also a writing of literary history, inasmuch as it inevitably fixes and presents in a particular way the traditions it draws upon. That there are disagreements within literary history, or violent oppositions, does not affect this point, any more than a conflict between characters keeps a story from being the one story that it is. That literary history uses material gleaned from other types of history does not affect this point, any more than the allusion to real political events affects the status of *L'Education sentimentale* as a novel.

Furthermore, the type of perfection approached by literary history includes a perfect activation of the individual with respect to the whole. There are no strictly passive victims, no strictly objective observers; even mere reading, in order to belong to literary history in the first place, must become an act. The imperial tendency in literary history, its ambition to become history as such, is thus but an aspect of the literary ethics we have repeatedly seen operate in drama, an aspect of the striving to assert human dominion in history, to have done with the idea or possibility of an organic historical closure as imagined in the mind of a perfectly receptive anonymous reader. The trouble, however, is that literary genres, by their nature, *themselves* manifest history in the form of a continuous organic unfolding. Hence the importance of the defective, contaminated genre, the genre that has no history and must make its own, the genre of drama, which thus provides the only possible scene for literature's striving toward the status of history as such. Drama is the church of literature, now in the sense (by comparison with other genres) of a space that is defined in gross material terms but must then become a vessel of the spirit's dreaming.

This idea is not yet an argument. But of the thought that would be needed to make it an argument, enough is present to be carried at least one step further. Namely, the inherent historical aspiration of literature inevitably makes nonsense of itself in practice, a nonsense that becomes almost enjoyable in *Die Physiker*. For if literature were ever to achieve its aim and simply become history, it would thereby also absorb into itself its own outside—precisely that outside, that domain of the referent, which drama insists on in its literary function—and the result would be the hegemony, the becoming-history, not of literature, not of a self-emancipated humanity, but of *writing*. The result would be not merely the "autonomy," but the tyranny of the signifier; and literature, by way of drama, thus finds itself in the absurd situation of having to institute a boundary with (or against) writing as such. Literature no longer has a boundary with drama, but now uses drama in the attempt to *escape* its own inescapable condition as writing. We can perhaps begin to speak of Dürrenmatt/Artaud. At least Artaud and Pirandello now come back into the picture. For in the absurd situation at which dramatic history necessarily arrives, the only possible alternative to the radically negative strategy of *Die Physiker* seems to be precisely a direct assault upon the structure of signification, an apparently essentialist importing of semiotic reversibility (hence of the dethroning of language) even into the content of drama, that bodies might now become ghosts, and trees sentences, in very earnest. The self-violating quality of the boundary—which is necessary so that the literary can encounter an "outside" that retains its full outsideness—now obtains *only* in the semiotic sense of Pirandello/Artaud.

The discussion of drama in relation to history thus moves along two different paths, two separate arguments, which are not only irreconcilable with each other, but also each deeply erroneous in itself. The essentialist error in the argument on the inherent semiotic function of drama is exposed by the concrete historical application of just that argument (and of its assumption that drama does operate as a literary genre), which produces the picture of a type that has nothing "inherent" about it, but possesses identity only in the repeatedly unprecedented boundary effects it creates for itself. But this second argument, when its consequences are traced, develops its own imperial or totalitarian error, the swallowing of history by literary history; and this error is exposed by its relation to the first argument's model of a tenable semiotic boundary of the literary. Dramatic history, in other words, presents us with two erroneous and irreconcilable positions, plus the recognition, nevertheless, that the combination of these positions, their impossible reconciliation (which includes the impossible affirmation of each), is what we

mean by drama—in the same way, as we saw earlier, that the combination of irreconcilable hermeneutic positions (which we associated with Gadamer and Hirsch) is also what we mean by drama,
"l'art même du paradoxe."

5.

This, then, is what I mean by *the* theory of drama, which is prevented from becoming *a* theory by its own internal dynamics. And
the reader must therefore be prepared, so to speak, to supply quotation marks where they are needed, as a reminder that the foregoing
arguments never reach far enough, but always only stand for arguments yet to come, which will be more complex and penetrating—
and paradoxical. For at the least, I think I have shown that the
theater, in its relation to literature by way of the genre of drama, *is* a
problem, the exploration of which cannot but continue to open ec-
centric and disturbing perspectives upon literature in general.

In any case, let us finish by turning things around and glancing at
the manner in which the idea of the theater as a problematizing
force, an opening of difficult perspectives, *has* operated in literary
thought, especially by way of its use as a metaphor. We think perhaps first of the work of Frances A. Yates, and of the relations she
exhibits among entities of such disparate nature as the metaphorical
linking of theater and world; theatrical architecture, including actual
examples; and a curious construct, never definitively either material
or mental, called the memory theater.[3]

Or we think of certain extremely compact perceptions with extremely far-reaching consequences, for instance Marian Hobson's use
(or discovery) of the theater metaphor as a kind of hinge on which
philosophy makes its huge swing from Descartes to Hume and
beyond.[4] The theater has an inherent totalizing tendency that is at
once both fruitful and dangerous. By materializing the difference or
distance between scene and spectator, by insisting, in the realm of
material fact, on what is otherwise the categorical difference between
reader and fiction, the theater also makes the reader/spectator available as an *object* that can now be incorporated into the artistic proceeding; and once this step is taken, its replication—in the form of an

---

[3]Frances A. Yates, *Theatre of the World* (Chicago, 1969).
[4]Marian Hobson, "Du Theatrum Mundi au Theatrum Mentis," *Revue des Sciences
Humaines*, n.s., no. 167 (1977). Quotations by page in parentheses.

inclusion (not merely a representation) of the whole world, or of history, in the theatrical event—is opened as a possibility. This quality of the theater as a kind of expanding universe is then, in its turn, reflected in drama's abstract relation to the literary, where it begins as a mere material accident, but soon turns the tables, becoming the unique site of literature's happening *as* literature. And if Hobson now shows that a crucial turn in Western philosophy can be grasped with special appropriateness as the difference between a *theatrum mundi,* strictly limited with respect to the Divine Eye that presides over it, and a *theatrum mentis* that has no "hors théâtre" whatever, how shall we understand *the availability of this argument?* Is it our own quasi-divine perspective that thus enables us to compare inherently disparate phenomena? Or is it rather, perhaps, that the dramatic theater not only illuminates, as a metaphor, but also actually infects the literary in a sufficiently broad sense to include the structure of problem setting in philosophy?

In this connection, Hobson is illuminating even when she is wrong. She opens her essay by saying:

> Le théâtre n'est pas théâtral. "Théâtralité" porte en soi deux termes: le théâtre et quelque chose, autre chose, que ce soit une autre forme d'art ou le contenu d'une situation réelle. Ainsi la formule "théâtralité hors du théâtre," dans la mesure où elle suggère la transgression d'une barrière—séparation des genres ou des catégories art/vie—établit en fait deux lieux bien distincts, qu'elle fait communiquer et qu'elle tient séparés dans le moment de la transgression même. [P. 379]

> The theater is not theatrical. "Theatricality" contains two terms: the theater, and something different, whether another form of art or the content of a real situation. Thus the formula, "theatricality outside of the theater," to the extent that it suggests transgression of a barrier—a separation of genres or of the categories art/life—in fact establishes two clearly distinct positions between which it communicates, and which it keeps separate in the very moment of transgression.

The reasoning is correct, but the opening statement is false. The theater *is* undeniably "theatrical"—in just the sense Hobson means— and is accordingly always *itself* "deux lieux bien distincts"; it always both is and is not itself, is itself and yet also more than itself—as the vessel of a literary type, which, as theater, it has no business being. Hobson goes on to ask, "But is a generalized theatricality possible, a theatricality in the form of universal contamination?" The answer is, Yes, and with reference to theatricality not merely as a general cultural force that must be pieced together out of text-analyses, but concretely, as a *real* site of infection, of problem, of paradox, in the bosom of an intellectual and cultural life that by its nature always threatens to evaporate into the merely systematic.

Or let us turn, finally, to the concluding pages of Suzanne Gearhart's *The Open Boundary of History and Fiction:*

> It is not by accident that the theater is a problem that recurs in this study as a whole. . . . If the theater is evoked at key moments of my analysis, it is no doubt because it seemed to be the best means of articulating the continual transgression of the boundary between the literary and the historical, the fictional and the real. . . . As I have used it, "the theater," or rather the theatrical, is neither simply a metaphor nor a concept. It points to a textuality that is not simply of the text; that is, it underscores the fact that textuality is not of necessity and in essence a positive or empirical concept. The theater signifies the irruption of what is posited as the nontextual in the textual, while, at the same time, it reveals the fictive, theatrical characteristics of the historical event. Though the notion of theatricality is central to the argument of this study, it should be stressed that the term clearly has potential abuses: the most obvious being a conflation of history and fiction in which the political and the historical are neutralized. Such a general theory of fiction as theatricality questions everything except its own concept of fiction; it ignores the way in which that concept, even as it claims to obliterate the distinction between history and fiction, depends itself on an unquestioned and naive view of history to which it opposes itself in order to assert its own singularity and preeminence. Theatricality in this study, on the contrary, functions to challenge not only attempts to fix the boundary between fiction and history, but also efforts to erase it.[5]

Even when thus torn out of its place in the larger work that it summarizes, this passage raises interesting questions. Does what it says apply *only* to the theater as a counter in critical study, as "metaphor" or "concept"? Or is that entity which Gearhart means, and which is not quite either metaphor or concept, not after all, at a couple of removes, simply the operation of the dramatic theater itself, as empirically as one wishes to take it? In any case, the abuse that Gearhart warns against is a danger in my work as well. *A* theory of drama is not my goal, and is in fact not a goal to begin with, but only a trap. This book is about *the* theory of drama.

[5] S. Gearhart, *Open Boundary* (Princeton, 1984), pp. 291–92.

Index

Aeschylus, 69
Apollinaire, Guillaume, 145
Aristotle, 3, 126, 160–62
Artaud, Antonin, 5, 76, 79n., 94, 175, 189, 206–7, 215–19, 252, 253, 257–58, 261–62, 264
Audience, 88–89, 150–59, 211; and spectator, 151–59, 161–63, 169–70, 180, 184, 185, 259
Author, 21–22, 28, 81–82, 183–84, 187, 210–11, 213; authorial function, 28, 66, 186–89, 211, 261

Bakhtin, M. M., 63–64n.
Barthes, Roland, 1, 10–11n., 131n.
Baudrillard, Jean, 238n.
Baumgarten, Alexander Gottlieb, 161n.
Beckett, Samuel, 74, 76, 78–79, 88, 91, 140, 142–44; *Endgame*, 143; *Waiting for Godot*, 70–73, 138, 143, 186–87, 199–200, 202, 214–15, 259
Benjamin, Walter, 161n., 254n.
Blanchot, Maurice, 217
Boccaccio, Giovanni, 166
Boundary effects, 56–57, 59–81, 89–92, 93, 133, 170, 190–95, 198, 254–55, 258–62, 264
Brecht, Bertolt, 91, 137, 141, 145, 162, 187, 242, 253, 261; "Lehrstücke," 86–89
Brustein, Robert, 27n.

Calderon de la Barca, Pedro, 69
Camus, Albert, 145
Cézanne, Paul, 19

Chekhov, Anton, 250–51
Churchill, Winston, 236–40
Cinema. *See* Drama
Cocteau, Jean, 141
Communication, 25–29, 70–72, 74, 78, 84, 90–92, 93, 130, 168, 185–86, 187; ethics of, 27–29, 31, 33, 43–52, 58, 84–85, 133–34, 177, 257; and the other, 39, 46–51, 84, 139, 168, 261
Copernicus, Nicolaus, 236
Corngold, Stanley, 241n.
Crane, Hart, 67
Culler, Jonathan, 10, 186n.

Dada, 145
Dante Alighieri: *Commedia*, 196
Davé, Sveta, 65n.
Deleuze, Gilles, 186n.
de Man, Paul, 63–64n., 132–33n., 191
Derrida, Jacques, 10–11n., 63n., 184, 186, 206, 217–19, 246–47n., 253
Descartes, René, 265
Diderot, Denis, 74
Dilthey, Wilhelm, 156n.
Discrimination. *See* Boundary effects
Drama: absurd, 137–45, 148–50, 155–59, 163, 171, 186; ancient Greek, 3, 18, 69, 89, 160, 171, 254n.; and cinema, 65–73, 75–77, 85, 89–91, 177, 194, 255, 258; French classical, 18; German Classical, 18, 65, 69, 85, 91, 133n., 254n., 255; Italian comedy, 111; as a literary type, 1–5, 14–16, 57–68, 90, 133–34, 137, 159–63, 169–71, 179, 190–219, 250–52, 254–67;

Drama (*cont.*)
  and opera, 75–77, 86, 89–90, 134,
  194, 255; Renaissance, 18; text of, 2–
  5, 61–64, 67–68, 72–81, 90–91, 93–
  98, 107–10, 112–13, 118, 126, 133,
  151–53, 194, 199–204, 256–57. *See
  also* Theater
Dürrenmatt, Friedrich, 220–52, 253,
  256–61, 264; *Die Physiker*, 94, 220–52,
  253, 257–62, 264

Eco, Umberto, 199n., 200n., 214
Einstein, Albert, 227
Elam, Keir, 12–13, 15
Eliot, T. S., 1, 141, 249
Euripides, 69

Fascism, 15, 137, 140–41, 148–49, 155–
  71, 203–5, 215, 246, 256–62
Flaubert, Gustave: *L'Education sentimen-
  tale*, 263; *Madame Bovary*, 195–96
Foucault, Michel, 218–19
Freud, Sigmund, 112, 219, 237
Frisch, Max, 177; *Biedermann und die
  Brandstifter*, 88–89
Frost, Robert, 93
Frye, Northrop, 4–5, 56

Gadamer, Hans-Georg, 64n., 81–85,
  89, 265
Galileo Galilei, 227
Gasché, Rodolphe, 132–33n.
Gearhart, Suzanne, 6–7n., 132–33n.,
  267
Genet, Jean, 258; *Le Balcon*, 172–84
Ghelderode, Michel de, 145
Giraudoux, Jean, 141
Giudice, Gaspare, 204n.
Goethe: *Faust*, 24, 52n., 138, 176n.,
  249n.
Goodman, Nelson, 6
Greimas, A. J., 11

Hamburger, Käte, 56, 190–95, 210–11
Handke, Peter, 150–51, 154–55, 170
Hartman, Geoffrey, 191
Hauptmann, Gerhart, 94
Hegel, Georg Friedrich Wilhelm, 7–8,
  63, 131–33, 144, 161, 164, 174
Heidegger, Martin, 82–83, 201–3, 206–
  8
Herder, Johann Gottfried, 84, 161
Hermeneutics, 4, 57–58, 67–91, 132,
  144, 174, 177, 193, 195, 265. *See also*
  Interpretation; Reversibility

Hirsch, E. D., Jr., 58n., 77–79, 81–83,
  89, 265
History, 15, 131–34, 141, 144, 155, 169–
  71, 174–75, 185, 215, 241–42, 245,
  249, 257–65; of drama, 7–9, 11, 15,
  33–34, 89, 134, 144–45, 194, 253–58;
  and experience, 234–40; literary, 1,
  5–6, 257–59, 262–65; of style, 33–34,
  91, 142, 144, 257
Hobson, Marian, 6–7n., 265–67
Hofmannsthal, Hugo von, 75n., 108,
  110, 122, 241n.
Hume, David, 265

Ibsen, Henrik, 17–54, 55, 58, 84–85,
  90–92, 93, 130, 133–34, 139, 141–42,
  168, 170–71, 175, 177, 187, 257;
  Ghosts, 35; *Hedda Gabler*, 19, 23–24;
  John Gabriel Borkman, 22, 24–25; *The
  Lady from the Sea*, 19, 23–24; *Little
  Eyolf*, 22, 23–25; *The Master Builder*,
  19, 22, 24–25; *Peer Gynt*, 23, 24;
  Rosmersholm, 19; *When We Dead
  Awaken*, 22–23, 26–27, 91; *The Wild
  Duck*, 19
Interpretation, 72–89, 91, 107, 113,
  144, 151, 154–59, 166–69, 172, 176n.,
  211; performance as, 66–68, 73–81,
  85–88, 152–53, 193, 208, 210, 213;
  and understanding, 73–89, 91, 116,
  130, 139, 151–55, 162. *See also* Hermeneutics; Reversibility
Ionesco, Eugène, 74, 76, 78–79, 88, 91,
  140–41, 142–50, 155–64, 167–71, 178,
  179–80, 183, 184, 187, 246, 253, 256–
  61; *Amédée ou Comment s'en débarrasser*, 148; *La Cantatrice chauve*, 138,
  140, 148; *Les Chaises*, 148; *L'Impromptu de l'Alma*, 149, 187; *Jacques ou
  la soumission*, 148; *La Leçon*, 71–73,
  148, 161–62; *Le Piéton de l'air*, 148;
  Rhinocéros, 140, 145–46, 148–50, 155–
  64, 167–71, 175–76, 246, 257–60;
  Tueur sans gages, 148, 157; *Victimes du
  devoir*, 138–39, 148–49
Iser, Wolfgang, 62n., 118
Issacharoff, Michael, 70n., 195n

James, Henry, 62, 118
Jarry, Alfred, 145
Jesus Christ, 237
Johnston, Brian, 27n.
Joyce, James, 2

Kafka, Franz, 140
Kant, Immanuel, 63, 164, 234, 236

Keller, Gottfried, 242
Kelly, Walt, 237
Kermode, Frank, 176n.
Kleist, Heinrich von, 65n., 69
Knodt, Eva, 63n.
Kristeva, Julia, 10n., 63–64n., 195n.

Lessing, Gotthold Ephraim, 74n., 111n.
Lévi-Strauss, Claude, 218
"Longinus," 82
Lubbock, Percy, 118

Mach, Ernst, 112
Mann, Thomas, 141; *Mario und der Zauberer*, 164–71, 258–60
Marx, Karl, 236
Mautner, Franz H., 96n., 104n.
Molière, 69, 149

Narrative, 2, 5, 20, 22, 28, 56, 58, 63–64n., 110–11, 139–40, 169–71, 186, 188, 190–96, 198, 210, 249–50, 254–55, 258–60, 263; and cinema, 66–68, 89, 255; narrative function, 192, 198, 210
Nestroy, Johann, 94–110, 112–13, 119, 122–24, 126, 130–31, 134–36, 140, 141, 168, 170, 175, 187, 257–58; *Freiheit in Krähwinkel*, 96–97, 100–101, 104–5; *Häuptling Abendwind*, 96, 102, 104; *Einen Jux will er sich machen*, 96, 99, 101; *Liebesgeschichten und Heiratssachen*, 109; *Lumpazivagabundus*, 96, 104; *Der Talisman*, 96, 102; *Der Unbedeutende*, 96; and Wagner, 96, 106; *Weder Lorbeerbaum noch Bettelstab*, 94–96, 99; *Der Zerrissene*, 96–97, 99–101, 104; *Zu ebener Erde und erster Stock*, 98–99
New Criticism, 132–33n.
Newton, Isaac, 227
Nietzsche, Friedrich, 36, 48, 55, 89, 103, 131, 164, 172, 224–25, 248

Parade, 76
Pavis, Patrice, 13
Peirce, Charles Sanders, 9–10, 197n., 201–4, 207–8, 213
Performance. *See* Interpretation; Theater
Picasso, Pablo, 236–40
Pico della Mirandola, Giovanni, 234
Pirandello, Luigi, 74, 76, 78–79, 88, 91, 108, 149, 178, 179–90, 192–93, 200–205, 208–19, 253, 257–59, 261–62,

264; *Ciascuno a suo modo*, 192–93; *Così è (se vi pare)*, 180, 193; *Enrico IV*, 193; "La Favola del figlio cambiato," 218; *I Giganti della Montagna*, 208–9, 211–13, 216–18, 257–58; *Lazzaro*, 200–201, 203–4, 209–10; *La nuova colonia*, 204–5, 209–10, 215, 218; *Quando si è qualcuno*, 179–90, 193, 211, 215; *Questa sera si recita a soggetto*, 192–93; *Six Characters*, 69, 180, 183, 192–93; *Trovarsi*, 193
Pirandello, Stefano, 213
Plato, 198, 242
Pogo Possum, 237

Quigley, Austin E., 6–9, 13, 59–60n.

Reader, 66, 71, 73–74, 118, 131, 152, 168, 177, 249–50, 257, 261; anonymous, 63, 131–36, 263; virtual, and actual spectator, 73–81, 87–88, 93, 102, 107, 109, 118, 123, 135–36, 139, 151–54, 161–62, 170, 205, 214, 250. *See also* Theater
Reference, 11, 69–73, 195–212, 260. *See also* Reversibility; Semiotics
Reinhardt, Max, 76
Reversibility, 14, 173; of frame relations, 171, 174, 179–86; of reference, 199–201, 205–8; of signification, 207–8, 212–15, 218–19, 264; temporal in Strindberg, 41–42, 179; of understanding and interpretation, 76–81, 85–91, 130, 155, 185, 207–8
Rosenzweig, Franz, 254n.
Rougemont, Denis de, 148, 159
Rousseau, Jean-Jacques, 63n.

Salzburg Festival, 76
Sartre, Jean-Paul, 145
Saussure, Ferdinand de, 10, 139, 186, 207
Schiller, Friedrich, 122, 244–45, 247, 252
Schleiermacher, F. D. E., 58, 84
Schnitzler, Arthur, 110–36, 140, 168, 170, 175, 206, 246, 257; *Anatol*, 110–19, 121–24, 128–30, 155; *Der grüne Kakadu*, 124–30, 135, 257; *Reigen*, 119–25, 128–30, 136
Schopenhauer, Arthur, 164
Semiotics, 9–15, 57, 68–73, 139, 175–76, 179–90, 193–219, 258–62, 264; and literary language, 9–12, 14, 139–41, 194–208, 211–16, 218–19; of personal identity, 181–85, 189–90; semi-

Semiotics (*cont.*)
  urgic indeterminacy, 196–98, 202–6,
  209–10, 256. *See also* Reference; Re-
  versibility; Signification
Shakespeare, William, 4, 7–8, 69;
  Hamlet, 66, 74–75, 85, 131, 155, 170,
  173–74, 215, 254n.; *King Lear*, 201;
  Measure for Measure, 86; *Richard II*,
  146, 153, 195–96, 206
Shaw, George Bernard, 55, 93–94, 141
Signification, 11, 12–13, 139, 183, 185–
  86, 195–215, 260, 264. *See also* Reversibility; Semiotics
Sokel, Walter H., 34n.
Sophocles: *Ajax*, 69; *Oedipus at Colonus*,
  69; *Oedipus the King*, 18
Spectator. *See* Audience; Reader
Staiger, Emil, 56
Strawson, P. F., 196–97n.
Strindberg, August, 17–54, 55, 58, 84–
  85, 90–92, 93, 130, 133–34, 139, 141–
  42, 168, 170–71, 175, 179, 187, 190,
  246, 257, 261; *Creditors*, 19–20; *The
  Dance of Death*, 20, 35; *A Dream Play*,
  21, 29, 31–32, 34, 39–40, 49–50, 53,
  128; *Easter*, 31; *The Father*, 19; *The
  Ghost Sonata*, 35–37, 39–40, 46, 48,
  54, 117n.; *The Great Highway*, 37–54,
  90–91, 115, 134; *Miss Julie*, 19; *To
  Damascus*, 20, 21, 29–32, 34, 44–45,
  46–47, 49–50, 53
Style, 91, 141–44; cubist, 20, 32–53,
  139, 179, 261; and decorum, 5; dramatic, and painting, 17–51; and ethics, 27–29, 30–32, 33, 36–37, 42–52,
  91, 139, 141; mimetic, 20–29, 52, 91,
  177, 187. *See also* Communication;
  History

Surrealism, 145
Szondi, Peter, 7–9, 11, 13, 21, 28, 54,
  187

Theater: as ceremony, 53–54, 74–76,
  83–91, 130–32, 174; as defining
  drama, 2–4, 9, 14, 58–62, 64, 68, 90–
  91, 177–78, 194–95, 208–19, 254, 262;
  as event, 9, 153, 175; as model of
  society, 53, 90–91, 101–2, 105; nondramatic, 2–4; of readers, 15, 28–29,
  34, 54, 55, 65, 91–92, 133–34, 170–
  71, 257, 261–62; as scenic space, 12,
  107, 170, 207; textless, 15, 94–98,
  107–10, 112–13, 118, 123–24, 126–31,
  134–36, 137, 140, 163, 168, 257; Viennese, 94–96, 110, 119, 124; within-
  theater, 68–69, 108, 124–28, 192–93,
  209, 256–57, 258. *See also* Drama
Todorov, Tzvetan, 110

Ubersfeld, Anne, 3–4, 11–12, 63n.,
  70n., 79n., 139, 170, 195n., 207
Uniformity of response. *See* Fascism

Wagner, Richard, 96, 106
Wedekind, Frank, 187
Wehle, Peter, 95n.
Wilamowitz-Möllendorff, Ulrich von,
  254n.
Wittgenstein, Ludwig, 6, 13
Wolff, Christian, 160–61
Wunberg, Gotthart, 112n.

Yates, Frances A., 6–7n., 265
Yates, W. E., 134n.

Library of Congress Cataloging-in-Publication Data

Bennett, Benjamin, 1939–
    Theater as problem : modern drama and its place in literature / Benjamin
Bennett.
        p.   cm.
    Includes index.
    ISBN 0–8014–2443–7 (alk. paper). —ISBN 0–8014–9730–2 (pbk. : alk. paper)
    1. Drama—19th century—History and criticism.   2. Drama—20th century—
History and criticism.   3. Drama.   4. Theater.   I. Title.
PN1851.B38   1990
809.2'034—dc20
                                                                        90–55115